The Complete Guide to Blender Graphics

The Complete Guide to Blender Graphics

Computer Modeling and Animation

John M. Blain

CRC Press
Taylor & Francis Group
Boca Raton London New York

CRC Press is an imprint of the
Taylor & Francis Group, an **informa** business

AN A K PETERS BOOK

Cover image courtesy of Kevin Hays.

CRC Press
Taylor & Francis Group
6000 Broken Sound Parkway NW, Suite 300
Boca Raton, FL 33487-2742

Printed in the United States of America on acid-free paper
Version Date: 20120216

International Standard Book Number: 978-1-4665-1703-5 (Paperback)

Library of Congress Cataloging-in-Publication Data

Blain, John M., 1942-
   The complete guide to Blender graphics : computer modeling and animation / John M. Blain. -- 1st ed.
       p. cm.
   Includes bibliographical references and index.
   ISBN 978-1-4665-1703-5 (pbk. : alk. paper)
   1. Computer animation. 2. Three-dimensional display systems. 3. Computer graphics. 4. Blender (Computer file) I. Title.

TR897.7.B573 2012
777'.7--dc23   2012000422

Visit the Taylor & Francis Web site at
http://www.taylorandfrancis.com

and the CRC Press Web site at
http://www.crcpress.com

Table of Contents

Introduction

Computer Modeling and Animation

Blender is an open source freeware program maintained by the Blender Foundation. The program can be downloaded, free of charge, from www.blender.org.

Blender is a challenging program to learn but it has limitless possibilities and will give you an understanding of computer animation. Due to the complexity of the subject, it is not possible to cover everything. This manual is designed for beginners to help with the very basics of computer animation using Blender. The subject matter in this book is aimed at removing some of the frustration from the learning process. Blender is a wonderful application but one major drawback has been the lack of up-to-date basic instruction; documentation has always lagged behind development. There is a multitude of free information available on the Internet from various sites in the form of tutorials. Much of the information is relevant to earlier versions of the program and since there has been a dramatic change to the interface, with the introduction of version 2.50+, I believe that a new student would find learning Blender difficult without a current written instruction. This manual is an attempt to remove some of the pain and relieve frustration by introducing the basics.

The manual has been written through trial and error by navigating the way between Blender 2.49 and Blender 2.50+. I trust you will find the information informative and useful.

Blender Versions

Blender has been around for a considerable time. Upon starting the program, the graphical user interface (GUI) shows a panel with the version number in the center of the screen. On each release, this panel has been changed to identify the version. Blender has developed over time and as that development has evolved, new releases (or versions) of the program have been made available. The developers considered that a complete overhaul of the GUI was necessary; at the time of writing, version 2.60 is the current one. The GUI of 2.5+ is completely different than 2.49 and the frustration of learning the new interface without documentation has prompted the writing of this manual.

Graphical User Interface

The GUI is the arrangement of windows, panels, and buttons that allow you, the user, to interact with the program. The interaction takes place through inputs via the computer keyboard and mouse.

By giving instructions with reference to keyboard and mouse actions, a series of commands has evolved. The list of commands is extensive and it is not recommended that a new user attempts to memorize the list without understanding the meaning. As you progress through this manual many of the commands are repeated and you'll soon find that it becomes second nature. Of course, you might forget the obscure commands, therefore a listing is provided in Appendix A.

Evolution

Blender will continue to evolve and change. New versions of the program will inevitably be released with additions and changes incorporated, but the basic operation of the interface and the majority of the functions will remain unchanged. If you care to assist in maintaining this manual, your comments and suggestions are welcome. Please email your comments to silverjb12@gmail.com. Good luck and I hope you enjoy the experience.

Acknowledgments

Many thanks to Neal Hirsig for his encouragement and support, and to Helen for her infinite patience.

—John M. Blain

How to Get Blender

Blender can be downloaded from www.blender.org.

Installation instructions

To install Blender, download the appropriate package for your platform to your computer. The Windows version comes with an optional self-extracting installer, for other operating systems you can unpack the compressed file to the location of your choice.

Provided the Blender binary is in the original extracted directory, Blender will run straight out of the box. No system libraries or system preferences are altered.

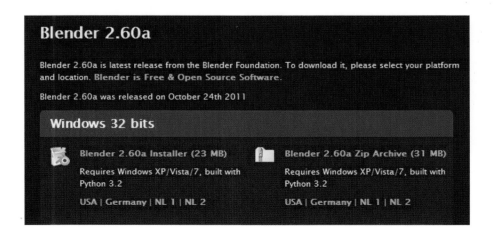

Blender 2.60a

Blender 2.60a is latest release from the Blender Foundation. To download it, please select your platform and location. Blender is Free & Open Source Software.

Blender 2.60a was released on October 24th 2011

Windows 32 bits

Blender 2.60a Installer (23 MB)

Requires Windows XP/Vista/7, built with Python 3.2

USA | Germany | NL 1 | NL 2

Blender 2.60a Zip Archive (31 MB)

Requires Windows XP/Vista/7, built with Python 3.2

USA | Germany | NL 1 | NL 2

Windows 64 bits

 Blender 2.60a Installer (27 MB)

Requires Windows XP/Vista/7 64bit

USA | Germany | NL 1 | NL 2

 Blender 2.60a Zip Archive (36 MB)

Requires Windows XP/Vista/7 64bit

USA | Germany | NL 1 | NL 2

Linux x86–32

 Blender 2.60a (37 MB)

Requires glibc 2.7, includes Python 3.2, FFmpeg
Suits most recent Linux distributions

USA | Germany | NL 1 | NL 2

Linux x86–64

 Blender 2.60a (39 MB)

Requires glibc 2.7, includes Python 3.2, FFmpeg
Suits most recent Linux distributions

USA | Germany | NL 1 | NL 2

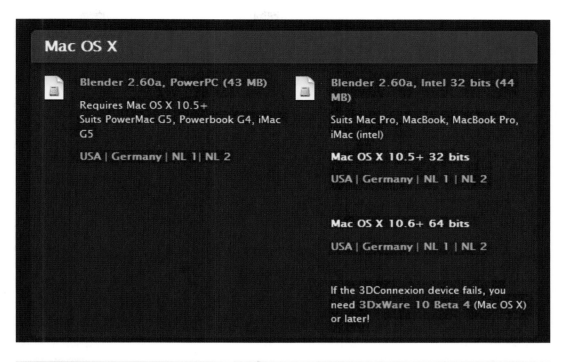

Mac OS X

Blender 2.60a, PowerPC (43 MB)

Requires Mac OS X 10.5+
Suits PowerMac G5, Powerbook G4, iMac G5

USA | Germany | NL 1| NL 2

Blender 2.60a, Intel 32 bits (44 MB)

Suits Mac Pro, MacBook, MacBook Pro, iMac (intel)

Mac OS X 10.5+ 32 bits

USA | Germany | NL 1 | NL 2

Mac OS X 10.6+ 64 bits

USA | Germany | NL 1 | NL 2

If the 3DConnexion device fails, you need 3DxWare 10 Beta 4 (Mac OS X) or later!

FreeBSD

Blender 2.60a i386 (21 MB)
USA | NL

Blender 2.60a amd64 (16 MB)
USA | NL

Note: The download information above is referring to version 2.60a of the Blender program. Blender is always under review but the download site will reflect the most current version release and it's expected that the download procedure and installation will remain unchanged.

Recommended Viewing

Blender 3D Design Course: Tufts University

The Blender 3D Design Course provided by Neal Hirsig of Tufts University is a self-paced online educational facility providing a comprehensive series of video tutorials, PDF tutorials, and learning exercises. It can be found at www.gryllus.net.

The video tutorials are short and concise, providing the student with an introduction to the many facets of the Blender program. The tutorials are presented in an ordered structure that lead the student gently into the complex and fascinating world of computer modelling and animation using the Blender program. Where you see this logo throughout the manual gives an approximate reference to the relevant Learning Unit and Video Tutorial provided on the Blender 3D Course website.

To access the 3D Design Course video tutorials, go to the website address shown above. Click on the "Learning Units" heading to open a selection menu for Learning Units 1 to 5 and Learning Units 6 to 10. Clicking on the Learning Unit headings will in turn open a selection menu for the individual unit, which then provides access to the video tutorials.

1

The Blender Interface

1.1 The Blender Screen

When Blender first opens, the screen displays the graphical user interface (GUI), as shown in Figure 1.1. On some operating systems, the screen may not display full size upon start up. Left click on the expansion button in the upper RH corner of the screen. The Blender screen opens with the version panel in the middle (there are webpage links included here). Left click anywhere on the screen to remove this panel.

The default Blender screen displays with five windows opened (Figure 1.2). Besides the windows displayed, there are 15 other window types available for selection. Look

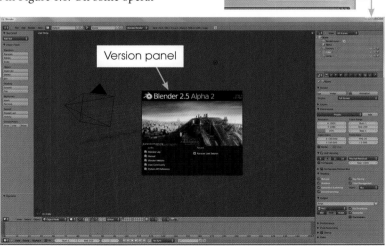

Expansion button

Version panel

Figure 1.1

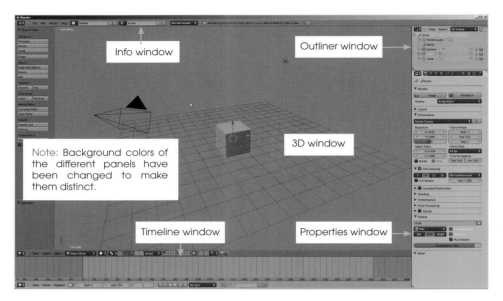

Info window

Outliner window

Note: Background colors of the different panels have been changed to make them distinct.

3D window

Timeline window

Properties window

Figure 1.2

at the lower LH corner of the 3D window and note the icon. This is the icon representing the 3D window. Each window has an icon displayed in the upper or lower LH corner of the window representing the window type.

Clicking on a window type icon displays a drop down selection menu for selecting a different type of window (Figure 1.3). Selecting a different window from the menu changes the current window into the type selected.

1.1.1 Interface Input

The user input to the program is described in this manual using a standard keyboard and a three-button or wheel mouse. Blender is designed to be operated with one hand on the mouse and the other on the keyboard. Laptop users will have to adapt to the instructions provided as notes throughout this manual.

Here's an example. In the lower LH corner of the 3D window, click on the icon with the mouse cursor. Select "Graph Editor," and the window changes to the graph editor window. Click on the graph editor icon and select "3D View"—the window reverts to the 3D window. Any window may be changed to a different window type in this way.

Editor type:

- Console
- File Browser
- Info
- User Preferences
- Outliner
- Properties
- Logic Editor
- Node Editor
- Text Editor
- Video Sequence Editor
- UV/Image Editor
- NLA Editor
- DopeSheet
- Graph Editor
- Timeline
- 3D View

Figure 1.3

Every window and panel within a window may be resized. Place the mouse cursor on a window or panel border and it changes to a double headed arrow (see right). Click and hold with the LH mouse button (referred to as LMB from now on) and drag the arrow to resize the panel or window. This works on both horizontal and vertical borders.

Every window may be divided to form a new window. In opposite corners of each window there is a small cross hatched triangle, which is a splitter widget (Figure 1.4). When the mouse cursor is placed on the cross hatching, the cursor changes to a white cross. Click, hold, and drag the cross into the window and the window divides in two to form identical copies of the original window. One copy may then be changed to another window type as previously described.

Learning
Unit 1

Splitting/Joining/
Extending
Windows

To cancel a window, place the mouse cursor on the cross hatching (it changes to a cross) and drag it out of the window into the window to be canceled (Figure 1.5). A large arrow appears pointing into the window to be canceled. Release the LMB and the window cancels. Before releasing, you can move the cursor from one window to the other and the arrow changes direction accordingly. Releasing the LMB cancels the window into which the arrow is pointing. The individual windows will be explained as you progress through the book but first you need to understand the components of a window in general terms (Figure 1.6).

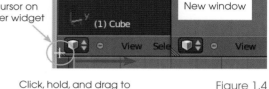

Mouse cursor on the splitter widget

New window

(1) Cube

View   Sele   View

Click, hold, and drag to make a new window.

Figure 1.4

One of the great features of Blender is that the GUI may be modified to suit the preferences of individual users. I have mentioned how to resize windows and panels and how to split and cancel windows, but there are many other features that can be changed. At this stage I will demonstrate an example just to show how this is done. The possibilities are endless, so like many things in Blender, you will have to experiment and try these options for yourself. The following example will introduce you to the user preferences window.

Figure 1.5

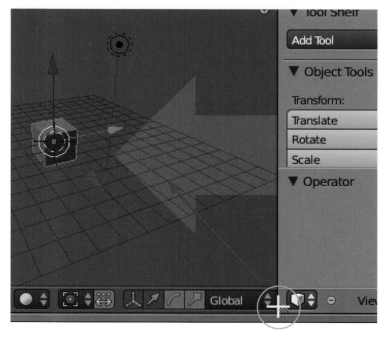

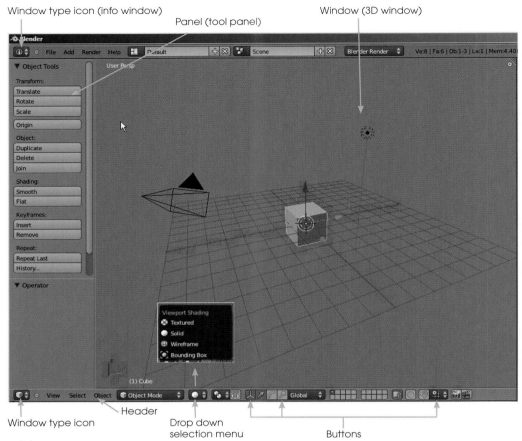

Window type icon (info window)

Panel (tool panel)

Window (3D window)

Window type icon

Header

Drop down
selection menu

Buttons

Figure 1.6

1.2 The User Preferences Window

If you find it difficult to see things on the screen, especially against Blender's sultry dark 3D window background, you can fix it. Divide the 3D window in two (see the previous instructions) and make one part the user preferences window by clicking the window type icon; or, you can go to the info window header, click on "File" then click on "User Preferences Window." In the latter scenario, Blender opens an overlapping version of the user preferences window—this is the only time that Blender opens one window over another.

Go to the top of the window (Figure 1.7) and click on "Themes." At the LHS of the window you can see a list of the different windows. Click on "3D View." You will see a series of colored panels with headings next to them. At the bottom of the first column you will see "Window Background." This is a gray colored panel, which is the color of the 3D window background. Click on the panel and a color picker will display (Figure 1.8).

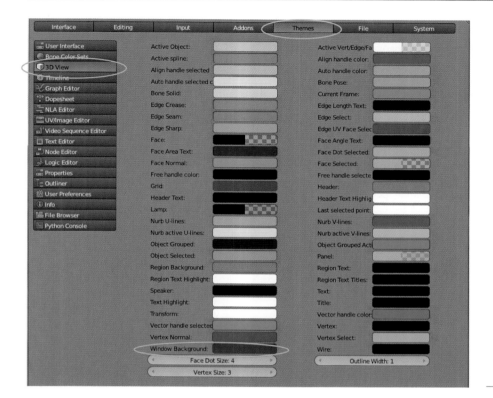

Figure 1.7

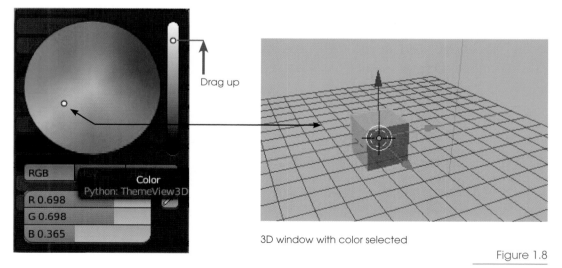

3D window with color selected

Figure 1.8

At the RHS of the picker is a vertical bar showing a color gradient from white at the top to black at the bottom with a white dot in the middle. Click the LMB on the dot and drag, while holding the button. Move the dot upwards, and you'll see the background color of the 3D window lighten up (the color picker also lightens up). You can click the LMB anywhere in the colored circle to change the 3D window background to any color you like. You can also change the color by altering the RGB values (click the LMB on either the R, G, or B value and the text changes to white, which indicates that it is editable). Press delete to delete the value and retype a new value. A second click before deleting will place a blue text cursor, which allows individual numbers to be edited. You may also click and drag the slider. The background color will remain set for the remainder of the session. You can now close the user preferences window. If you want to set the background color permanently, click on "Save As Default" at the bottom of the user preferences window; this will change the background color for the next time you start Blender.

> Note: When you press "Save As Default" in the user preferences window, you obviously have the user preferences window open. Blender takes the command literally and assumes that you want the user preferences window displayed the next time you open Blender. If you don't want this to happen, close the user preferences window without clicking "Save As Default" by clicking and dragging on the cross hatch in the corner as previously described. In the info window header click on "File" then "Save User Settings."

If you nose around the user preferences window, you will see that there are many options. Feel free to experiment. If you goof up when changing the themes, just press "Reset to Default Theme" at the bottom of the window—this puts everything back to square one. Remember to close the user preferences window and click "Save User Settings" in the info window header. *If you change settings in other panels of the user preferences window, make sure you record the changes you have made. The other panels do not have a reset button.*

1.3 Preset Interface Arrangements

While still on the subject of GUIs I will point out that Blender has some preset arrangements for working on different aspects in the program.

In the info window header at the top of the default screen arrangement to the RH of the "Help" button, there is a little window button with "Default" in the panel. "Default" is referring to the default Blender screen arrangement or GUI. Placing the mouse cursor over the window button displays "Choose screen layout." Clicking on the button displays a drop down selection menu with a choice of screen arrangement options. You will see that "Default" is highlighted in blue (Figure 1.9). Clicking on any of the options changes the screen arrangement with window types appropriate for the named aspect of the program.

Figure 1.9

Window button

Search bar: type in a word to search

1.4 The 3D Window

Learning Unit 1

3D Editor Viewport Window

Before we can actually create anything in Blender we should understand the 3D window. First, we should understand the basic concept of creating something with computer graphics. A scene is created; the scene may be static or animated. In either case, the scene is rendered. The render produces a computer image in the case of a static scene or a computer animation in the case of an animated scene. Images are rendered to a number of file formats such as JPEG or PNG while animations are rendered into video files. The scene is set up in the 3D window.

The default 3D window in Blender is shown in Figure 1.10. The widow panels have been colored to distinguish them. The 3D window comprises a main window panel and a side object tools panel. The 3D window header is the strip across the bottom of the window with all the buttons. The default 3D window contains a cube object, a lamp, and a camera. Without the lamp or camera, nothing will render.

The object tools panel can be hidden from view by pressing the T key on the keyboard. Press the T key again to show the object tool panel; this process is referred to as toggling. You can also drag the edge of the panel to close it.

Besides the object tools panel, there is the object properties panel, which by default is hidden. Press the N key or the expansion icon to show the panel. Here you will see values pertaining to the object that is selected in the 3D window (Figure 1.11).

Note: With the objects tool panel and the objects properties panel hidden, a small tab with a cross is displayed in the upper corners of the 3D window; this is the expansion icon. Clicking the LMB on these will also display the panels.

Object tools panel →

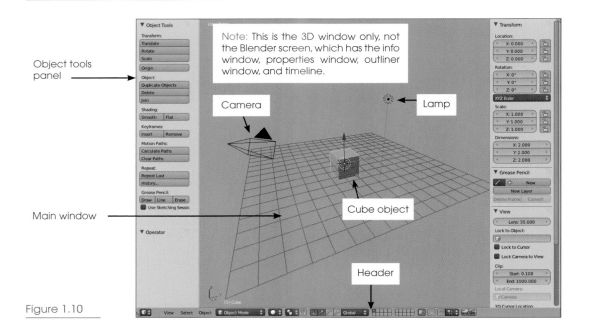

Note: This is the 3D window only, not the Blender screen, which has the info window, properties window, outliner window, and timeline.

Camera

Lamp

Main window →

Cube object

Header

Figure 1.10

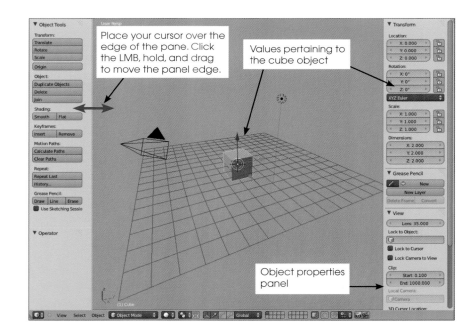

Place your cursor over the edge of the pane. Click the LMB, hold, and drag to move the panel edge.

Values pertaining to the cube object

Object properties panel →

Figure 1.11

1. *The Blender Interface*

By default, the cube is selected as shown by the orange outline around the cube. An object is deselected by pressing the A key and selected by clicking on it with the right mouse button (RMB). Note that if you deselect an object, then press the A key a second time, you will select everything in the 3D window.

Try it out: Press the A key to deselect. Click the RMB on the camera. Press the A key to deselect again. Click the RMB on the cube (this selects the cube again).

Note also that with the object properties panel displayed, the values change according to which object you have selected. At this stage do not be concerned with the values; we are just becoming familiar with the broad outline of the interface.

Remember that in the 3D window we are seeing a 3D representation of a world. The squared grid in the scene represents the horizontal mid-plane of the world on the x- and y-axis. The green line on the grid is the y-axis and the red line is the x-axis. The vertical axis is the z-axis. If you look at the lower LH corner of the window you see these axes displayed. You also see in white the name of the object selected.

The red, green, and blue arrows on the cube object are a 3D manipulator for moving the object around on the scene (Figure 1.12).

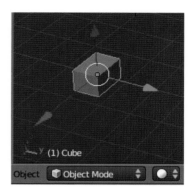

Figure 1.12

This will be discussed in detail later but for now we will use it to move the cube. Click on the green arrow and, while holding the mouse button down, drag the mouse to the right. The cube outline turns white in the process indicating that it is in "Grab" mode. Release the LMB and the cube will stay where it is placed.

We moved the cube so that you can see the small circle with the crosshairs at the center of the world. This is the 3D cursor, not the mouse cursor (Figure 1.13). If you click the LMB anywhere in the scene with the mouse, the 3D

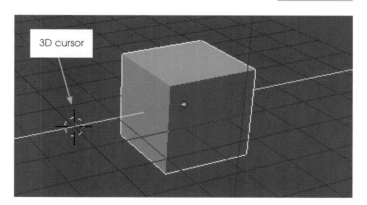

3D cursor

Figure 1.13

cursor relocates to wherever you clicked. If you were to add another object into the scene, that object would be located at the point of the 3D cursor.

The cube object is called a primitive, which is one of ten basic shapes available in Blender from which to commence modeling (Figure 1.14). Click on "Add" in the info window header then place the mouse cursor on "Mesh" in the drop down menu to see the list of primitives.

Learning
Unit 1

Primitive Mesh
Objects

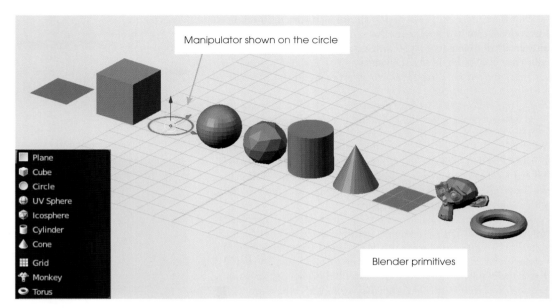

Manipulator shown on the circle

Plane
Cube
Circle
UV Sphere
Icosphere
Cylinder
Cone
Grid
Monkey
Torus

Blender primitives

Figure 1.14

You can click on one to add it to the scene. Another way to do this is to press Shift + the A key on the keyboard to display the same list.

1.5 Window Modes

The 3D window, by default, is opened in object mode. You will see this in the window header. By clicking on the drop down selection menu you are able to select one of the other modes (Figure 1.15). At this stage, we only need be concerned with the edit mode option. Object mode allows us to move, rotate, and scale an object in the scene while edit mode allows us to change the shape of the object.

To change between the two modes, you can select the mode from the drop down in the header. Since it is common to switch between object and edit mode, pressing the Tab key toggles between modes.

Mode:
Weight Paint
Texture Paint
Vertex Paint
Sculpt Mode
Edit Mode
Object Mode

(1) Cube

Object   Object Mode

Click for the drop down menu.

Figure 1.15

With the cube selected in the 3D window and the mouse cursor positioned in the window, press Tab. You will see the object shown with its edges drawn in orange with dots at each corner; these are called vertices (Figure 1.16). The significance of this will be discussed in detail later. For now, toggle back to object mode.

1.6 Layers

Like many other graphics programs, Blender uses layers to aid in constructing complex scenes. Note the display in the 3D window header; this represents 20 separate layers. Imagine sheets of transparent drawing paper with different items on each sheet being placed one on top of the other. Each square represents one sheet. The orange dot in the first square indicates that an object is on the first layer (Figure 1.17). The fact that the first square is shaded tells us that we are looking at the first layer.

To move to another layer, click on one of the squares. It becomes shaded indicating that the layer is being seen in the window. If you click on square 2, the screen shows an empty layer. The orange dot remains in square 1 indicating that there is an object in layer 1 (it is not necessarily selected). Go back to square 1.

To move the cube object to layer 2, first select the cube in the 3D window. Press the M key and the "Move to Layer" window appears. Click on square 2 and the cube is moved to layer 2 as indicated by the orange dot displayed in square 2 in the window header (Figure 1.18). Note there is still a dot in square 1. This shows that there are objects on layer 1 (namely, the camera and the lamp).

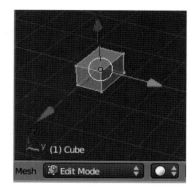

Figure 1.16

Learning Unit 2

Blender Layers

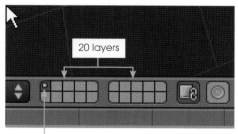

20 layers

The orange dot indicates that an object is in the first layer.

Figure 1.17

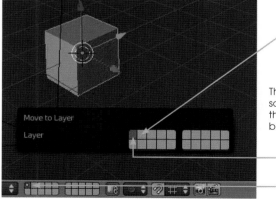

Move to Layer

Layer

Click on square 2 to move the cube to layer 2.

The shaded square indicates that layer 1 is being viewed.

The orange dot shows that the object is on layer 1.

The orange dot will display here when the cube is moved to layer 2.

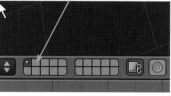

Figure 1.18

To replace the cube in layer 1, click on square 2 in the header, select the cube in the 3D window, press the M key with the cursor in the 3D window, and click on square 1 in the "Move to Layer" window.

1.6.1 Object Tools Tab (Tool Shelf Panel)

The object tools tab contains tools for manipulating objects in the 3D window. What tools are displayed depends on which window mode you are in (e.g., object mode or edit mode). Not all tools are displayed—this is simply to save screen space.

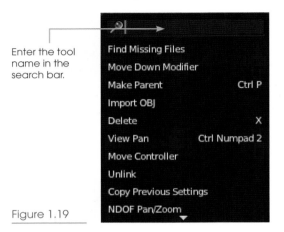

Enter the tool name in the search bar.

Figure 1.19

In earlier versions of Blender 2.5, there is a search bar at the top of the tool shelf where you can enter the name of a tool and it is added to the shelf. In later versions, the tool shelf has become the object tools tab and the search bar has disappeared. The search bar is now accessed by pressing the space bar with the cursor in the 3D window. This displays a drop down menu with the search bar at the top (Figure 1.19).

1.7 Moving in 3D Space

In a 3D program, not only do you have to worry about where you are in two dimensions (height and width), but you also need to consider depth (how close or far away). Before you can work in 3D space, it would be beneficial if you had some skills in 2D drawing and layout. Moving around in the 3D window is controlled by the mouse and the keyboard number pad.

Learning Unit 1

Maneuvering About in 3D Space

The Blender default scene opens in what is termed the user perspective view, which allows you to move objects around in the 3D window. Sometimes it is more convenient and easier to see how far objects are separated by using separate orthographic views. Think of a standard three-view orthographic drawing: top, front, and right side views. These views match up with the 7, 1, and 3 keys on the number pad. Put your cursor in the 3D window and try pressing those numbers keys.

Learning Unit 1

Blender for Laptops

Note: Some laptops do not have number pad keys. In the user preferences window, click on "Input" at the top of the window and then, at the LHS of the window, click "Emulate Numpad." You can now use the number keys on your laptop to emulate the number pad on a standard keyboard.

When moving from the user perspective view to either of the orthographic views, at first you'll get a top, front, or end perspective view (Figure 1.20). Look at the lamp and you should see a line pointing towards the cube. Press on the number pad 5 to get the true orthographic view. Pressing the number pad 5 again toggles back to the perspective view.

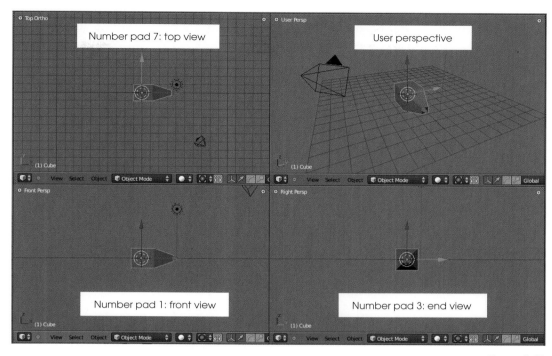

Number pad 7: top view

User perspective

Number pad 1: front view

Number pad 3: end view

Figure 1.20

Pressing the number pad 0 will put you into camera view (which is what the camera sees). To get back to the user perspective view, press the number pad 5 twice. One press gets a user orthographic view and the second press gets the user perspective view. However, you'll notice that it's not quite the same as what we had in the default scene. We need to rotate the view a bit. Click and hold the middle mouse button and wiggle it slightly; you'll see the scene rotating in the window. Wiggle and practice is the best way to learn. This all sounds a bit complicated, but you will soon get used to it.

When you go to camera view (number pad 0), most of the window becomes shaded leaving a small window in the middle with a dotted line around it (Figure 1.21). This is the part that will actually render to an image. Right click on the outer line and it turns orange—this means you have the camera selected. You can now move and rotate the camera like any object in any view. The shading in the camera view is called passepartout and can be removed to let you have a clear view of everything in the scene. I will show you how to do that later.

Learning
Unit 2

Camera View

The number pad arrow keys (2, 4, 6, 8) will rotate you around in 3D space (not in camera view). The + and - keys on the number pad will zoom in and out. The number pad . (period) key will center your view on the selected object on your screen.

The mouse serves a number of functions. Clicking the LMB in the 3D window repositions the 3D cursor in the scene. Wherever the 3D cursor is positioned is where the next

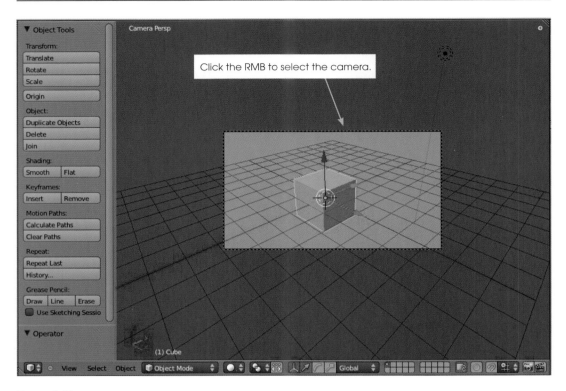

Figure 1.21

object you add to the scene is located. Clicking the RMB on an object selects that object. Similarly, in edit mode, clicking the RMB on a vertex will select that vertex. Pressing the B key on the keyboard then clicking the LMB and dragging a rectangle over an object will select that object. Click the LMB to cancel. Pressing the C key on the keyboard changes the mouse cursor in the 3D window to a circle. Scroll the mouse wheel to change the size of the circle. Position the circle over an object and click the LMB to select the object. Press the Esc key to cancel the circle selection. Click and hold the middle mouse button or mouse wheel and drag to rotate the 3D view. Scrolling the mouse wheel zooms in and out on the scene.

Don't attempt to memorize all the combinations; they will become second nature with practice since they are used over and over again.

1.8 The Blender View Menu

The Blender view menu shows the full range of options to manipulate the view ports (Figure 1.22).

Note: Clicking on the "Toggle Quad View" option displays all four orthographic views in separate windows as shown in Figure 1.20. The keyboard shortcut to select this option is to press Ctrl + Alt + the Q key. Pressing this combination a second time toggles to the front orthographic view. To return to the user perspective view, press the number pad 0 (camera view) then press the number pad 5 twice and rotate the view.

The view menu also shows the shortcut keys for the right, front, and top orthographic views. These are the number pad 1, 3, and 7 keys previously mentioned. Besides these views, the following views are also available:

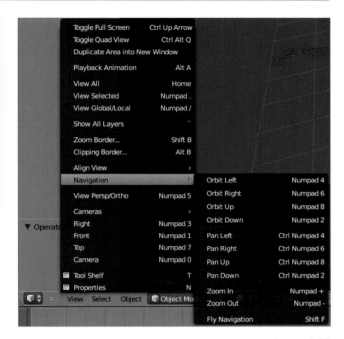

Figure 1.22

- Number pad 7: top
- Number pad 1: front
- Number pad 3: right side
- Number pad 0: camera view
- Ctrl + 7: bottom
- Ctrl + 1: rear
- Ctrl + 3: left side
- The number pad 2 and 8 keys rotate the view about the x-axis.
- The number pad 4 and 6 keys rotate the view about the z-axis
- The number pad period key (.) centers the selected object.
- The number pad forward slash key (/) zooms in on the selected object.
- Hold the Shift + the F key and move the cursor to fly around the scene. Click the LMB to stop.

Note: The numeric keys at the top of the keyboard change the active layers not the viewports, unless the "Emulate Numpad" function has been set for a laptop computer.

1.9 The Properties Window

The 3D window is the place where you set up your scene to see what you are creating and where you are going. The properties window on the other hand is the engine room

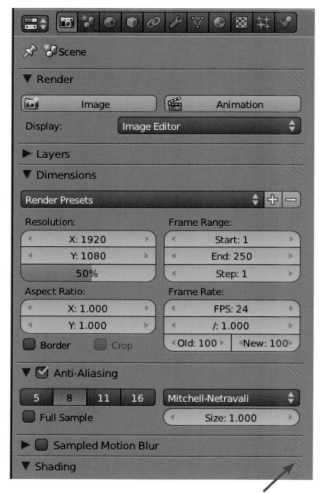

Figure 1.23

Click, hold, and drag the crosshatching up or down to reposition the tabs.

with all the controls that drive everything (Figure 1.23). The properties window is the main part of the vertical panel at the RH of the default screen. It controls what you see in the 3D window, how objects move and behave, and finally how the scene renders. It controls how your artificial world is configured, and how everything in the scene appears, moves, and interacts with everything else.

To get an insight into the properties window in practical terms, look at the row of buttons displayed in the window header. These buttons are the starting point for everything that happens.

Note: In the 3D window, the default cube object is selected as seen by the orange outline. Buttons available in the properties window header vary depending on what is selected in the 3D window. Try clicking the RMB on the camera then the lamp and back on the cube—you will see the buttons in the header change.

By default, Blender opens the properties window in the default screen arrangement with the render button active and with the window containing all the render buttons and values. The render button is seen highlighted in blue. The diagram on the opposite page shows the default properties window header (Figure 1.24).

It is not my intention to describe the function of every button and value in the properties window. The specific operation of buttons and controls will be demonstrated as you progress through this book and even then it will be up to you to experiment and record as you go.

Clicking on each of the buttons in the header changes the display of buttons and controls in the main window. The buttons and controls are separated into panels called tabs. Some tabs are open and some are closed. Clicking on the little triangle in front of the tab name toggles the tab open or closed. With some buttons selected there are too many tabs to fit in the window. When this happens, a scroll bar appears at the RHS of the window.

Figure 1.24

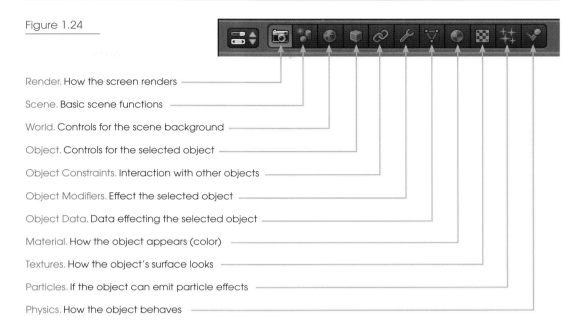

Render. How the screen renders

Scene. Basic scene functions

World. Controls for the scene background

Object. Controls for the selected object

Object Constraints. Interaction with other objects

Object Modifiers. Effect the selected object

Object Data. Data effecting the selected object

Material. How the object appears (color)

Textures. How the object's surface looks

Particles. If the object can emit particle effects

Physics. How the object behaves

The properties window may be resized by dragging the border and may be changed to another window type if required. The location of the tabs in the properties window can be rearranged by clicking and holding the crosshatched area at the upper RHS of the tab and dragging it up or down in the stack.

1.10 Blender Controls

Up to this point I have assumed that you are familiar with the use of the keyboard and mouse and the input of data to the computer via these devices. Blender uses a system of controls employing the keyboard and mouse as follows:

Learning
Unit 1

Blender Controls

- Button control. Activated by positioning the mouse cursor over the button and clicking the LMB. Button controls either perform a direct action or activate a secondary function. For example:
  – With an object selected in the 3D window, clicking on the delete button in the tool panel requires you to click on a "Delete – OK" button to delete the object.
  – Clicking on the scale button in the tool panel requires you to drag the mouse cursor in the 3D window to scale the selected object.

Most button controls are duplicated by keyboard shortcut keys. For example:

- Pressing the X key on the keyboard with an object selected prompts the "Delete – OK" button.

- Pressing the S key and then dragging the mouse cursor scales the object.

Checking (ticking) the button controls require you to click the LMB in a small square to place a tick, which activates a function. Clicking a menu selection button displays a drop down menu that requires a selection by clicking the LMB on an option. This activates a function.

- Slider controls. Activated by three separate methods:
  - Click the LMB with the mouse, hold, and drag right or left to change a value.
  - Click the LMB on the arrows at either side of the slider to incrementally alter a value.
  - Click the LMB on the value displayed in the slider, press the Delete key, retype a new value, and press Enter.

1.11 Blender Windows

The application of the Blender windows will be explained as you progress through the different sections of the manual (Figure 1.25). There are some windows however that require special mention since they have a more general application rather than applying to a specific topic. For that reason, when sticking to the basics, they can be overlooked. They are worth mentioning here to make you aware.

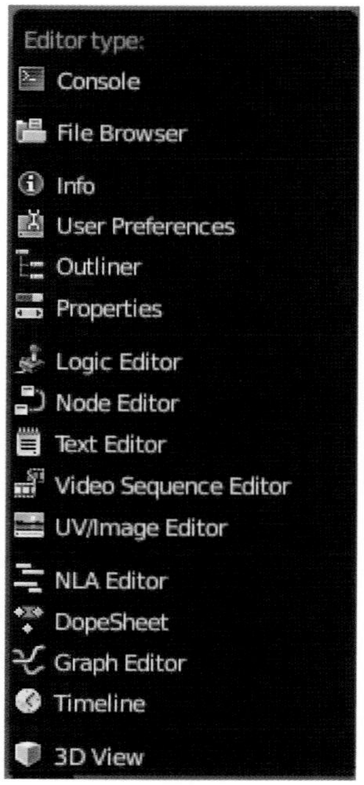

Editor type:
- Console
- File Browser
- Info
- User Preferences
- Outliner
- Properties
- Logic Editor
- Node Editor
- Text Editor
- Video Sequence Editor
- UV/Image Editor
- NLA Editor
- DopeSheet
- Graph Editor
- Timeline
- 3D View

Figure 1.25

1.11.1 Console Window

The console window is where you go if you want to modify the Blender program using Python script (Figure 1.26). Python is the programming language of Blender.

1.11.2 Outliner Window

The outliner window gives you a visual display of everything in your scene and shows how the different items are connected (Figure 1.27). For example, if you click on the little cross next to "Cube" you get "Cube" and if you click again you see that it has a material.

1.11.3 Text Editor Window

The text editor is just that: a text editor (Figure 1.28). When you create something in Blender and save the .blend file to use later, you can write yourself notes in the text editor and what you write will be saved in the .blend file. This is very handy for anyone with a bad memory.

Console window

Figure 1.26

Learning
Unit 2

Outliner Editor

Outliner window

See the website's supplements
page for more details about
the outliner window.

Figure 1.27

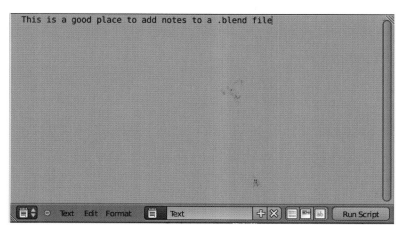

Text editor window

Figure 1.28

1.12 Add-Ons

In order to minimize some of the selection options in various parts of the Blender interface, some features have been put aside in a repository. You could say they have been hidden away, so I will tell you where to go looking if you can't find something. These features are listed in the add-ons directory in the user preferences window and may be activated and deactivated depending on what you are doing (Figure 1.29).

Figure 1.29

See the supplements page for more detailed information on installing add-ons.

This example shows the activation of an add-on. In the 3D window, Shift + the A key is pressed to add an armature. Without the add-on, only "Single Bone" is available. With the add-on ticked, "Human (Meta-Rig)" is added to the selection. "Rigging: Rigify" is the name of a Python script that adds "Human (Meta-Rig)" to the program. Python is the programming language for Blender.

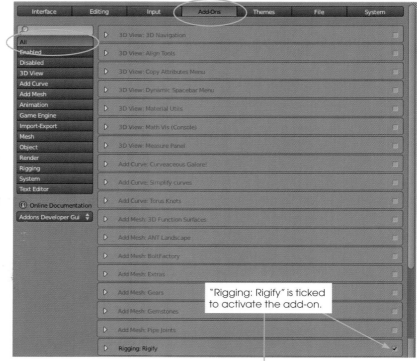

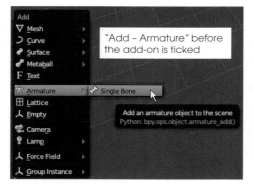

"Add – Armature" before the add-on is ticked

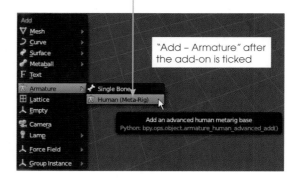

"Add – Armature" after the add-on is ticked

2

Navigation

2.1 Navigate and Save

This section has been titled "Navigate and Save" since it is most important to understand where you are saving your work. As with all computer work, being organized will save you a lot of frustration down the road when you have created many files and want to find something. Blender is all about building up your own library of things that you have created or things that you have downloaded and want to use in future Blender masterpieces.

Learning Unit 2

Opening – Saving – Autosaving Files

It is impossible to teach everything so I will assume that you know how to navigate around your computer system and create places where you store your files (if you are unfamiliar with this, see Section 2.2 on Windows Explorer). In a Windows system, Windows Explorer is an invaluable tool for doing just that. It is recommended that you become familiar with your computer's file system. At some stage you will want to save files, images, web pages, audio files, and obviously your Blender files and movie files.

We will discuss how you navigate in the Blender file browser and save your work to a location of your choice. The assumption is that you have created a file to save and a folder in which to save it. The creation of the folder is where Windows Explorer comes in. As a demonstration, we will use the default Blender scene with the cube object, the lamp, and the camera. I know that is not very exciting but we haven't learned to do anything yet at this stage.

Open Blender with the default scene. In the info window header, click on "File." In the drop down menu that is displayed, you will see "Save" and "Save As" (Figure 2.1).

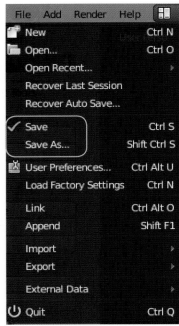

- Use "Save" to save a new file or to save work you have added to a file.
- Use "Save As" to save a copy of a file. You will have to give this a new name if you are saving it in the same folder as the original.

With our new default scene, click on "Save." The Blender file browser window should open with the option "Save Blender File" in the top RH corner of the window. Where you see "untitled.blend" is the name of your file (Figure 2.2). Blender automatically names the file untitled.blend. Click on the name to highlight it, press Delete on the keyboard, then type in a new name and hit Enter. I have named my file Demo.blend. It is good practice to add the ".blend" suffix—older versions of Blender did not automatically add it.

Just above where you have typed the name you will see the file path to where your file will be saved. On my computer this is "c:\temp\." Blender has automatically decided that if I do not say otherwise my file will be saved in the temp folder on the C: drive. You can see there is a previous .blend file already saved to this folder. The temp folder is

Figure 2.1

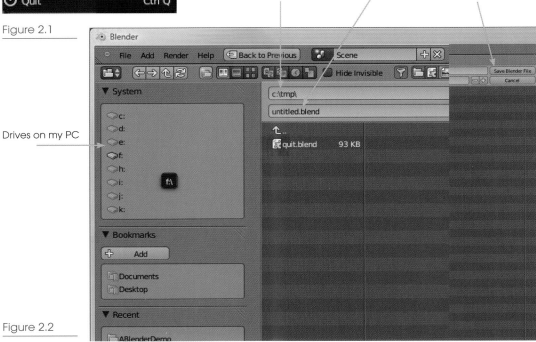

Figure 2.2

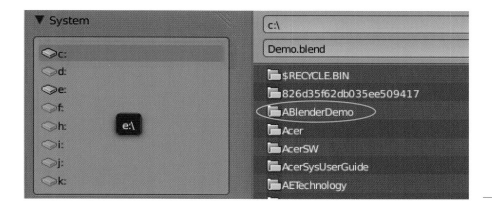

Figure 2.3

not where I want my file to go, so I have made a new folder named "ABlenderDemo" on my C: drive for this new file (Figure 2.3). To navigate to this folder, I go into the system panel at the top LH side of the screen. In the panel you should see all the drives on my computer listed, the top one being the C: drive.

When I click on the "c:" in the panel all the folders on my C: drive display in the main browser window. ABlenderDemo is third from the top of the list. Note that just above where I typed in my file name Demo.blend, "c:\" is displayed. This tells me that I am looking at the C: drive. To put my new file into ABlenderDemo I click on it in the window. The main window is now showing the contents of folder ABlenderDemo, which is empty as it should be since I haven't put anything into it. Now I click on "Save Blender File" at the top RH side of the screen. Blender displays the default blender scene again.

If you have followed these directions on your computer and want to prove that you have saved your file, change the window type to the file browser window. Click on the 3D window header icon and choose "File Browser." And there's Demo.blend in the c:\ABlenderDemo\ folder (Figure 2.4)!

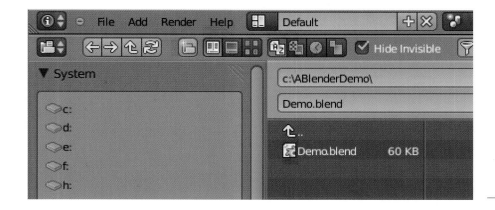

Figure 2.4

Choose how the
files are displayed.

Thumbnails

Figure 2.5

Note: In the Blender default 3D window, the 3D window button/icon is in the lower LH corner of the window in the window header. In the file browser window, the button is in the header at the top of the window at the LHS.

That should keep us out of trouble for the time being as far as saving our work, but it is a good idea to play around and find out what all the buttons in the file browser window do. If you hit on one that says "Create a New Directory," Blender just names it "New Folder," which isn't all that helpful. With "New Folder" newly created, press Delete and retype a new name, then press Enter.

This has been a brief insight into navigating in the file browser window as well as showing how to save your work. Of course you can use the file browser to find other stuff as well. Just click on a folder in the window and it opens showing what's inside. There are some buttons at the top of the window that let you choose how the contents of the folders are displayed (Figure 2.5). One helpful button lets you see files as thumbnails (pictures) so if you have photo images you can see them from within Blender (Figure 2.6).

Figure 2.6

2.2 Windows Explorer

Let's make a folder where we can save our stuff. Open Windows Explorer. There are several ways of opening Explorer depending on what version of Windows you are using. You can usually find the application by clicking the "Start" button, clicking open "All Programs" and going to "Accessories." Windows Explorer is usually in Accessories. You could have a quick start icon somewhere else.

If your computer is like mine it persists in opening Widows Explorer showing my "Documents" folder (Figure 2.7). You can save your stuff there but it will soon accumulate and get all mixed in with your letters to Grandma and the Tax Man. This is not a good thing.

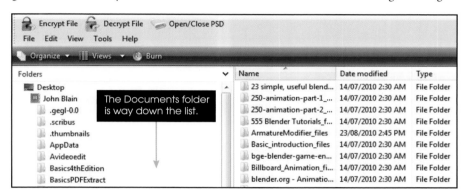

Figure 2.7

We will make a new folder in the C:\ drive. Close the folder list and get back to the basic directory (Figure 2.8). Right click on your C:\ drive and in the drop down that displays, click on "New" and then click on "Folder" (Figure 2.9). Windows enters a new folder and names it "New Folder." At this stage you can edit the name. Press Delete to delete "New Folder" and type in your

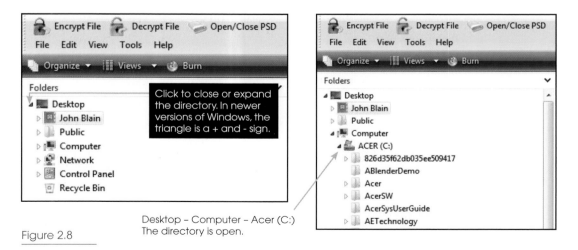

Figure 2.8

Desktop – Computer – Acer (C:)
The directory is open.

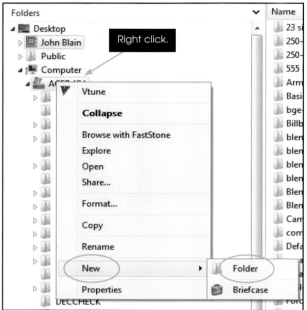

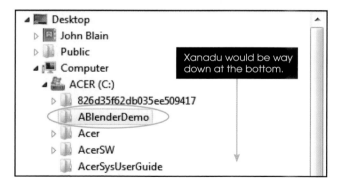

Figure 2.9

Figure 2.10

Learning Unit 5

Appending and Linking Blender Files

new name. I have named my folder "ABlenderDemo" (Figure 2.10). I have put the A at the beginning of the name so that Windows will put it at the top of the directory list. If I named it "Xanado" it will go way down the bottom. When you have typed in your name, press "Enter" and you have a new folder.

IMPORTANT: Remember your folder name and where it is located. This will make your life easier later on.

2.3 The Append or Link Command

When you want to insert elements from one Blender (.blend) file into another, you can select the "Append" or "Link" commands from the file pull-down menu in the info window header (Figure 2.11).

"Append" takes data from an existing file and adds it to the current file. "Link" allows you to use data from an existing file in the current file but the data remains in the existing file. The data cannot be edited in the current file—if the data is changed in the existing file, the changes show in the current file the next time it is opened.

Selecting "Append" or "Link" opens the file browser window allowing you to navigate to the Blender file you wish to select elements from. You can append anything from cameras, lights, meshes, materials, textures, scenes, and objects. For most purposes, use the object option. By appending objects, any materials, textures, and animations that are linked to that object will automatically be imported with the object. Clicking the LMB on an object will select it. Pressing the A key will deselect. After you select your objects to append, click

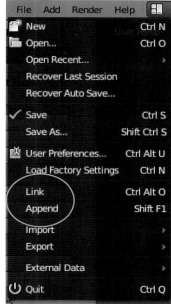

Figure 2.11

the "Link/Append from Library" button in the upper right corner of the screen (Figure 2.12).

2.4 Packing Data

If you plan to open a Blender file on other computers, you will need to select the "Pack into .blend file" option in the file menu under "External Data" (Figure 2.13). Textures and sounds are not automatically included in your Blender file in order to keep the file size down. Every time your file opens, the textures and sounds are placed into your file. If the files can't be found, you won't have any textures and sounds. If you pack the data, those files are included with the .blend file so they can be opened anywhere. Remember, your file size may become very large. When data is packed, a small package shows up on the top of your screen letting you know that the file is packed. You can also unpack data to bring the file size back down.

1. Click on C:.
2. Click on ABlenderDemo.
3. Click on Object.
4. Click on Cube to select.

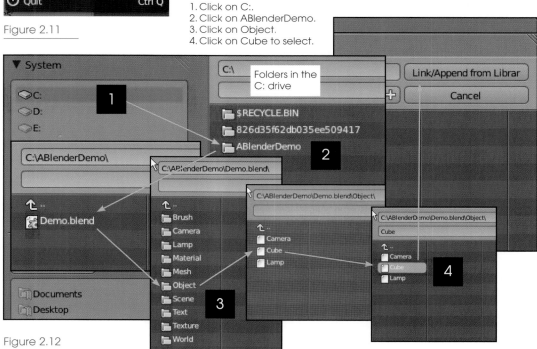

Figure 2.12

Figure 2.13

2.5 Importing Objects

One of Blender's strong points is its ability to accept several generic types of 3D files from other programs. Two examples are:

- The .mxh file format used by the Make Human program, which creates models of the human figure, and
- The .dxf file format used by the Elefont program, which creates 3D solid text models.

Both the Make Human and Elefont programs are freely available.

Other programs save files in one format but also give the option to export in another format. You will have to find the "Export" command in the program and match up the file type with one of the file types in Blender's import add-ons. With every new release of Blender, the import/export format options list changes. This makes Blender compatible with a variety of other 3D modeling and animation software programs.

Note: There are only a few file type options shown in the default selection menu. MXH and DXF are not shown. To conserve space in the GUI, Blender has limited the file type display. MXH and DXF as well as several other file types are available as add-ons in the user preferences window.

To import a MXH or DXF file into a Blender scene, open the user preferences window and click on "Add-Ons" at the top of the window. In the list at the LHS of the window select "Import-Export." A short list of the import/export file types will display (Figure 2. 14). Find the file type you require and place a tick in the box at the RHS of the panel. The ticked file type will now be available in the "Info Window – File – Import" selection drop down menu (Figure 2.15).

Note: When importing Blender files into other Blender files, remember to use the "Append" command instead of "Import." In the "Append" command, select the file, then select what you would like to bring into the current file. You will usually want the objects option.

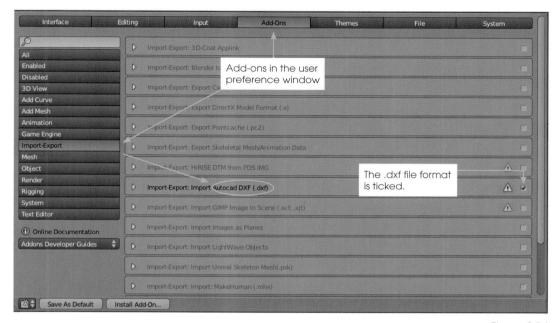

Add-ons in the user preference window

The .dxf file format is ticked.

Figure 2.14

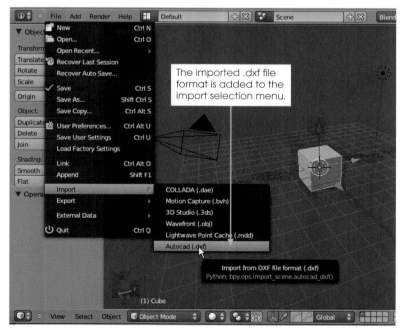

The imported .dxf file format is added to the import selection menu.

Figure 2.15

3

Creating and Editing Objects

3.1 Working with Basic Meshes

Now that we know how to move around in Blender, let's start doing some basic building and shaping. In this section we will talk about creating basic shapes and using modifiers to form them. There are a lot of different types of things to make in Blender; right now we will only discuss meshes.

Start a new scene in Blender and save it in your "Documents" folder. Name it something meaningful and write down the name. You can save your work wherever you like as long as you remember what you named the file and where you saved it. In Windows the "Documents" folder is usually accessible from the desktop so it's easy to find. It's best to be familiar with saving and creating files and folders, so go back and read the section on that subject if necessary.

Note: Blender will not prompt you to save your file when exiting the program. Remember to always save your work often and don't forget the .blend suffix!

3.2 Placing Objects on the Screen

The 3D cursor's location is used to place new objects. Click with the LMB where you want your object located and the 3D cursor locates to that position. When you have the cursor

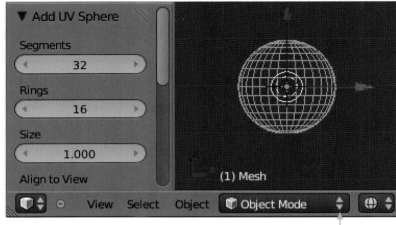

Figure 3.1

Window modes

in a good location, press Shift + the A key to bring up the insert menu. Select "Add," then "Mesh," and select "UV Sphere."

Note: I previously stated that we were discussing meshes. An object in Blender is a mesh object. Think of a sphere made out of chicken wire or fishing net and you get the idea. A sphere in Blender has a mesh with vertical and horizontal divisions called segments and rings: vertical segments like the inside of an orange and horizontal rings (Figure 3.1). The default UV sphere has 32 segments and 32 rings. You can change these by altering the values in the panel at the bottom of the tool shelf, which displays when you add the sphere to the scene. You can keep it at 32.

3.3 Edit Mode and Object Mode

Learning Unit 1

Modeling Modes – Viewport Shading

When you place an object in Blender, it enters the scene in object mode and is selected as shown by its orange outline. There are basically two states in Blender: edit mode and object mode (Figure 3.2). Edit mode is intended for modifying the shape of the object by selecting vertices on the object (vertices are the joining points of the mesh). Object mode affects the object as a whole. The Tab key toggles you between the two modes.

Before entering a new object into your scene, make sure any other objects are not in edit mode, otherwise the objects will be joined. Another way to switch between modes is to use the mode selection drop down menu in the window header. You will see that besides object and edit, there are other modes available (Figure 3.3). The default display mode is solid. In Figure 3.1, which shows the UV sphere with segments and rings, the sphere was drawn in wireframe display mode (Figure 3.4).

3. Creating and Editing Objects

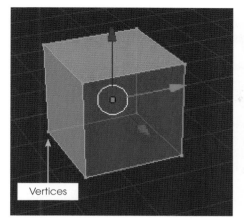

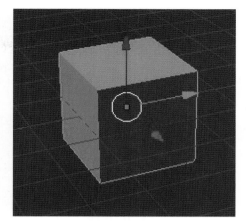

Edit mode   Object mode   Figure 3.2

Window modes

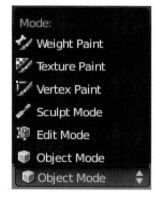

Figure 3.3

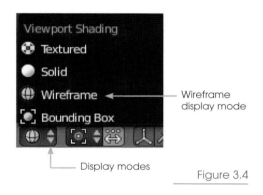

Wireframe
display mode

Display modes

Figure 3.4

3.4 Mesh Types

Press Shift + the A key to reveal the mesh types selection menu. The available mesh types (or primitives) are in Figure 3.5. Primitives are basic shapes from which you can start modeling.

Learning
Unit 1

Primitive Mesh
Objects

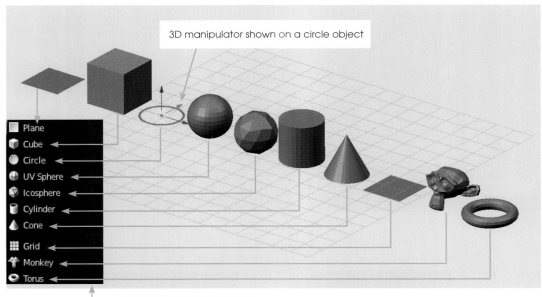

3D manipulator shown on a circle object

Plane
Cube
Circle
UV Sphere
Icosphere
Cylinder
Cone
Grid
Monkey
Torus

Figure 3.5   Mesh types selection menu

Learning
Unit 2

Undo/Redo,
Adding Mesh
Objects in Edit
Mode,
Naming Objects,
Deleting Objects

Learning
Unit 3

Duplication

Figure 3.6

Learning
Unit 1

Moving Objects,
Blender Grid –
Units – Scale,
X, Y, and Z Axis

3.5 Cursor Placement

To precisely place the 3D cursor, use Shift + the S key for options to move the cursor to objects, grids, etc. (Figure 3.6).

3.6 Moving Objects

The three basic controls for moving an object are: G key (grab), S key (scale), and R key (rotate). To move an object freely in the plane of the view, press the G key with the object selected and drag the mouse. To lock the movement to a particular axis, press the G key + X , Y, or Z (Figure 3.7).

Snap

Selection to Grid
Selection to Cursor
Selection to Origin

Cursor to Selected
Cursor to Center
Cursor to Grid
Cursor to Active

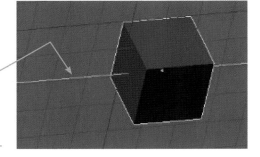

Movement is locked to the
x-axis.

Figure 3.7

3. Creating and Editing Objects

3.7 Scaling Objects

To scale an object freely, press the S key and drag the mouse. To lock the scale to a particular axis, press S key + X, Y, or Z (Figure 3.8).

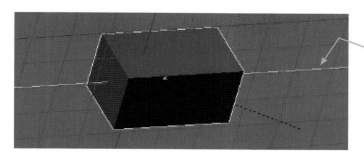

Scale is locked to the *x*-axis.

Figure 3.8

3.8 Rotating Objects

To rotate an object, press the R key and move the mouse about the object's center. To lock the rotation to an axis, press the R key + X, Y, or Z. To rotate a set number of degrees, press R + 30, which rotates the object 30 degrees. R + X + 30 rotates the object 30 degrees about the *x*-axis.

3.9 Precision Manipulation

To manipulate an object in the scene to a precise location, scale, or angle of rotation, alter the values in the object data numeric panel. By default, the panel is hidden in the 3D window. The N key toggles between hide and display. The panel displays at the RH side of the 3D window and the values therein pertain to the object selected in the window (Figure 3.9). To change a value in the numeric panel

- click on the value with the LMB, press Delete, retype the value, and press Enter, or
- repeatedly click on one of the little arrows on either side of the value, or
- click and hold the LMB in the value box and drag the mouse right or left.

3.9.1 Snap and Align Tool

Sometimes it is desirable or essential to accurately position the object or your cursor to a center or grid location. Blender provides a quick shortcut tool for performing these operations. You can view the options from a drop down menu in the 3D window header. Click on "Object – Snap" (Figure 3.10). Alternatively, you can press Shift + the S key to display a selection panel. The selection menu is self-explanatory.

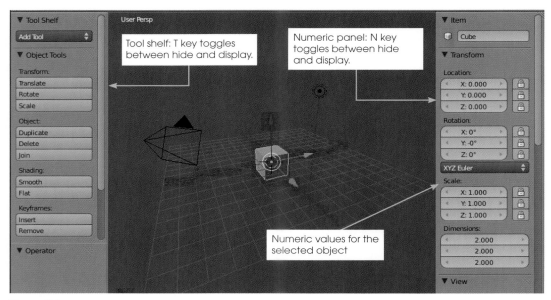

Tool shelf: T key toggles between hide and display.

Numeric panel: N key toggles between hide and display.

Numeric values for the selected object

Figure 3.9

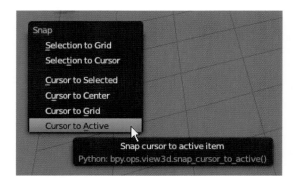

Figure 3.10

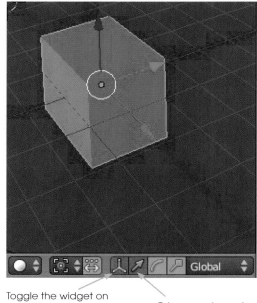

Toggle the widget on and off.

G key = grab mode

Figure 3.11

3. Creating and Editing Objects

3.10 The Transformation Widget

The transformation widget is a handy way of performing the manipulation operations of the G, S, and R keys described previously. By default, the widget is displayed in the 3D window in grab mode (Figure 3.11).

Learning Unit 2

Global & Local Orientation, Center Point (Object Origin), Pivot Points

Clicking on the red, green, or blue handles with the LMB and holding while dragging the mouse moves the object in the window. The widget sometimes obstructs the view but it can be turned off in the window header. The rotate and scale modes are also accessed in the window header (Figure 3.12).

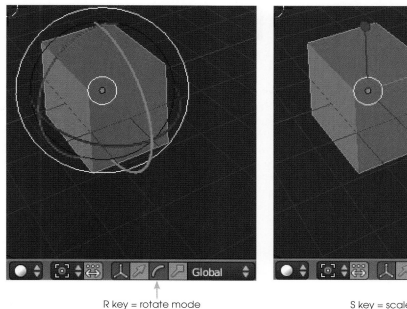

R key = rotate mode

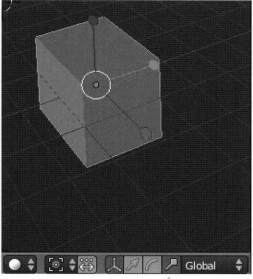

S key = scale mode

Figure 3.12

3.11 Mesh Vertex Editing

After you have added a mesh to your scene in object mode, you can enter edit mode (by using the Tab key) and change its shape (Figure 3.13). In edit mode, you can work with the shape's individual vertices (mesh intersections) to create the shape you want. You know you're in edit mode when you see orange lines and dots on the selected object. When you tab into edit mode, the whole of your selected object is in edit mode with all the vertices selected. By default, edit mode is in vertex select mode.

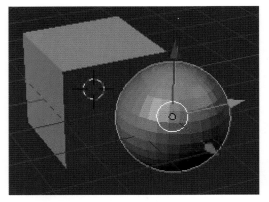 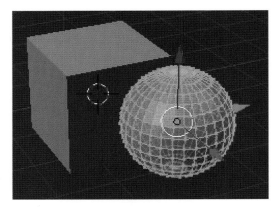

Figure 3.13   Object mode   Edit mode

Learning Unit 3

Selecting Vertices

3.12 Selecting Vertices

While in edit mode, to select a single vertex, first press the A key to deselect all the vertices. In edit mode this does not deselect the object, only the vertices. Click with the RMB on a vertex to select it. To select multiple vertices, hold down the Shift key while using the RMB to click on them. You can also drag a window around the vertices. Press the B key and drag a window to select a group of vertices. Pressing the C key will bring up a circular selection tool. Holding the LMB and dragging the circle selects vertices on the move. The circle can be sized by pressing the + or - keys on the number pad or scrolling the center mouse wheel. Pressing Esc will get you out of the circular selection tool. In order to select all vertices or deselect currently selected ones, press the A key once or twice.

Learning Unit 3

Vertices, Edges, & Faces

3.13 Edit Mode Selection Options

By default, in edit mode, the selection mode is "Vertex." You can also select "Edge" or "Face" (Figure 3.14). These options are available in the window header.

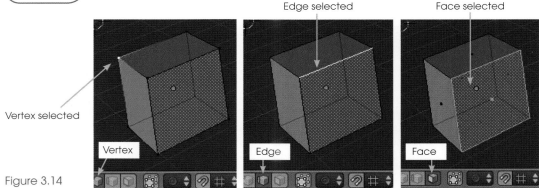

Figure 3.14

3. Creating and Editing Objects

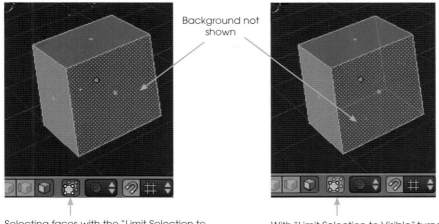

Background not
shown

Selecting faces with the "Limit Selection to
Visible" on will only select the front three
faces of the cube.

With "Limit Selection to Visible" turned
off, all six faces can be selected.

Figure 3.15

Also, by default, only visible vertices or faces are available for selection. This means that you can only select the vertices or faces on the front of an object. Blender has a "Limit Selection to Visible" function, which allows you to only see the front surface and only select vertices or faces on the front (Figure 3.15). This function is toggled on and off in the window header.

Learning Unit 3

Selecting Edges, Selecting Faces, Vertex – Edge – Face Menus & Search

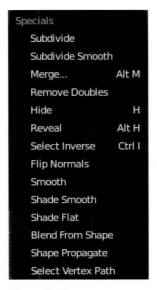

Figure 3.17

3.14 Creating Vertices

Sometimes you need to add more vertices to some or all of the mesh in order to create detail. To do this, you must first select all the vertices in an area that you wish to add vertices to, then go to the tool shelf at the LH side of the screen (using the T key toggles between hide and display) and find the "Subdivide" button (Figure 3.16). Click it as many times as you need to divide the area selected. You can of course subdivide the whole mesh object in this way.

To add individual vertices, in edit mode simply click the LMB while holding Ctrl.

3.14.1 Specials Menu

In edit mode, pressing the W key will bring up a shortcut menu that will give you a variety of editing options (Figure 3.17). Most of these options can also be selected in the tool shelf.

Learning Unit 3

Subdivide

Figure 3.16

3.14. Creating Vertices

Figure 3.18

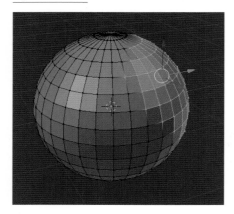

Figure 3.19

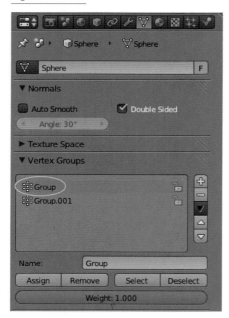

3.14.2 Creating Vertex Groups

Sometimes you will want to manipulate a group of vertices. You can select multiple vertices on an object and manipulate them, but once deselected you may have trouble selecting the exact same group the next time you want them. You can assign multiple vertices to a designated group for reselection. Working through this example will give you the idea.

Start the default scene and replace the cube with a UV sphere. Zoom in on the scene to give a better view (press the number pad + sign). Tab to edit mode and then press the A key to deselect the vertices. Press the C key for circle select (scroll the mouse wheel to adjust the circle size) and with the mouse drag the circle over the sphere to select a bunch of vertices (Figure 3.18). Press Esc to cancel the circle selection. The vertices remain selected.

In the properties window – "Object Data" button – "Vertex Groups" tab, click on the + sign to create a vertex group data slot. By default, this will be named simply "Group" (Figure 3.19). You can change the name to something meaningful if you wish by clicking on "Group" in the "Name" slot, deleting it, and retyping a new name. With the bunch of vertices still selected on the sphere, click on the "Assign" button in the "Vertex Groups" tab—this assigns the selected vertices to "Group." By clicking on the "Select" and "Deselect" buttons, you will see the vertices on the sphere being selected or deselected, respectively. Deselect the vertices and repeat the circle select with a different bunch. Click on the + sign again in the "Vertex Groups" tab and you should see a new data block created named "Group.001." Click the "Assign" button to assign the new bunch of vertices to "Group.001." Deselect the vertices on the sphere in the 3D window, and you can now select "Group" or "Group.001."

3.15 Center Points

Every object you create in Blender has a small dot somewhere in the center (by default, usually in the center geometry of that object). This is the object's center, or pivot point (Figure 3.20). Beginners in Blender often move these center points to locations other than where they want them. This happens because

they move all the vertices of the object in edit mode, but the center point fails to move. If you want to move an entire object, hit Tab to get out of edit mode and into object select mode. Using the G key to move the object in object mode will move the center point along with the object.

     3. Creating and Editing Objects

Figure 3.20

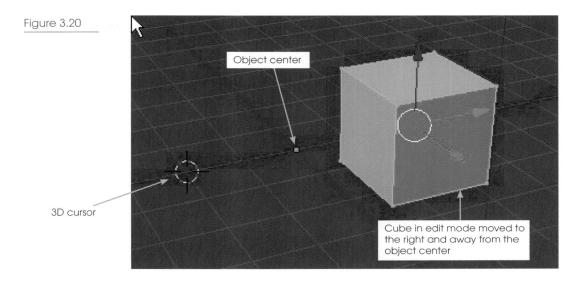

Figure 3.21

If you ever need to relocate an object's center point, move the 3D cursor to the desired center location. In object mode, click on "Object" in the window header, then "Transform," then "Origin to 3D Cursor" (Figure 3.21). This will move the center point to the cursor. Now repeat the process selecting "Geometry to Origin," which moves the vertices to the center.

3.16 Object Display

Usually by default, the selected object in the window is set to "Solid Shading." Many times, you will need to work with your objects in wireframe mode. All shading does is change the way you see your objects. Shading also affects the way you can select vertices in edit mode. In solid shading, only visible vertices can be selected. In wireframe, all vertices can be selected. To change between solid and wire modes, press the Z key or select the shading mode from the header toolbar (Figure 3.22). You will notice several other shading options in the menu; experiment with the other options.

Figure 3.22

3.17 Smooth and Flat Shading Options

As you add objects and view them in solid shading, you will notice that circular objects are not displayed smoothly. In the tool shelf you will see two buttons under the heading "Shading." Clicking these buttons either smoothes the object or reverts it to flat shading (Figure 3.23). These buttons not only affect the way things look on the screen, but how they will be rendered in a final image. Be aware that the appearance of objects on the screen are not displayed at the same quality as a final rendered image. The computer needs to conserve memory because 3D applications can be very memory intensive. There are other smoothing options available in the tool shelf.

Figure 3.23

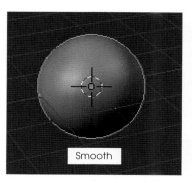
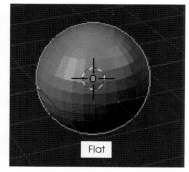

3.18 Extruding Shapes

Shapes can be altered by selecting either a single vertex or a group of vertices (click the RMB, B key, or C key), then clicking the G key to move the vertices, the S key to scale, or the R key to rotate. Click the LMB to leave them in position. Scaling and rotating are relative to the object's center. The G key, R key, and S key are the basic modifiers.

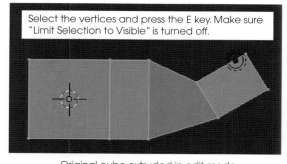

Original cube extruded in edit mode

Figure 3.24

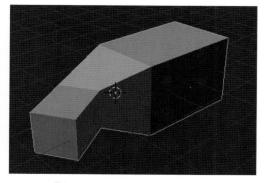

Extrusion rotated in object mode

3. Creating and Editing Objects

A more refined method of altering a shape is by extrusion. Select the vertices as in Figure 3.24 and press the E key while in edit mode. The selected vertices are duplicated and by default placed into grab mode, ready to be moved. Also by default, the movement is confined to a line normal to a plane defined by the selected vertices. This line displays on the screen. Moving the mouse moves the vertices along the line. If you want to freely move the vertices, click the middle mouse button (MMB) and then move the mouse—the MMB might be a scroll wheel, but it should also be clickable. The vertices will follow wherever you go. You can constrain the extrusion to the *x*-, *y*-, or *z*-axis of the scene by pressing the E key + X, Y, or Z. Clicking the LMB when you have finished moving releases the vertices from grab mode, but they remain selected. You can now rotate and scale them; but, in this case, the rotation and scaling takes place about the midpoint of the selected vertex group.

Figure 3.24 is an example of a cube, extruded from the right side several times using scale and rotate. "Basic Extrude" is a great command for making long tubes and tunnels. It is also good when you don't want to subdivide an object too much in order to add detail.

3.19 Proportional Vertex Editing

Proportional vertex editing is used to create a flow in the shape when editing vertices. To turn proportional vertex editing on, press the O key while in edit mode or by selecting the small circle button on the toolbar (Figure 3.25).

Learning Unit 8

Proportional Editing

Note: You will only be able to select this option while in edit mode.

Figure 3.25

You have several options for affecting vertices in proportional editing. I usually use sharp or smooth fall off, but feel free to experiment with the other options.

Turn proportional editing on/off.

Select the type of fall off.

3.20 Creating Ground

You can use proportional vertex editing to create a landscape easily (Figure 3.26). The first thing you need to do is create a plane in the top view (number pad 7). While in edit mode, make sure all vertices are selected (the vertices should be orange)—you can use the A key to select them all. Press the W key for specials menu, then select "Subdivide" or click subdivide in the tool shelf. Do this a few times. Select a single vertex somewhere near the center. Next, switch to a front view (number pad 1) and press the O key to enter proportional vertex editing mode. Select sharp or smooth fall off depending on what effect you want. Press the G key to grab (move) the vertex or drag the arrows on the manipulation widget. Use the scroll mouse wheel to change the size of the proportional selection if you have used the G key. Experiment with different size selections and different fall offs. To see your final work in a smooth display, exit edit mode (Tab key) and, with the object selected, go to the tool shelf and find the "Set Smooth" button. This will smooth the mesh in the display and final output.

Figure 3.26

Ground terrain can be created by subdividing a plane, then selecting a single vertex and moving it up the *z*-axis with the proportional editing tool on with random fall off.

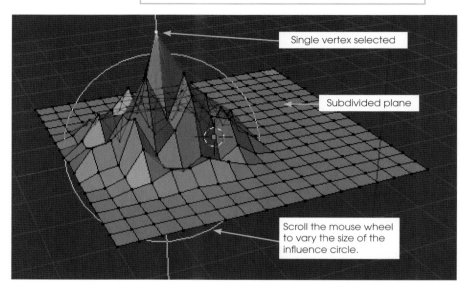

Single vertex selected

Subdivided plane

Scroll the mouse wheel to vary the size of the influence circle.

Learning Unit 4

Loop Cut and Slide

3.21 Edge Loop Selection

When working with vertices, it is sometimes useful to be able to select edge loops. To demonstrate this procedure you will have to create an object like the one shown in Figure 3.27.

Add a circle mesh object to the 3D window and tab to edit mode—the mouse cursor should change to a white cross. Press the E key to extrude but do not move the mouse

Figure 3.27

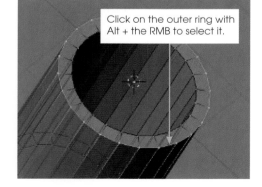

Click on the outer ring with Alt + the RMB to select it.

cursor. Click the LMB on the mouse. You have created a duplicate set of vertices. Now press the S key to scale the duplicated vertices and move the mouse cursor towards the center of the circle. This produces an inner circle. Press the A key twice to deselect the inner circle then select all the vertices. With both circles selected, press the E key (extrude) and move the mouse cursor away from the mesh. By default, the extrusion takes place normally (at right angles to the plane of the selected vertices, which in this case is along the *z*-axis). You should have a mesh object similar to the one shown in Figure 3.28 (left).

To select a circular edge loop from this object, perform the following steps in edit mode: click on the outer ring with Alt + the RMB to select it; press Shift + Alt + the RMB

Figure 3.28

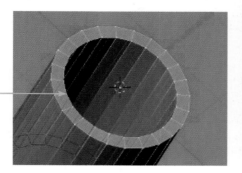
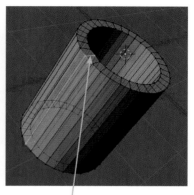

Press Shift + Alt + the RMB to add the inner circle of vertices to the selection.

Click on the edge with Alt + the RMB to select the loop.

to add the inner circle of vertices to the selection. To select a longitudinal edge loop, click on the edge with Alt + the RMB to select the loop, as seen in Figure 3.28 (right).

3.21.1 Basic Modifiers

After selecting vertices, edges, or faces, you can use the basic tools we talked about earlier (G to grab or move, S to scale, and R to rotate) (Figures 3.29 and 3.30).

> Note: An alternative to the G key + mouse drag is to click on one of the transformation widget handles, hold the mouse button, and move the mouse (Figure 3.29).

Figure 3.29

Widget handle: red, green, or blue arrow

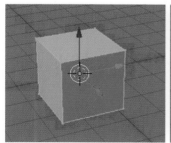
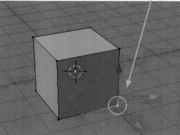
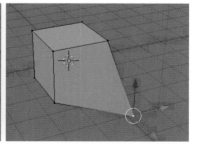

Default cube object: all vertices are selected

Single vertex selected: click the RMB on the vertex

Single vertex translated: press the G key + drag the mouse or click and drag the widget handles

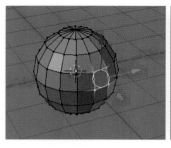

Four vertices selected in a UV sphere: hold Shift + click the RMB

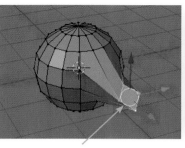

Vertices translated: G key + drag the mouse, or click on the translation widget

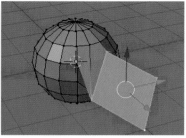

Vertices rotated: R key + move the mouse

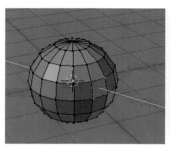

Vertices are extruded along an axis normal to the plane of the selected vertex group.

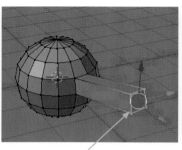

Four vertices selected: E key to extrude + drag the mouse

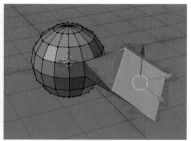

Vertices rotated: R key + move the mouse

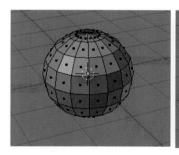

UV sphere in face select mode

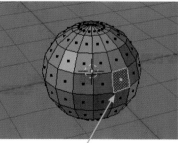

Single face selected: click the RMB

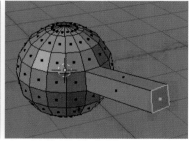

Face extruded: E key + drag the mouse

Note: The transformation widget is turned off in this face select mode example.

Figure 3.30

3.22 Joining and Separating Meshes

To join two or more meshes together, hold down the Shift key and click the RMB to select them, then press Ctrl and J to join them. They will retain any materials you have placed on them, but they will be one object (Figure 3.31).

In order to break up a mesh, you need to be in edit mode (Tab key) and select the vertices you wish to separate from the rest of the mesh (Figure 3.32). With the vertices selected, type the P key (partition) and click on "By Selection." You also have an option to separate "By Loose Parts," which means separating objects that were added while an object was in edit mode. "Separate By Material" separates vertex groups with different colors assigned.

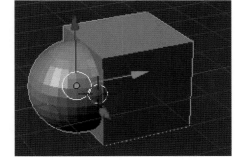

> Note: Pressing the P key in object mode deletes the scene background. Press Esc.

Figure 3.31

Figure 3.32

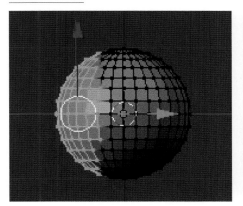

Vertices selected

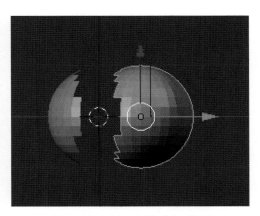

Separated: P key + "By Selection"

3.23 Deleting Vertices, Edges, or Faces

If you want to make a hole in a mesh, select the vertices, edges, or faces you wish to remove, then hit the Delete key.

3.24 Adding Faces

Learning Unit 4

Rip Tool

Sometimes you need to fill in holes in a mesh by creating your own faces. To do this, go into edit mode and select the vertices you wish to face together (you are limited to four vertices in

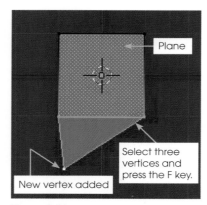

Plane

Select three
vertices and
press the F key.

New vertex added

Figure 3.33

a group). With vertices selected, hit the F key; a face will be formed. Figure 3.33 is an example. A simple plane object has been added to the scene. In edit mode, a single vertex is added (Ctrl + click the LMB). Shift select or box select two vertices on the plane and the new vertex and press the F key (face).

3.25 Modifiers

Mesh objects can have their shape modified by using Blender's modifiers. Modifiers are accessed from the properties window on the RH side of the screen. With the object selected in the 3D window, go to the properties window – "Object Modifiers" button and click on "Add Modifier" to display the modifier selection menu (Figure 3.34). A modifier may be selected from the menu to change the shape of an object. As you can see, there are a number of modifiers to choose from. At this stage we will demonstrate a few; for more on modifiers, see Chapter 12.

Note: After selecting a modifier and adjusting values to produce the desired effect, click on the "Apply" button to permanently apply the modification to the object. The modifier panel in the properties windows cancels.

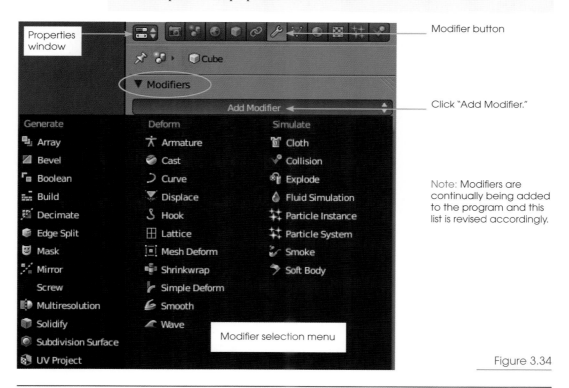

Figure 3.34

Figure 3.35

Cube with a bevel modifier added

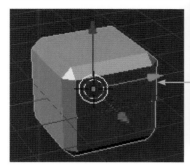

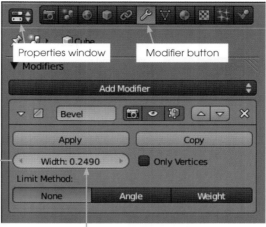

Change the value to increase/decrease the bevel.

3.25.1 Bevel Modifier

The bevel modifier replaces edges and/or vertices with an angled slice that "rounds" them (Figure 3.35).

Learning Unit 6

Bevel Modifier

3.25.2 Subdivision Surface Modifier

The subdivision surface, or subsurf, modifier subdivides the faces of an object to make it appear smoother/rounder (Figure 3.36).

Figure 3.36

Cube with a subsurf modifier added

View: 1 = 4 divisions

View: 0 = cube

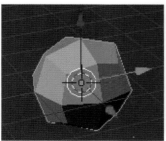

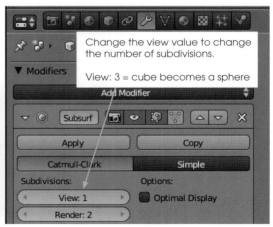

Learning Unit 8
Mirror Modifier

3.25.3 Mirror Modifier

Sometimes when creating a complex shape, you want it to be symmetrical on either side of a centerline. The mirror modifier is a very useful tool for achieving this. Start a new scene and place the default cube in the front orthographic view (number pad 1 followed by number pad 5). Tab into edit mode and in the tool shelf click on "Subdivide" once.

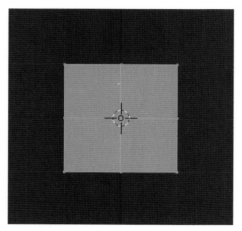

The surfaces of the cube have been subdivided into four squares (Figure 3.37). It is important to note that only the surfaces of the cube are subdivided, not the cube itself.

Still in edit mode, deselect all vertices (A key). Turn off "Limit Selection to Visible." Box select (B key + drag a rectangle) over one side of the cube and delete the selected vertices (X key) so that you are left with half of the cube (Figure 3.38). Tab to object mode. If you rotate the scene (click and hold the center mouse wheel and drag) you will see that you have half an empty box with one side missing. Hit the number pad 1 to get back to front view.

Remain in object mode and go to the properties window – "Object Modifiers" button. Click on "Add Modifier" and select "Mirror" in the drop down menu (Figure 3.39). And you have the solid cube back again! Any modifications you make to the one side of the cube in edit mode will be duplicated on the other side (Figure 3.40). For more on modifiers, see Chapter 12.

Figure 3.37

Learning Unit 6
Boolean Modifier

3.25.4 Boolean Modifier

Boolean operations allow you to cut and join meshes by using other meshes. The operations are implemented by employing Boolean modifiers.

An object selected in the 3D window has a modifier applied to it and the modifier is given the instruction to use another mesh to perform an operation. The operations performed are described as intersection (Figure 3.41), union (Figure 3.42), and difference (Figure 3.43).

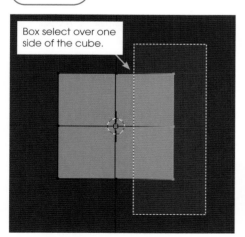

Box select over one side of the cube.

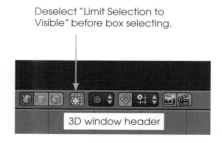

Deselect "Limit Selection to Visible" before box selecting.

3D window header

Figure 3.38

3. Creating and Editing Objects

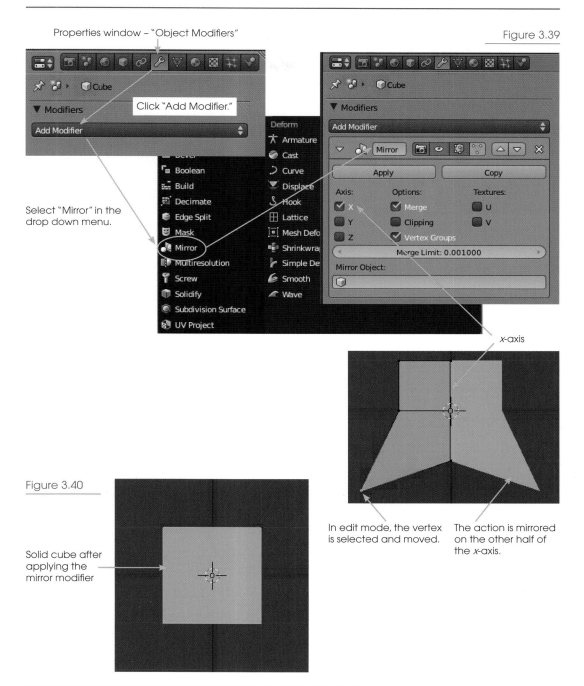

Properties window – "Object Modifiers"

Figure 3.39

Click "Add Modifier."

Select "Mirror" in the drop down menu.

x-axis

Figure 3.40

Solid cube after applying the mirror modifier

In edit mode, the vertex is selected and moved.

The action is mirrored on the other half of the x-axis.

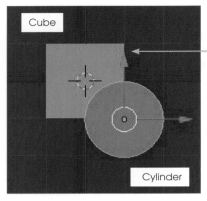

Cube

Cylinder

1. The default cube is in the 3D window with a cylinder object added and positioned as shown.

2. The default cube is selected in the 3D window.

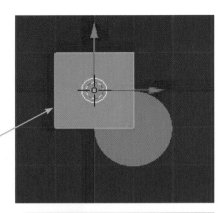

3. With the cube selected, a Boolean modifier is added and the operation type "Intersect" is selected.

4. Click on the little cube and click on "Cylinder" in the drop down menu to select the modifying object.

5. Click the "Apply" button.

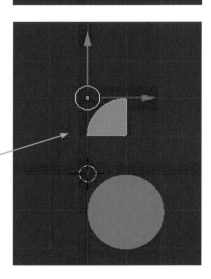

6. Here is the result after applying the modifier and separating the meshes. The original cube has been modified to the shape of the intersection (overlap).

Figure 3.41

3. Creating and Editing Objects

Figure 3.42

The Boolean union type is selected. ────

Here is the result after applying the modifier.

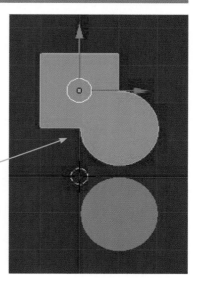

Here is the result after applying the modifier and separating the meshes. The two meshes are joined together.

Figure 3.43

Here is the result after applying the Boolean difference modifier.

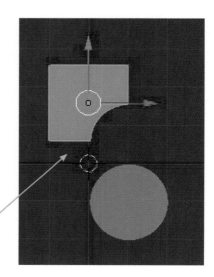

Here is the result after separating the meshes. The overlap of the meshes is subtracted.

Learning
Unit 4

Knife Cut Tool

3.26 The Knife Tool

As Blender is developing, some things seem to disappear from the interface. One such useful tool is the knife tool. The knife tool is used to create additional vertices on the surface of an object while in edit mode. It allows you to add vertices by drawing a line across a series of edges much like subdividing, but limiting the subdivision to a specific region.

As an example using the default cube, tab into edit mode and leave all the vertices selected (the vertices and edges should be orange). Hold down the K key and click and hold the LMB. The mouse cursor turns into a neat little knife (Figure 3.44). Drag the knife over some of the edges on the cube. Release the mouse button and the vertices on the plane are deselected except for new vertices, which have been created where your knife cut the edges. The new vertices may now be manipulated to modify the surface of the cube object.

Figure 3.44

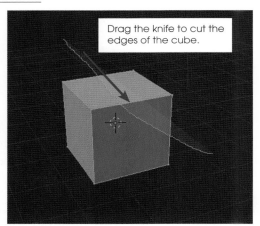
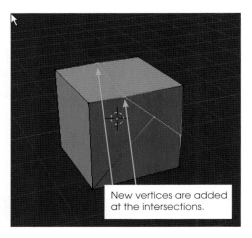

Drag the knife to cut the edges of the cube.

New vertices are added at the intersections.

Learning
Unit 6

Bezier Curve and
Circle – Handles,
Bezier Curve and
Circle – Extrusion,
Bezier Curve
and Circle – Loft
Bevelling Along
a Path,
Bezier Curve and
Circle – Lathe
Bevelling Along
a Path

3.26.1 Bezier Curves and Circles

Blender uses curves—or, to be precise—curve paths in a variety of ways. Objects can be made to follow a curve path in an animation, they can be extruded following the shape of a curve path, or they can be duplicated in a scene and placed along a path. The speed of an object in an animation can be manipulated by altering the shape of a curve in a graph. There are many applications for curves and in particular Bezier curves. The Bezier circle is simply a circular curve joined at the ends.

Curves are added to a scene by pressing Shift + the A key in object mode and selecting "Add – Curves" (Figure 3.45). Bezier curves and circles are of particular importance since they have control handles attached, which facilitate the reshaping of the curve. At first, the method of controlling the shape of the curve can be tricky to grasp especially without some instruction. Run through the following tutorial to get the idea.

In the default Blender scene press the X key followed by "OK – Delete" to delete the cube object. Change to the top orthographic view (number pad 7 followed by number pad 5). Press Shift + the A key and select "Add – Curve – Bezier" to add a Bezier curve to the scene.

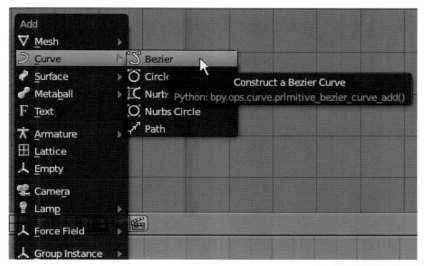

Figure 3.45

Figure 3.46

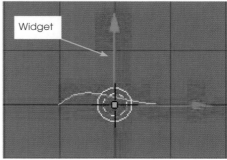

Bezier curves are always added to a scene drawn on the *x,y*-plane—that is, in top view. If you add a curve in front view, all you will see is a straight line. As it is, in top view you see a curved orange line (Figure 3.46); you will have to zoom in to see it properly (press the number pad + key two or three times). As with any object in Blender, the line is selected as shown by the orange color and the transformation widget is active by default. Turn the widget off (Figure 3.47).

To fully appreciate the Bezier curve, we need to be in edit mode; press the Tab key. The curve is now displayed as a black line with a series of chevrons along its length and

Figure 3.47

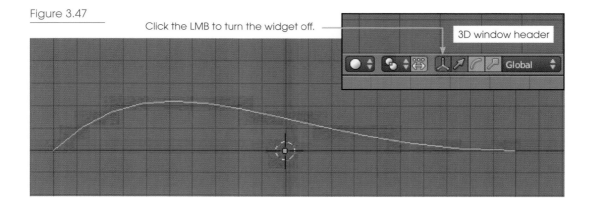

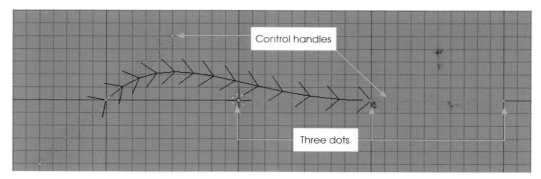

Figure 3.48

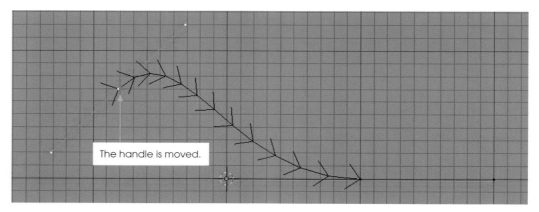

Figure 3.49

colored straight lines located at either end (Figure 3.48). These colored lines are control handles and they are drawn tangential to the curve. The handles are selected as shown by the bright color. Note that each handle has three dots: one at the center and one at either end.

Press the A key to deselect the handles then press the A key again to select. In edit mode, you are selecting and deselecting the handles only, not the curve. Press the A key to deselect the handles and right click on the center dot of the left handle. The whole handle is selected as indicated by the bright color (make note of the white dots). Press the G key and drag the mouse—the handle is moved, reshaping the curve (Figure 3.49). Click the LMB to cancel the movement.

Press the A key to deselect the handle. Right click on the dot at the end of the handle; only one half of the handle is selected as indicated by the bright color. Press the G key + drag the mouse to move the end of the handle rotating about the handle's midpoint and reshaping the curve (Figure 3.50). Click the LMB to cancel the operation.

Right click on the handle's midpoint to select. Press the E key (extrude) and drag the mouse, moving the handle away from the curve (Figure 3.51). The curve is extruded, pro-

Figure 3.50

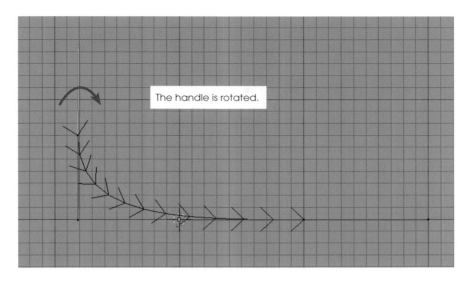

The handle is rotated.

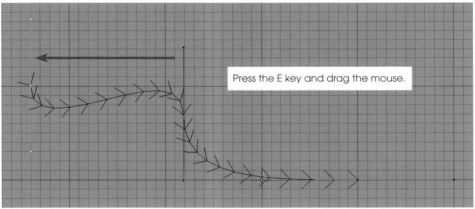

Press the E key and drag the mouse.

Figure 3.51

ducing a curve with three control handles. Press the A key twice to select all handles (the whole curve). In the tool panel at the left side of the window, click on "Subdivide." The curve is subdivided and control handles are added (Figure 3.52).

Any of the handles may be selected and manipulated to change the shape of the curve. Tab to object mode and the whole curve may be translated, scaled, and rotated in the scene.

3.27 Sculpt Mode

The 3D window sculpt mode allows the manual manipulation of mesh vertices. Object surfaces are constructed from a mesh of vertices; by pulling and pushing the mesh, you

Figure 3.52

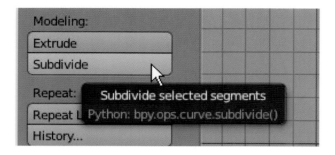

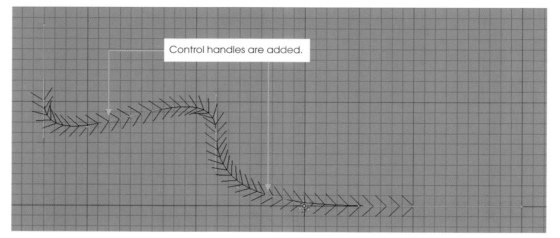

Control handles are added.

modify the surface. It's a bit like modeling a piece of clay or plasticine, only there's no inside to the lump.

To get you started, let's consider a UV sphere. Add a UV sphere object to your scene. Tab into edit mode and in the tool panel at the LHS of the window, click "Subdivide" three times. This will provide plenty of vertices on the surface of the mesh to manipulate. Tab back to object mode.

Change the 3D window from object mode to sculpt mode and change the viewport shading to "Textured" (Figure 3.53). The "Textured" viewport shading lets you see the effect of your sculpting a little better; it has nothing to do with applying a texture. Zoom in to get a nice big view of the sphere (number pad + key).

Take a look at the 3D window in sculpt mode. The only difference between object mode and sculpt mode is that the tool panel at the LHS of the window has changed and the cursor has a circle attached to it (Figure 3.54). For want of a better word, the circle attached to the cursor is called the brush. It is in fact a sculpting tool.

▶ Tab closed

▼ Tab open

The tool panel contains a series of tabs with buttons and sliders for controlling the brush (Figure 3.55). By default, the "Brush Tab" is open. Clicking on the little triangles adjacent to each tab name toggles the tab open or closed (see left). This is purely a space-saving mech-

3. Creating and Editing Objects

Figure 3.53

Tool panel

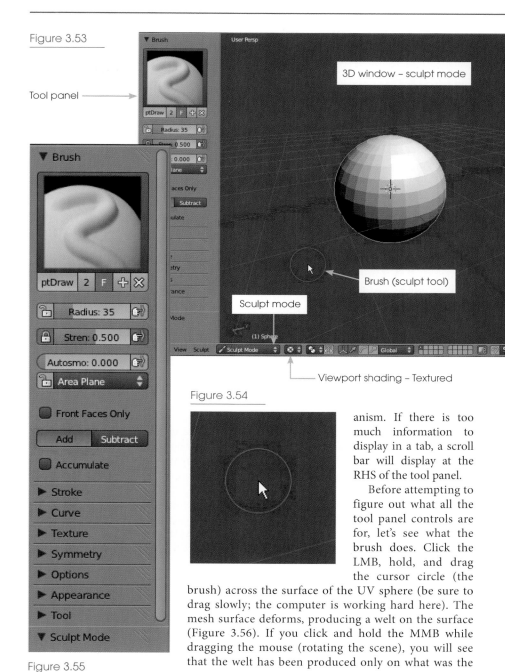

▼ Brush

ptDraw 2 F ➕ ✖

🔒 Radius: 35 ▣

🔒 Stren: 0.500 ▣

(Autosmo: 0.000 ▣

🔒 Area Plane ▲▼

⬤ Front Faces Only

Add | Subtract

⬤ Accumulate

▶ Stroke

▶ Curve

▶ Texture

▶ Symmetry

▶ Options

▶ Appearance

▶ Tool

▼ Sculpt Mode

Figure 3.55

3D window – sculpt mode

Brush (sculpt tool)

Sculpt mode

Viewport shading – Textured

Figure 3.54

anism. If there is too much information to display in a tab, a scroll bar will display at the RHS of the tool panel.

Before attempting to figure out what all the tool panel controls are for, let's see what the brush does. Click the LMB, hold, and drag the cursor circle (the brush) across the surface of the UV sphere (be sure to drag slowly; the computer is working hard here). The mesh surface deforms, producing a welt on the surface (Figure 3.56). If you click and hold the MMB while dragging the mouse (rotating the scene), you will see that the welt has been produced only on what was the

Figure 3.56

Figure 3.57

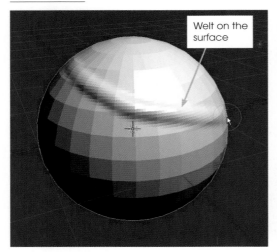

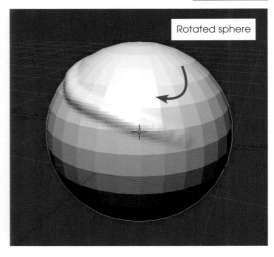

visible surface (Figure 3.57). That is how the brush works, but of course there is much more to it than that.

At the top of the "Brush" tab there is a small window showing part of a sphere with a welt on the surface. By clicking the LMB on the window, a second panel displays showing 19 brush type options (Figure 3.58). You will see that type "F Sculpt Draw" is highlighted in blue, which is the default brush type. Clicking on any of the different types selects that particular type, making it active.

Go to the tool panel and open the "Tool" tab. You should see that the tool type "Draw" is shown as being active. The tool type "Draw" is the same as "F Sculpt Draw." Where you see "Draw" is a drop down menu that lists the same 19 brush type options as before (Figure 3.59). You can select a brush type here as well. Note that below the drop down menu button there are four options for brush selection. Since we are in sculpt mode, the "Brush for Sculpt Mode" is active.

I will attempt to explain some of the control options for the brush. To do this, we will use the default tool type "Draw." There are many combinations of control options for the brush, for which, unless we maintain a common baseline, an explanation would be impossible. Experimenting is the only way to achieve proficiency.

3.27.1 The Brush Tab

The radius slider controls the size of the brush circle. Another way to change the size of the brush circle is to press the F key and drag the mouse (Figure 3.60). Click with the LMB when you have finished dragging.

The strength slider controls the strength of the brush influence on the vertices, the "Add" button pulls vertices away from the surface, and the "Subtract" button pushes vertices into the surface. (See Section 3.27.2 and Figure 3.62.)

Figure 3.58

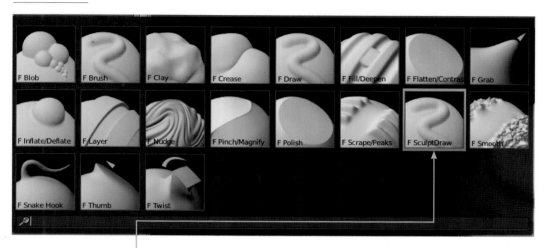

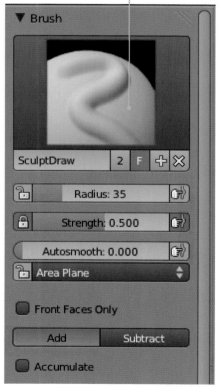

Figure 3.59

Figure 3.60

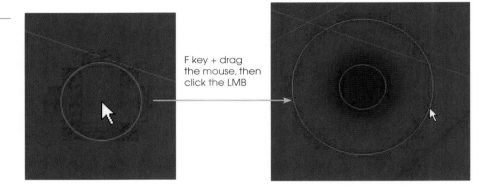

F key + drag
the mouse, then
click the LMB

Figure 3.61

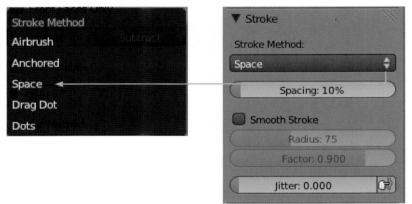

3.27.2 The Stroke Tab

The stroke method drop down menu provides different options (Figure 3.61). Remove the UV sphere and add a plane object to the scene. Subdivide five or six times to produce vertices. You must be in object mode to delete the sphere and then tab to edit mode to subdivide the plane. After subdividing, change back to sculpt mode—make sure you have viewport shading type "Textured" selected.

Clicking the LMB and dragging the brush across the surface of the mesh with "Add" selected in the brush tab deforms the mesh in the positive direction as the brush is moved (Figure 3.62). This applies to all stroke methods. In most cases, dragging over a deformed area produces an accumulative effect even though the "Accumulate" box in the brush tab is not ticked (Figure 3.63). In these screenshots, the brush strength value is 0.963.

Clicking the LMB and dragging with any stroke method produces a deformation with the exception of the "Drag Dot" and "Anchored" methods. With "Drag Dot," the initial deformation upon clicking is duplicated and moved to a new location when the mouse is dragged (Figure 3.64). With "Anchored," the deformation is produced (increased) on the same spot (Figure 3.65).

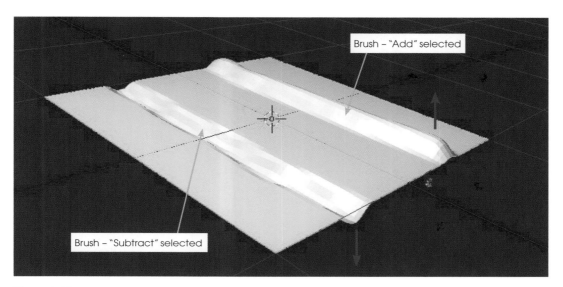

Brush – "Add" selected

Brush – "Subtract" selected

Figure 3.62

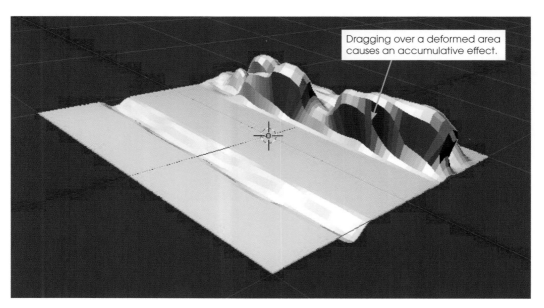

Dragging over a deformed area causes an accumulative effect.

Figure 3.63

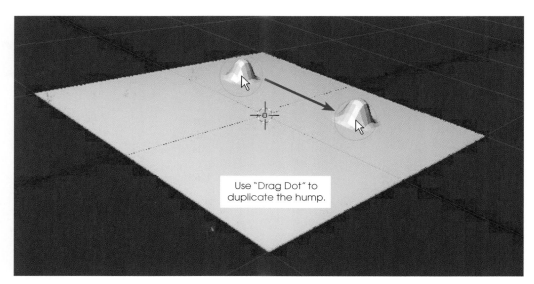

Use "Drag Dot" to duplicate the hump.

Figure 3.64

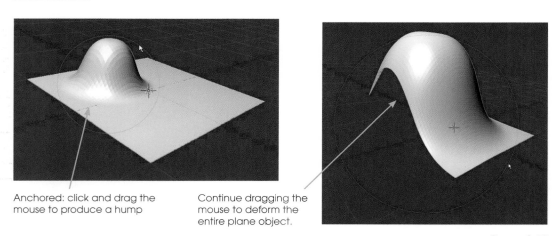

Anchored: click and drag the mouse to produce a hump

Continue dragging the mouse to deform the entire plane object.

Figure 3.65

3.27.3 The Curve Tab

The curve tab is a graphical method of controlling the brush effect. Click and drag the handles (dots) on the curve to reshape the curve or select from the array of quick select options displayed below the curve window (Figure 3.66).

3. Creating and Editing Objects

Figure 3.66

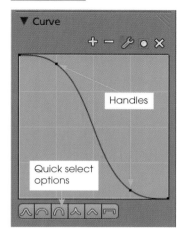

3.27.4 The Texture Tab

See Figure 3.67 for the texture tab drop down menu. Experiment with the different options.

3.27.5 The Symmetry Tab

Ticking X, Y, or Z under "Mirror" results in a deformation produced on one side of an object's axis being reproduced on the other side of the selected axis (Figure 3.68).

3.27.6 The Options Tab

See Figure 3.69 for the options tab drop down menu, which is something else you can explore on your own.

Figure 3.67

3.27.7 The Appearance Tab

Clicking either of the two color bars displays color pickers for changing the appearance of the brush circle in the 3D window (Figure 3.70). This depends on whether you have "Add" or "Subtract" selected in the brush tab.

Figure 3.68

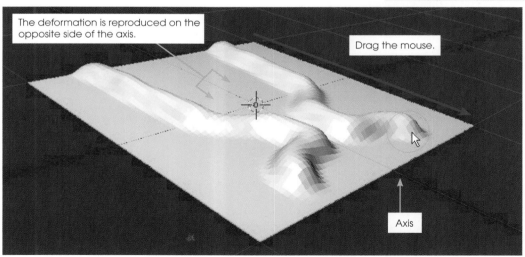

Figure 3.69

Figure 3.70

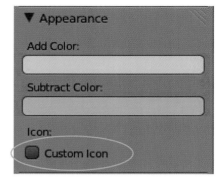

Ticking "Custom Icon" allows you to select an image to display for the tool type icon instead of Blender's default icon (Figure 3.71). This will add a new icon to the brush type options panel shown in Figure 3.58.

Figure 3.71

4

Materials

4.1 Introduction to Materials

What is a material in Blender? A material is a color but it is also much more than that. Think of the color red: it could be dark red or light red or any shade of red you could image. The color can be shiny or dull, it can be transparent, or it can gradually fade from one shade to another; the possibilities are endless. That is a material.

Learning
Unit 5

Colored
Materials

4.2 Material Settings

The default Blender scene has a cube object that displays as a dull gray color. Color is the way your eyes interpret the reflected light from an object's surface. If there is no light, you see nothing, so Blender has placed a white-light lamp in the default scene and assigned data to the cube that shows the cube as being gray in this color light. Every object added to the scene will also be given the same data as the cube, so you will see them as gray. Adding a material is done in the properties window with the "Material" button activated (Figure 4.1).

Properties window

Material button

Figure 4.1

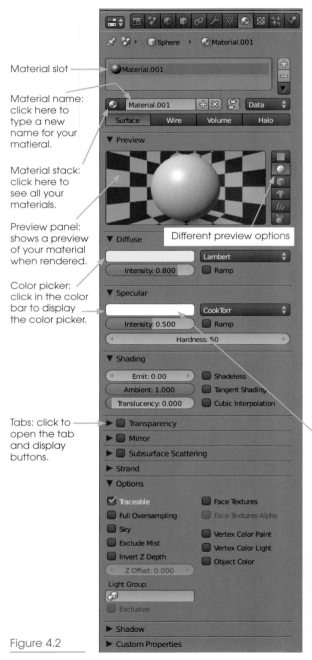

Material slot

Material name: click here to type a new name for your matieral.

Material stack: click here to see all your materials.

Preview panel: shows a preview of your material when rendered.

Color picker: click in the color bar to display the color picker.

Different preview options

Tabs: click to open the tab and display buttons.

Figure 4.2

Note: In the default Blender scene, the default cube object has been given a material as seen by the gray color of the cube object and the fact that the material buttons are displayed in the properties window. Subsequent objects added to the scene also display with this same color although the material buttons for a new object do *not* display. Clicking on "New" will display the buttons. For now, consider an object as *not* having a material unless the "Material" button displays all the tabs shown in Figure 4.2. Remember, the values in the properties window only apply to the object that is selected in the 3D window.

When you click on the material button for a new object, the properties window only displays the information in Figure 4.1. To add a material to an object, first select the object you want to work with (the default cube comes with a material added). In the properties window header, click the "Material" button, then click the "New" button. You will see the material properties tabs open up. The values will be the same as those for the default cube.

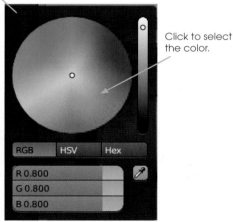

Click to select the color.

4.3 Material Buttons

The material panel is used to change some of the physical properties of the object's appearance (Figure 4.2). If you plan on using just straight color and no texture, this is where you set the object's color. This panel is also where you set other properties such as shading, transparency, glossy or flat, reflective, halo effect, etc. A brief example of setting a material will follow.

4.4 Material Colors

Each material can exhibit three colors:

- the basic diffuse overall color, which is seen when a surface reflects light,
- the specular color, which gives a surface highlights or a shiny appearance, and
- the mirror color, which is the color used to fake mirror reflections.

It is important to remember that the material color is only one element in the rendering process. The rendered color of an object is a product of the material color and the emitting light color. An object may have a yellow material color, but put it under a blue light or a red light and you'll see something else altogether.

4.5 Adding a New Material

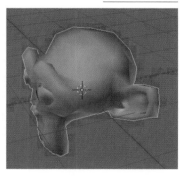

Figure 4.3

I will demonstrate the basics of adding a material by the following example. Start a new Blender scene and add a monkey object. Monkey always enters the scene lying on his back, so, with him selected, press the R key + X + 90 (to rotate him about the *x*-axis 90 degrees) (Figure 4.3). Hit the number pad + key and zoom in a bit. Go to the tool shelf and under "Shading" click on "Smooth." Make sure the monkey is selected then go to the properties window "Material" button (Figure 4.4).

Click on the "New" button to display the material properties buttons. When the monkey is added to the scene, Blender assigns it the properties for the gray color even though the material properties are not displayed. After clicking "New," you can modify the properties to achieve the look you want.

Note: We selected the smooth option from the tool shelf to better display the modifications to the material. Some of the effects are very subtle, so a nice smooth surface is best for this demonstration.

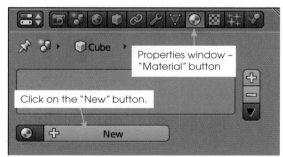

Figure 4.4

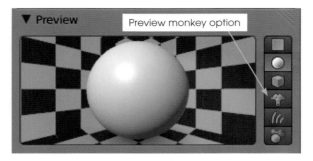

Figure 4.5

Color bar showing the diffuse color: click to display the color picker

Default color (gray)

Intensity slider

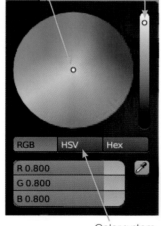

Color system options

Figure 4.6

4.6 The Preview Tab

Take a look at the "Preview" tab in the material properties window (Figure 4.5). This preview gives an indication of what you will see in a render of the 3D window. To save computer memory, Blender does not display everything in the 3D window. On the LH side of the "Preview" tab, there are options for viewing the preview in different formats. One of the options is "Monkey," but for simplicity, I have left my preview as the default sphere.

4.7 The Diffuse Tab

I previously stated that the monkey object had been assigned a gray color. This is the diffuse overall color of the material. Click the gray bar to display the color picker and note the R: 0.800, G: 0.800, and B: 0.800 values (Figure 4.6). These are the numeric values that denote the gray color in the RGB color system. RGB stands for "red, green, and blue," the primary colors. Mixing the three 0.800 values produces the gray color. There are three color system options available: RGB, HSV, and Hex.

What is intensity? The intensity of a color is the shade of the color going through a range from absolutely no light to maximum light. Figure 4.7, which demonstrates intensity, also serves to show that light has a major effect on a rendered image. When the monkey was added to the scene, it was added at the center of the world and then rotated on the x-axis by 90 degrees. This means that the position of the default lamp is above and behind the monkey's head, which explains why the monkey's face is in shadow. So how come we see the monkey when the intensity is 0.000 (no light)? We will come back to that a bit later. For now, let's make the monkey a bit more colorful.

Intensity = 0.000 (no light)   Intensity = 0.800

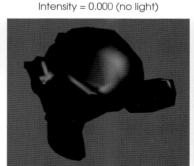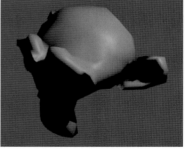

Figure 4.7

Open the color picker again and select a color you like. If you want to match my example exactly, enter the RGB values R: 0.800, G: 0.430, and B: 0.000—we now have a pretty golden monkey. The difference between what you see in the 3D window and the rendered image is shown in Figure 4.8. The 3D window has some shadowing effect so that you can see 3D features. This shadowing is evident in the render, but in addition you can see some shiny highlights. The shiny highlights are there because, by default, Blender has added specular color (discussed next) to the monkey; that's why we could see the monkey when we turned the diffuse color intensity down to 0.000 in Figure 4.7. In effect, we canceled the diffuse light reflection but there was still specular light reflection.

See Figures 4.9 and 4.10 for comparisons of 3D window objects and rendered images, respectively, when the intensity changes.

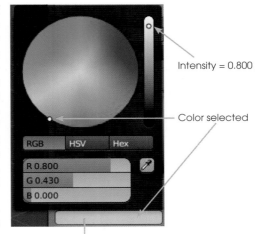

Intensity = 0.800

Color selected

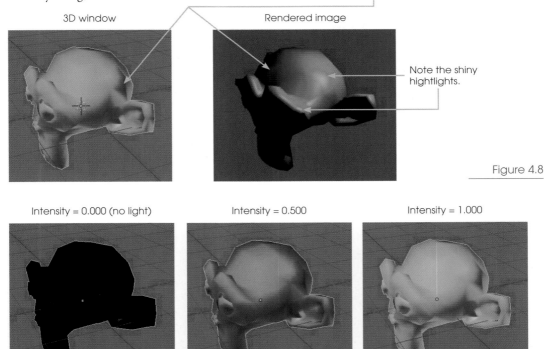

3D window

Rendered image

Note the shiny hightlights.

Figure 4.8

Intensity = 0.000 (no light)

Intensity = 0.500

Intensity = 1.000

Figure 4.9

Intensity = 0.000 (no light) Intensity = 0.500 Intensity = 1.000

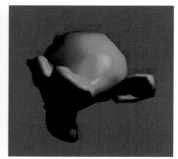

Figure 4.10

Hardness value

Selected specular color

4.8 The Specular Tab

The "Specular" tab is similar to the "Diffuse" tab with a color bar that, when clicked, displays a color picker. The difference between the two tabs is that the specular tab has a hardness value (Figure 4.11).

Click on the color bar and then slect the green color with R: 0.000, G: 1.000, and B: 0.450. Set the diffuse color intensity to 0.800. When you add a specular color to an object's material, there is no dramatic effect in the 3D window—the difference will be the specular highlights, which are more evident in the rendered image. Figures 4.12 and 4.13 demonstrate the differences with varying intensity values for 3D window objects and rendered images, respectively.

Figure 4.11

Intensity = 0.000 (no light) Intensity = 0.500 Intensity = 1.000

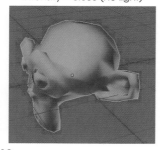
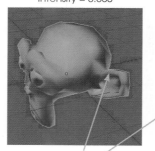
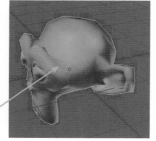

Figure 4.12

Specular highlights

| Intensity = 0.000 (no light) | Intensity = 0.500 | Intensity = 1.000 |

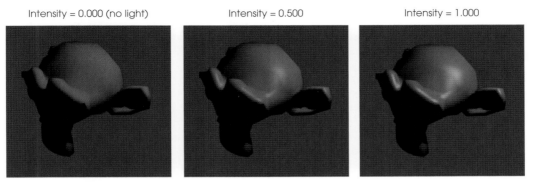

Figure 4.13

4.9 The Hardness Value

The best way I can describe the effect of the hardness value is to say that the effect spreads the specular color across the surface of the object (known as "soft light") or focuses it (known as "hard light"). The default hardness value is 50 and the value range is 1 to 115. The most visible effect when altering the value occurs in the lower region of the range. Figures 4.14 and 4.15 demonstrate this effect for 3D window and rendered images, respectively. Set both diffuse and specular color intensities to 0.800.

Learning
Unit 5

Multiple
Materials,
Blender
Materials – Mirror

| Hardness: 1 | Hardness: 50 | Hardness: 115 |

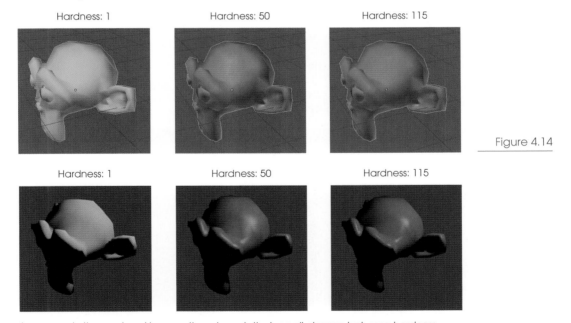

Figure 4.14

| Hardness: 1 | Hardness: 50 | Hardness: 115 |

As you see in the rendered images, there is a relatively small change between hardness value 115 and 50, but a huge difference between 50 and 1. It is especially hard to see the difference between 115 and 50 in the 3D window.

Figure 4.15

4.10 Ramp Shaders

Besides having control over diffuse and specular intensity and specular hardness, there is a ramp shader system to integrate color shading over a surface, sometimes known as gradient (Figure 4.16). I will not attempt to give instruction in its use here, only to point out its existence. Ramp shaders produce very subtle effects of color mixing, but it must be used in conjunction with lighting and lamp positioning.

4.11 Transparency

To make an object transparent, go to the properties window "Material" button and click the "Transparency" tab (Figure 4.17). Tick the "Transparency" box to display the controls.

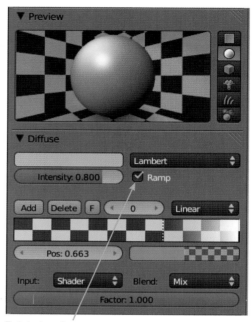

Tick to turn the ramp shader on.

Figure 4.16

With the sphere selected in the 3D window, tick "Transparency" and reduce the alpha value.

With the cube selected, untick "Receive" in the "Shadow" tab.

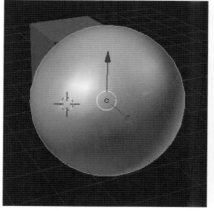

Figure 4.17   3D window view   Rendered image

Figure 4.18

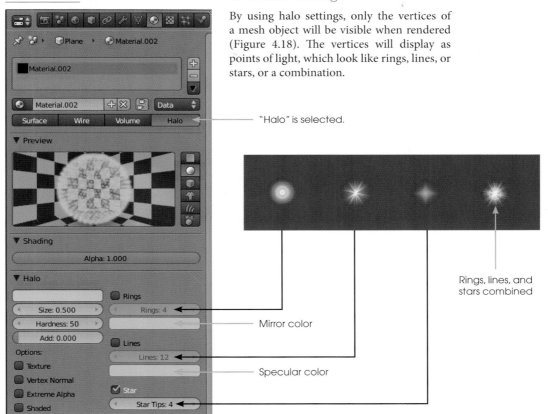

4.12 Halo Settings

By using halo settings, only the vertices of a mesh object will be visible when rendered (Figure 4.18). The vertices will display as points of light, which look like rings, lines, or stars, or a combination.

"Halo" is selected.

Rings, lines, and stars combined

Mirror color

Specular color

4.13 Vertex Painting

In addition to the options for adding materials to an object as described so far in this chapter, Blender also provides the "Vertex Paint" tool, which allows you to manually paint a material onto the surface of an object.

You can paint by changing the 3D window from object mode to vertex paint mode (Figure 4.19). You will be able to paint a selected object immediately, but before you can render an image with the paint showing, you must have a material added. A new object added to the 3D window displays with the default

Figure 4.19

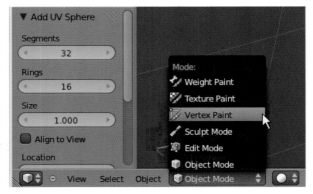

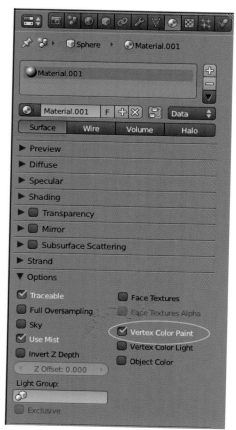

Figure 4.20

Blender gray color, but, as you can see in the properties window "Material" button, there are no control tabs displayed. With the new object selected in the 3D window, in the properties window "Material" button, press "Add Material." The new object still displays in the 3D window as the same gray color but now the "Material" button contains control tabs.

Go to the "Material" button – "Options" tab and tick "Vertex Color Paint" (Figure 4.20). "Vertex Color Paint" tells Blender to use the painted material instead of the base color when you render an image. It must be ticked before the paint color will render.

As vertex paint suggests, the process involves painting vertices. The default cube in the 3D window only has eight vertices, therefore it doesn't provide much scope for a demonstration. Delete the cube and add a UV sphere. The default UV sphere has 32 segments and 16 rings, which provides a vertex at each intersection point. If you would care to count the intersections, you will find there are a lot more vertices in the sphere than the cube. You can also subdivide in edit mode to add more vertices.

Change the 3D window to "Vertex Paint Mode"—the UV sphere looks like a white disk and your 3D cursor changes to an orange circle (Figure 4.21). The tool panel at the left of the window displays with the "Brush" tab open. In the "Brush" tab, you have a circular color picker for selecting the paint color with a bar across the bottom that shows the color selected (Figure 4.22). By default, the selected color is white. To paint, click in the colored circle to select a color then, in the 3D window, click, hold, and drag the brush across the UV sphere.

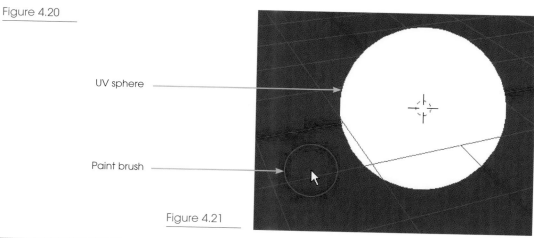

UV sphere

Paint brush

Figure 4.21

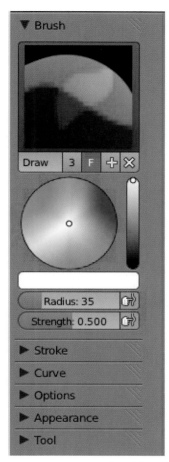

Figure 4.22

Immediately below the color bar are two sliders. "Radius" controls the size of the brush (the circular 3D cursor), and "Strength" controls how much paint color is applied. Another way of controlling the size of the brush is to press the F key and click and drag the cursor towards or away from the center of the brush circle (Figure 4.23). Click the LMB when finished. The size of the brush circle changes and the slider value in the tool shelf is reset.

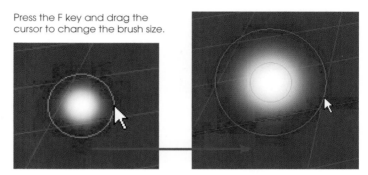

Press the F key and drag the cursor to change the brush size.

Figure 4.23

Besides the "Brush" tab, the tool panel contains five other tabs. Starting at the bottom:

- The "Tool" tab. Here you can select the tool specific to vertex paint and use a drop down menu for selecting the brush mode (Figure 4.24). The default mode is "Mix."
- The "Appearance" tab. Here you can see a color bar showing the color of the brush circle. Clicking on the bar opens a color picker for changing the color of the circle.
- The "Options" tab. This tab provides settings for how the brush operates. For example, with "All Faces" ticked, the brush will apply paint to all faces adjacent to the vertex being painted (Figure 4.25). Placing the cursor over each option displays a description of the function. Unfortunately, some of the descriptions are ambiguous.
- The "Curve" tab. This tab provides a graphical method for controlling how the brush applies paint. A small graph is displayed with a curve containing control handles (Figure 4.26). The handles may be manipulated, altering the curve shape and changing the brush paint application. There are also quick select buttons for changing the shape of the curve.

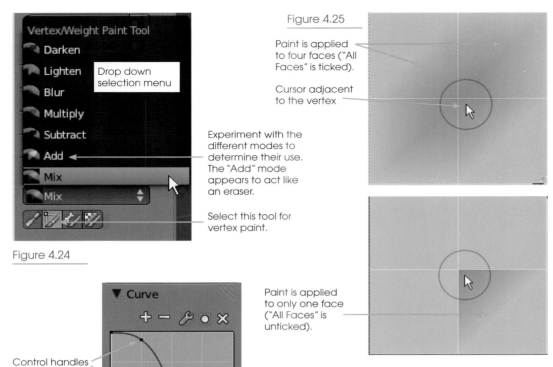

Vertex/Weight Paint Tool

Darken
Lighten
Blur
Multiply
Subtract
Add
Mix
Mix

Drop down selection menu

Experiment with the different modes to determine their use. The "Add" mode appears to act like an eraser.

Select this tool for vertex paint.

Figure 4.24

Figure 4.25

Paint is applied to four faces ("All Faces" is ticked).

Cursor adjacent to the vertex

Paint is applied to only one face ("All Faces" is unticked).

▼ Curve

Control handles

Quick select buttons

Figure 4.26

- The "Stroke" tab. This tab provides controls for brush application; you should experiment with the different effects.

Remember that although the UV sphere looks like a flat disc, it is in fact a 3D sphere. You can display the segments and rings and subsequently the vertices and faces of the sphere by activating the "Face Selection Mask" in the 3D window header (Figure 4.27). When painting, you can only paint the visible surface of the object. You have to pan the 3D view or rotate the object to paint the hidden surfaces (Figure 4.28). The vertex paint color can only be seen in vertex paint mode or in a rendered image (Figure 4.29).

There is plenty to experiment with regarding this topic and, now that you have grasped some of the basics, it's a good idea to look at some tutorials on the internet (see the References section of this manual for a starting point). Video tutorials pack in a lot of information and there are some good tips to be found:

Tips:
- In vertex paint, the default viewing mode is "Solid." I have mentioned turning on "Face Select Mask" to see the mesh vertices, but you can also

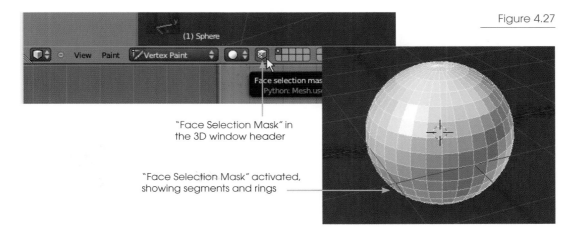

"Face Selection Mask" in
the 3D window header

"Face Selection Mask" activated,
showing segments and rings

Figure 4.27

The visible surface
is painted.

The 3D view is
rotated, showing
the unpainted
hidden surface.

Figure 4.28

Vertex paint mode

Rendered image

Figure 4.29

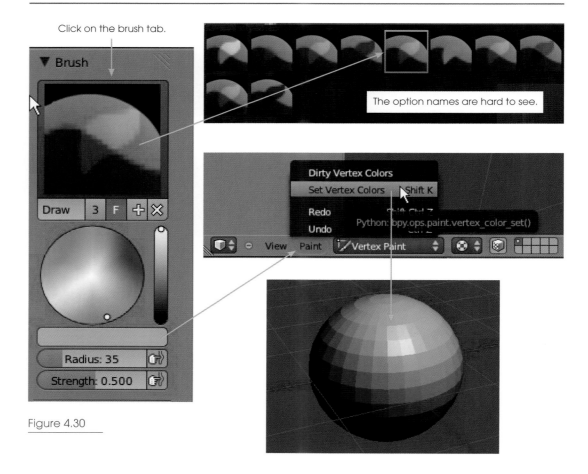

Figure 4.30

switch to "Textured Viewing" to see the actual surface of the mesh while you paint.

- Click on the icon in the "Brush" tab for the quick set brush options in the "Tool" tab (Figure 4.30).
- If you want to paint the entire surface of the mesh, go to the 3D window header (while in vertex paint mode) and select "Paint – Set Vertex Colors." Whatever color has been selected in the brush color picker will be applied to the whole mesh surface.
- Sometimes it is difficult to see what is being painted in the 3D window. Remember the default 3D scene only has a single point lamp in place. Therefore, you are going to have shadow that obstructs the paint view. Add some more light with additional point lamps or spot lamps (see Chapter 7 for more information).

4.14 The Application of Materials and Material Slots

Beginners should skip this section.

To simplify the understanding of the application of materials in Blender, it may be easier to think of materials as colors. The color of an object in a Blender scene is set by values entered using a color picker, typing RGB values, or moving sliders. A Blender scene may have multiple materials, and these materials are stored in a cache for use by any of the objects that are introduced to the scene or any object in any scene in the Blender file. A Blender file may contain multiple scenes.

To demonstrate the application of materials in Blender, set the screen to include the 3D view and the properties window with the "Material" tab active. When a new Blender scene is opened, the 3D view displays a cube mesh object, which has a dull gray color. The properties window opens with the "Render" button active. Change the properties window to set the "Material" button active (Figure 4.31).

With the "Material" button active, you can see that:

- a preview pane shows a dull gray color on a sphere,
- there is a material named "Material" in the unique data block ID name, and
- there is one material slot active showing the material named "Material."

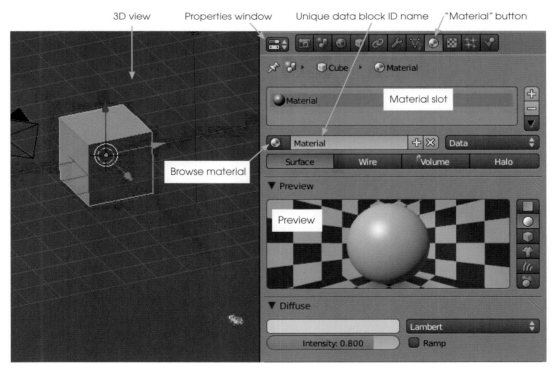

Figure 4.31

Figure 4.32

Clicking the "Browse Material" data button displays a drop down menu, showing the materials cache containing the single material named "Material" (Figure 4.32). The relationship between the material, the material slot, and the object in the 3D view is shown in Figure 4.33. Material data stored in the cache is entered in the material data block, which is linked to the material slot. The slot is assigned to the object selected in the 3D view. To further understand the relationship, continue with the following procedure.

Delete the cube in the 3D window, then add a new cube object. Observe that the properties window "Material" buttons now show no reference to any material data. The cube in the 3D window still displays as a dull gray color. By clicking the "Browse Material" data button, you can see that "Material" is still in the cache but it is named "0 Material" (Figure 4.34). It follows that there must be a hidden material slot with a "0 Material" data block linked to it and the slot is assigned to the cube in the 3D window. Click on "0 Material" in the cache to display the material properties in the slot.

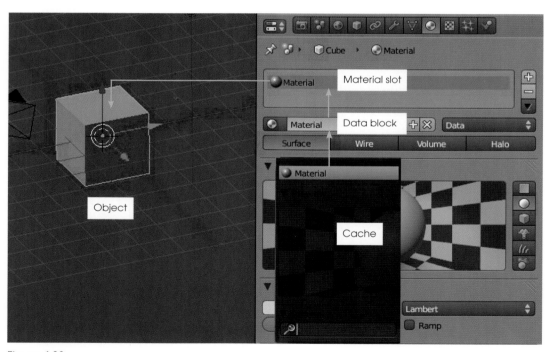

Figure 4.33

Figure 4.34

Material properties with no material data reference

No material data

No reference to the material

Click the "Browse Material" data button.

Material data added

Click on "0 Material."

Material properties with material data reference

0 Material

Material in the cache

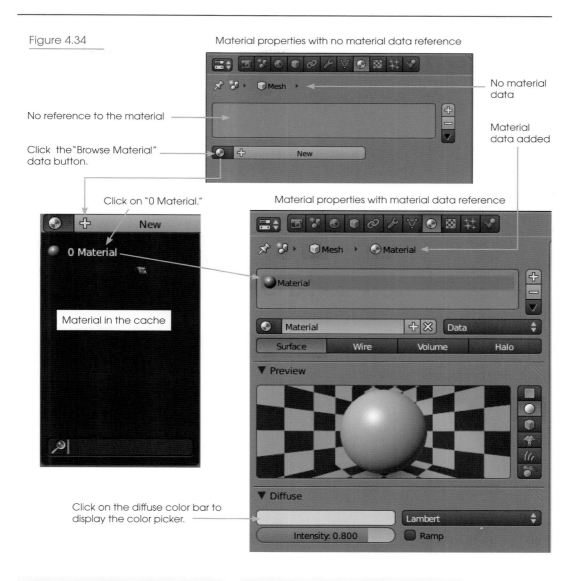

Click on the diffuse color bar to display the color picker.

Note: "0 Material" becomes "Material" in the cache, the data block, and the slot. The "0" prefix indicates that the material is not entered in a data block. In later versions of Blender, the default data is named "Material" and subsequent instances are named "Material.001," "Material.002," etc.

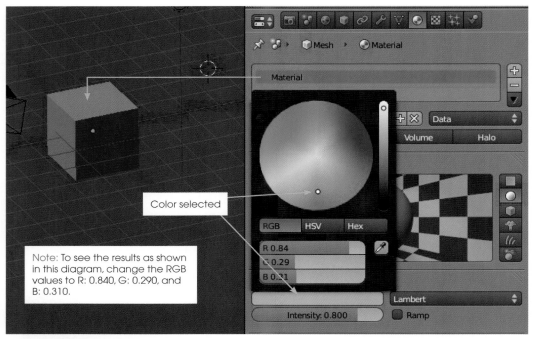

Note: To see the results as shown in this diagram, change the RGB values to R: 0.840, G: 0.290, and B: 0.310.

Color selected

Figure 4.35

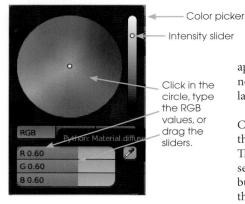

The relationship between the material and the object is applied whether the object is selected in the 3D window or not. If there is more than one object in the window, the relationship will be applied to the last object that was selected.

To demonstrate this, deselect the cube in the 3D window. Click in the diffuse color bar to display the color picker and then click in the multicolored circle to select a new color. The color of the cube changes despite the fact that it is not selected (Figure 4.35). The material is still named "Material" but it has been given new data. The material is still linked to the slot and the slot is still assigned to the cube object.

It is important to understand that with an object selected in the 3D window, the properties window shows the "Material" buttons and data that are relevant to the selected object only. Selecting a different object in the 3D window changes the properties window and the data from that of the previous object to the new object selected. This may seem to be expressing the obvious but the concept must be understood. The exception is that the materials cache and the materials contained therein are relevant to any object in any scene in the Blender file.

Multiple materials may be added to the cache. Click on the + sign, which is the "Add New Material" button, and a new material named "Material.001" will show in the "Browse Material" data block, which is linked to the slot and therefore assigned to the cube (Figure 4.36). Blender creates a duplicate of the previous linked material. "Material.001" is identical to "Material" in that it is the same color.

Click on the "Browse Material" data button to reveal the cache. "Material.001" is now stored in the cache. With the color picker, click and change the color. The color of the cube will change in the 3D window since "Material.001" is linked to the slot and assigned to the cube (Figure 4.37). Note that the cube is not selected in the 3D window.

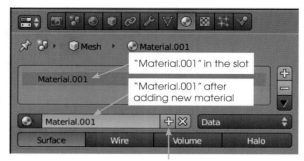

Figure 4.36

Note: A material in the cache that is not linked to an object has the "0" prefix.

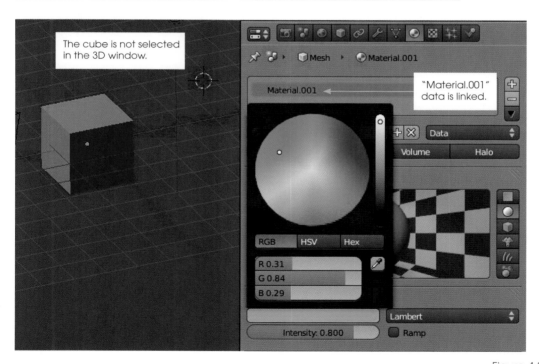

Figure 4.37

Go to the cache again and click on "0 Material." By using the color picker and changing the color, the material data has changed and therefore the color of the cube has changed. Clicking on "Material" has linked it to the slot; with the slot assigned to the cube, the color of the cube changes. Therefore, by selecting "Material" or "Material.001" from the cache linking the material to the slot, the color of the object cube can be changed at will.

Adding a new object to the scene creates a new material slot and by default the original material with its dull gray color is linked. As previously stated, when a new object is introduced into a scene, a new set of material data comes with it. The cache retains the material colors previously used and they may be selected and linked to the new slot, changing the color of the new object. Up to this point, only one material slot has been employed to link to an object.

Note: When a material from the cache is linked to more than one object, a number displays adjacent to the "Unique User ID name," indicating the number of users (Figure 4.38).

Figure 4.38

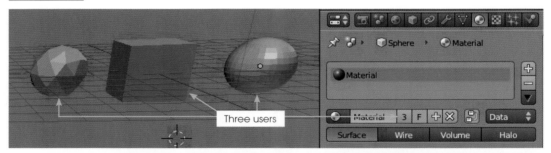

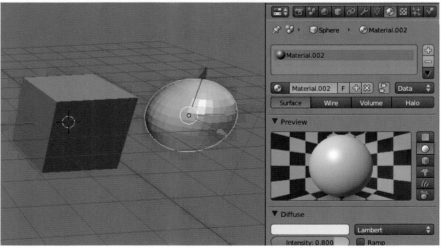

Figure 4.39

Multiple material slots may be introduced for each individual object in the scene. The application of multiple material slots can be demonstrated by showing how a single mesh object can have multiple colors. Follow this procedure, leaving the default cube in the scene.

Add a UV sphere mesh object to the scene. The sphere will be in object mode and selected in the 3D view. Have the properties window with the "Material" buttons active. The sphere will be the default dull gray color and the materials properties window will be blank. Remember the cache is still available for selecting materials if you wish.

Click on the "New" button to create a new material. By default, it is the dull gray color but note its data block ID name in the window: "Material.002" (Figure 4.39). Click on the "Browse Material" button and you will see the new name has been added to the cache. The name is "Material.002" since "Material" and "Material.001" already exist.

Now click on the "Add Materials Slot" button (Figure 4.40). A new slot

Figure 4.40

The upper slot is linked to the sphere.

Figure 4.41

is created but note that there is no material linked and the new slot is not assigned to the object selected in the 3D view. At this point, you can click on the "Browse Material" button and link a material to the new slot or you may click on "New" to create a new material data block. Remember, a new data block will be a duplication of the last data block selected, which in this case was "Material.002." Click on "New."

Since "Material.002" was the last in the list, Blender names the new material data block "Material.003" and it is identical to "Material.002" (Figure 4.41). Change the color of "Material.003"—notice that the sphere does not change color. There are now two color slots: one is linked to the sphere and the other is not linked. Remember, the information in the properties material window is only relevant to the object that is selected in the 3D view. If the sphere were deselected, the first slot remains assigned to the sphere since it was the last object selected. As a demonstration of the foregoing, select the cube then the sphere and note the change to the properties window.

We now have two slots assigned to the sphere: one is assigned and the other is not. To change the assignment, make sure the sphere is selected in the 3D window and tab to edit mode. All the vertices will be selected. Click on the new material slot (in this case, the slot with "Material.003" linked) and click on "Assign." Tab back to object mode and you will see

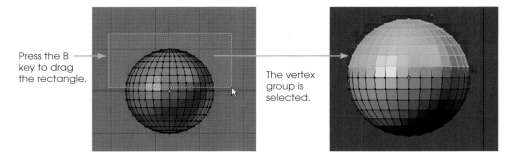

Press the B key to drag the rectangle.

The vertex group is selected.

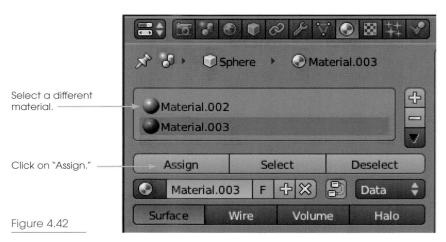

Select a different material.

Click on "Assign."

Sphere ▸ Material.003

Material.002
Material.003

Assign   Select   Deselect

Material.003   F   Data

Surface   Wire   Volume   Halo

Figure 4.42

that the sphere has changed color, showing that the material slot with "Material.003" linked is assigned to the sphere object. The material data block has also been assigned to the sphere since, in edit mode, you had all the vertices selected.

Change the 3D view to a side view (number pad 1 or 3) so the sphere is visible. Enlarge the view with the number pad + key. Tab to edit mode with the sphere selected (in edit mode, the sphere will have all its vertices selected). Press the A key to deselect the vertices. Press the B key and drag a rectangle around part of the sphere, selecting some of the vertices (a vertex group). Select "Material.002" and click on the "Assign" button (Figure 4.42). Blender assigns the slot and thus links the material to the selected group of vertices. Make sure that the color for the material linked to the slot is something different than the material linked to the first slot or this will not be evident (Figure 4.43). Tab to object mode in the 3D view to see the sphere with two colors.

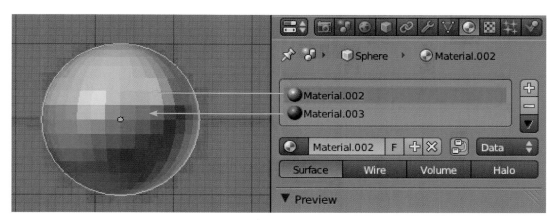

Figure 4.43

5

Textures

5.1 Introduction to Textures

In Chapter 4, we considered the effect of light reflecting off a smooth surface. Textures are the physical characteristics or imperfections of a surface such as the grainy surface of bricks, the fibrous pile of carpet, wood grain, etc.

Learning
Unit 5

Procedural
Textures –
Gradient Blend

In Blender, the visualization of these types of surface characteristics is created by mapping images on to the surface of a model in the 3D window. In this case, the images are called textures. In Blender, there are three texture modes: material, world background, and brush. Besides creating surface characteristics, textures are used to sculpt, paint, and deform objects. Textures are also used by several of Blender's modifiers.

It should be noted that textures do not display in the 3D window. An image of the scene must be rendered to see the texture; this is to save processing power.

5.1.1 Material Textures

Before you can add a texture to a surface you must first add a material because, by default, Blender textures are set to influence the material. Textures are applied to an object's surface using the options in the properties window – "Textures" button. Clicking the "Textures" button displays a panel where you can add a new texture. Blender comes with a series of built-in textures from which to choose or you can use any photo or image stored on your computer. Blender can also place movies on a surface and you can animate the textures.

Properties window   "Textures" button

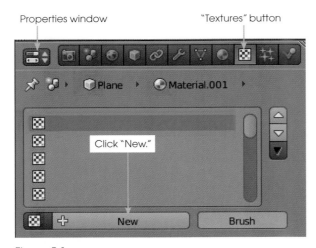

Figure 5.1

To demonstrate the placing of a texture, follow this example. Open a new Blender scene, replace the default cube with a plane, and scale the plane up by 5. Add a material with R: 0.800, G: 0.767, and B: 0.495 values. Go to the properties window – "Textures" button and click "New" (Figure 5.1).

Note: By default, material texture mode is active.

The texture buttons display with a default texture type "Clouds" shown in the "Preview" tab. Also notice that the properties window displays a "Clouds" tab (Figure 5.2, left). This tab contains settings for altering the characteristics of the texture, and the tab will change depending on what texture type is selected.

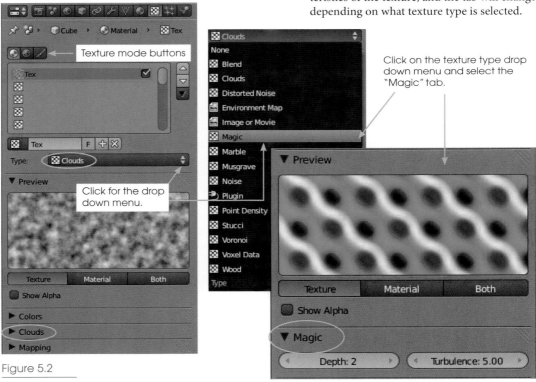

Figure 5.2

Click on the texture type drop down menu and select the "Magic" tab. The cloud texture is replaced by the magic texture and the "Clouds" tab is replaced by the "Magic" tab (Figure 5.2, right). This tab contains only two values for altering the characteristics of the texture: depth and turbulence. Note that the 3D window does not show the texture on the object. This is where Blender conserves memory. Render (press F12) to see the texture (Figure 5.3). Change the depth value to 4 and render again to see the alteration (Figure 5.4). Go back to the texture type drop down selection and select "Image or Movie." An "Image" tab displays instead of the "Magic" tab and the preview shows a black window—we haven't told Blender what image to use.

In the "Image" tab, click "Open" (Figure 5.5). The file browser window displays. Navigate to a file containing a picture (I have a picture named "Street.jpg" in my "Documents" folder). Click on the picture file then click "Open" at the top RHS of the screen.

You will see your picture in the preview panel (probably multiple images). Render to see your picture displayed on the surface of the plane (Figure 5.6).

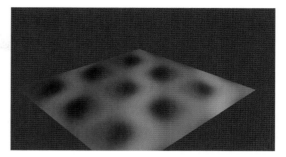

Figure 5.3

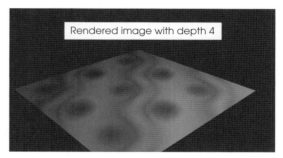

Figure 5.4

Click "Open."

Figure 5.5

Learning Unit 5
Image Textures

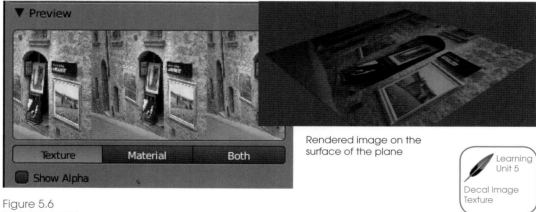

Rendered image on the surface of the plane

Figure 5.6

Learning Unit 5
Decal Image Texture

5.2 Texture Mapping

Whether you use one of Blender's built in textures or an image, you may want to adjust how the texture is positioned on the object. The "Mapping" tab is the place to do this (Figure 5.7). "Offset" and "Size" are self-explanatory, and can be controlled on either the x-, y-, or z-axis. The "Coordinates" drop down menu gives you a selection of coordinate systems, and the "Projection" drop down menu has a choice of mapping options to suit the shape of your object (Figure 5.8).

There are a lot of buttons and settings to experiment with in the "Texture" screen and the best way to find out what they do is to play around and record your results for future reference.

Figure 5.7

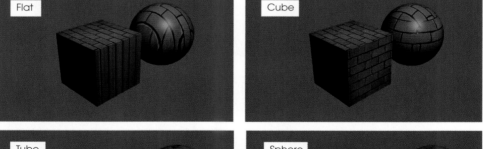

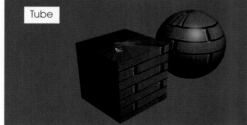

Figure 5.8

5.3 Displacement Mapping

Displacement mapping is using a texture to deform a mesh. You can make a cube or a sphere look wrinkled without having to move vertices around. Start a new Blender scene with the default cube. Make sure the cube has a material, then in edit mode, subdivide the cube six times. The texture is going to displace vertices, so you need a whole bunch of vertices to work with.

Learning
Unit 8

Bump Textures

Put a cloud texture on the cube then go to the "Influence" tab. Leave the "Diffuse: Color" ticked. Under the "Geometry" heading, tick "Displace" and alter the value as shown in Figure 5.9. Render to see the effect.

Figure 5.9

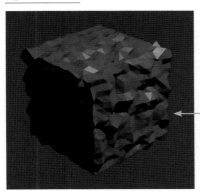

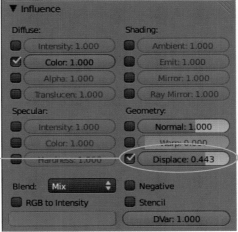

Moving the slider next to the "Displacement" box varies the amount of displacement. The "Blend" drop down menu displays options that influence the material. Try "Add" and "Subtract" and render to see the difference. Another example is shown in Figure 5.10. This time, a black-and-white image texture has been used on a plane. Don't forget to subdivide the plane. Negative displacement values raise the surface up, and positive values depress the surface. Experiment with other features and record the outcomes for future reference.

Black-and-white image

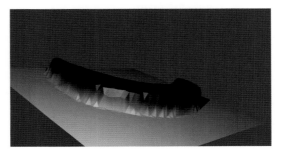

Rendered image with a negative displacement value

Figure 5.10

5.4 UV Texture Mapping

For complex models, regular flat, cubic, cylindrical, or spherical texture mapping is not sufficient to accurately place the texture on the surface. This is where UV mapping can help. The coordinates *u* and *v* are used simply to distinguish from the *x,y,z*-coordinates used in the 3D window.

UV mapping is accomplished by taking the surface of an object (the model), peeling it off as you would a skin from an orange, and laying it out flat on a 2D surface. An image is then superimposed as a texture over the flattened surface (this is known as mapping). The window for laying out the flattened object is the UV/image editor window. As with every basic instruction in Blender, it is best to begin with something simple. Although the process we are describing is for complex surfaces, anything other than simple is going to be confusing at first.

Start with a cube object in Blender's default 3D scene; delete the cube that is loaded automatically and add a new cube. The default cube comes preloaded with a material and a texture channel. In our previous discussion on material and textures, I stated that before a texture could be applied, an object had to have a material. Adding to the scene a new cube that does not have a material or a texture will demonstrate that neither are necessary to apply UV texture mapping (Figure 5.11).

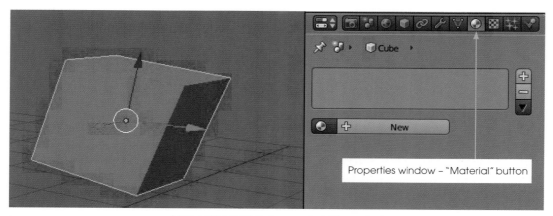

Figure 5.11   A new cube is added; no material is applied.

With the new cube added, split the 3D window in two and change one half to the UV/image editor. In the 3D window, zoom in on the cube—when you split the window, the cube is a little too small to see this process clearly. Change the 3D window to edit mode and select "Textured" as the viewport shading type; this will allow you to see the superimposed texture (Figure 5.12).

In the 3D window tools panel under "UV Mapping," click on "Unwrap" to display the menu for selecting the UV mapping unwrapping type (Figure 5.13). These options allow you to unwrap the surface of the selected object in a variety of ways. Some of the unwrap-

5. Textures

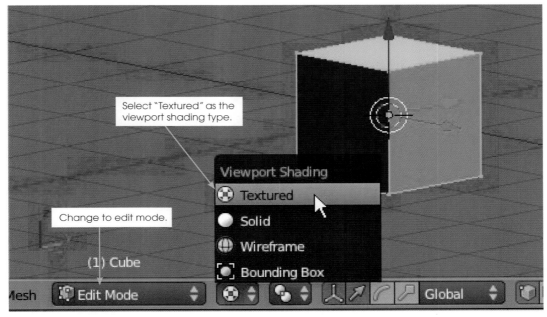

Select "Textured" as the viewport shading type.

Change to edit mode.

(1) Cube

Mesh · Edit Mode

Viewport Shading
- Textured
- Solid
- Wireframe
- Bounding Box

Global

Figure 5.12

Figure 5.13

Click on "Unwrap."

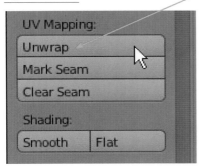

UV Mapping:
- Unwrap
- Mark Seam
- Clear Seam

Shading:
- Smooth | Flat

ping methods are difficult to visualize, so the only way to learn is to experiment and record your findings.

To keep things simple, select the "Follow Active Quads – Edge Length Mode – Length" method for unwrapping the cube and press "OK" (Figure 5.14). This method will lay out the surface of the cube as if you had unfolded a post office mailing box. The surface will consist of six squares. The UV/image editor window will probably require you to zoom out to see the whole arrangement (use the number pad minus key, the same as you do in the 3D window). Now that the flattened surface is displayed, it's time to load a texture image.

In the UV/image editor window header, click on "Image" and select "Open Image." This will display the file browser window where you can navigate and find an image to use as a texture. Once you have located your image file, click on it to select it and then click on "Open Image" (at the top RHS of the window). In my case, I have selected a picture file named "Chrysanthemum.jpg" in my C:\Users\Public\Pictures\SamplePictures\ directory (Figure 5.15). The image displays in the UV/image editor window.

Figure 5.14

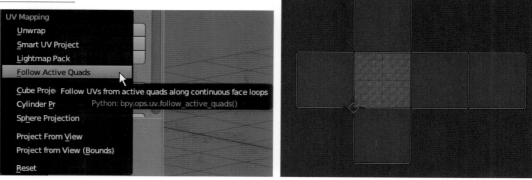

File browser window

Click to display the files as thumbnail images.

Figure 5.15

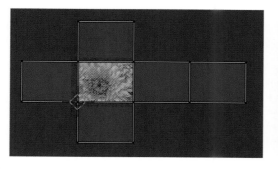

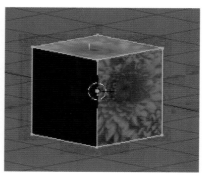

Figure 5.16

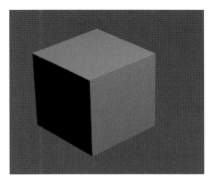

Figure 5.17

Figure 5.18

Zoom out again if the image is too large. The image shows in the center face, but you will see that it is mapped to each surface of the cube in the 3D window (Figure 5.16). With the cursor in the UV/image editor window, press the A key to select all the surfaces then the G key (grab) and move the selected surfaces around. As you move the surfaces, you will see that the image is repositioned on the surfaces of the cube in the 3D window. The outline of the surfaces in the UV/image editor can be scaled and rotated the same as you would edit a mesh in the 3D window. Individual vertices on the mesh may be selected then grabbed and moved also. As you see by manipulating the surface outline in the UV/image editor, you can accurately position the texture image.

If you were to render an image of the object (by pressing F12) at this stage, you would be disappointed to see that the image texture does not render (Figure 5.17). To render the image texture, activate "Face Textures" in the "Options" tab of the "Material" buttons in the properties window (Figure 5.18). Apply a material (the default dull gray color will do) and press F12 to see the rendered image.

5.5 Selective UV Texture Mapping

So far, the image texture has been mapped to all the surfaces of the object, but suppose you wish to place the texture only on one face of the object. Create a new scene and leave the default cube selected. Split the 3D window as before and set up the UV/image editor window. In the 3D window, tab to edit mode and select the "Textured" viewport shading.

In the 3D window, change from vertex select mode to face select mode (Figure 5.19). Deselect all faces then select only one face (right click on the face). In the UV/image editor window, select and enter an image for your texture as before, and you will see the image mapped to the face you selected in the 3D window. In this case, we didn't do any

---

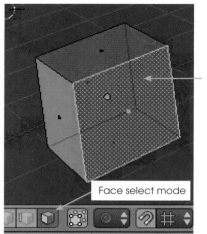

One face is selected.

Face select mode

Figure 5.19

unwrapping, but as soon as the image was entered in the UV/image editor, Blender automatically mapped the single face.

With the cursor in the UV/image editor window, press the A key to select the face. The white outline turns orange (Figure 5.20). You can then manipulate the face map to position your image the way you want. Remember, use the G key to grab, the R key to rotate, and the S key to scale (Figure 5.21). Note that the face map in the UV/image editor is in vertex select mode. There are also the options to select edge and face modes similar to the selections in edit mode in the 3D window. There is also a fourth option, which is island select mode (Figure 5.22). Some unwrapping operations divide the face mesh into separate parts, and island select allows you to select these parts.

The white outline turns orange.

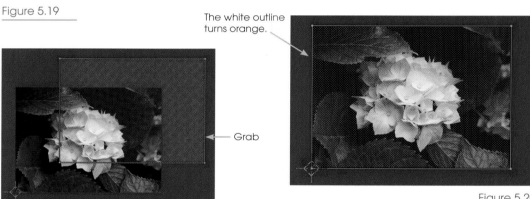

Grab

Figure 5.20

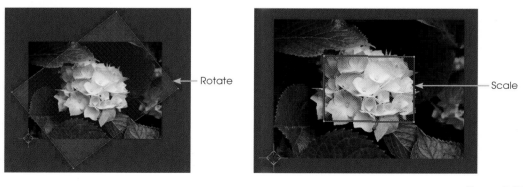

Rotate

Scale

Figure 5.21

By selecting different faces on the cube and adding different images to the UV/image editor, you can place the different image textures on the individual faces. You can also shift select multiple faces or shift select edges or vertices to tell Blender on which part of an object's surface you want the image texture placed.

Figure 5.22

5.6 Unwrapping with Seams

Let's go back and consider the mesh unwrapping. Pressing the "Unwrap" button gives you different options. In a new Blender scene, add an isosphere. An isosphere is chosen since, by default, it comes with just enough vertices for beginners to play around with.

Set up the UV/image editor window as we did previously. In the 3D window with the isosphere selected, tab to edit mode then press the A key to deselect all vertices. Change to edge select mode and shift select the edges, dividing the surface of the isosphere into three parts. It's best to zoom in on the isosphere and rotate the view while selecting the edges. With the edges selected, press "Mark Seam" in the tools panel; the selected edges will turn orange showing that a seam has been marked (Figure 5.23).

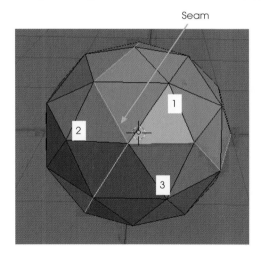

Figure 5.23

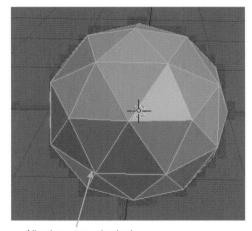

All edges are selected.

Figure 5.24

The next trick is to select all the edges of the faces of the isosphere, not just the edges marked as the seam. Use the A key to deselect the seam edges then the A key again to select all the edges (Figure 5.24). Having selected all the edges, press "Unwrap" in the tools panel then select "Unwrap" in the drop down menu (Figure 5.25). The separated parts of the isosphere's surface will be mapped in the UV/image editor window (Figure 5.26).

5.6. Unwrapping with Seams

Figure 5.25

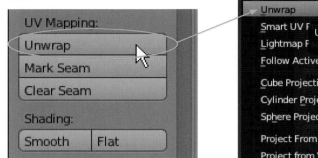

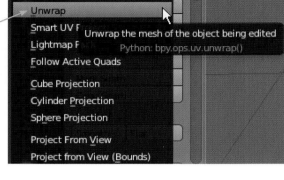

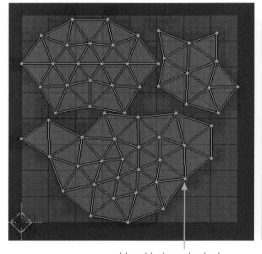

Figure 5.26

Island to be selected
(part 3 of the isosphere)

Figure 5.27

You can now open an image as a texture. In the 3D window in edit mode with "Textured" viewport shading selected , you will see the image on the surface of the isosphere mapped to the three parts you set up with the seam (Figure 5.27). In the UV/image editor window, select island select mode in the header (recall Figure 5.22). This will allow you to select separately each of the three surface parts. With a part selected, you can manipulate it to position the texture on that part (Figure 5.28).

Figure 5.28

The selected island is scaled down and positioned over the koala's ear.

The selection island has been moved and rotated.

5.7 Texture Paint

Texture paint is a built-in painting mode designed specifically to edit UV image textures. It is not a method for painting textures onto a surface. A UV texture is an image (picture) that is mapped to the surface of an object, providing color and surface definition (see Section 5.4).

With texture paint you can paint color over the image or directly onto the surface of the object once the image has been mapped. Before you can texture paint, the surface of the object must first be unwrapped to the UV/image editor window and an image must be applied as a texture (see Section 5.4).

The texture image is mapped to the surfaces of the cube in texture display mode.

UV/image editor window

3D window

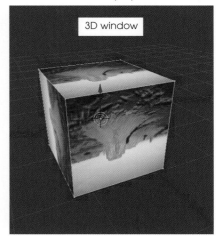

The cube is unwrapped using "Follow Active Quads" and the image is applied as a texture.

Figure 5.29

To demonstrate texture paint, use the default Blender scene with the default cube object. Remember that the default cube in the default scene comes with a material already applied. If you are introducing a new object to the scene, you must apply a material before you can introduce a texture. Select the cube and unwrap the surface to the UV/image editor window using the "Follow Active Quads" method; apply an image as a texture (Figure 5.29).

In the 3D window, change from edit mode to texture paint mode (Figure 5.30). The 3D window will now be very similar to the vertex paint window with the exception that there is a jitter slider in the "Brush" tab, a "Texture" tab, and a "Project Paint" tab.

In the UV/image editor window header, activate the "Enable Image Painting" button (Figure 5.31). In the 3D window with texture paint mode selected, you may now select a color from the color picker, set the brush size and strength, and set the type of stroke. Click, hold, and drag the brush to paint on the image in the UV/image editor window or on the surface of the object in the 3D window (Figure 5.32). Whichever window you paint in, the action is reflected in the other window. To see what you have painted when you render, you must tick "Face Textures" in the properties window – "Material" button – "Options" tab (Figure 5.33).

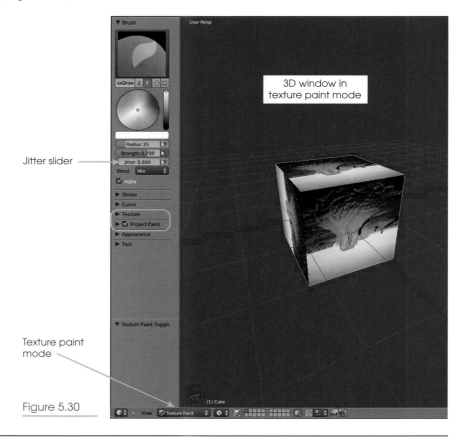

Figure 5.30

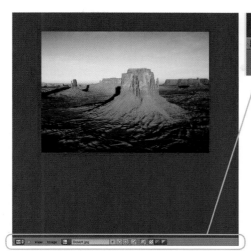

"Enable image painting" button

Figure 5.31

Figure 5.32

UV/image editor window

3D window

Figure 5.33

Once again, this is only a basic introduction. There are plenty of options for experimentation, and there are excellent tutorials on the internet covering this topic. To demonstrate that we have only seen the tip of the iceberg, look closely in the upper corners of the windows; you will see a small white circle with a plus sign inside it. These indicate that there are hidden tool panels. Clicking on these icons will display the panels, but you can also toggle the displays with the T key and the N key on your keyboard (Figure 5.34).

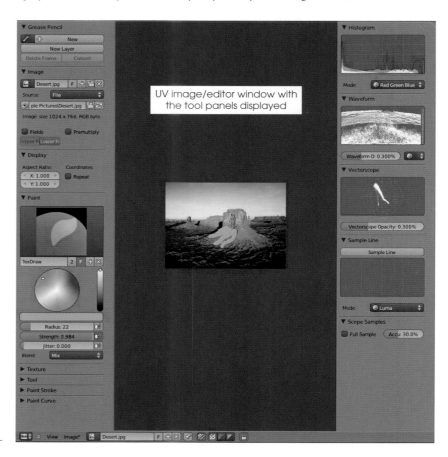

Figure 5.34

6

World Settings

6.1 Introduction to World Settings

The world settings allow you to set the background for your scene. The default world setup is the dull gray, which displays when an image is rendered. The background in the render is not the same as the background in the 3D window. The world button in the properties window displays the settings tabs, the first one being a preview panel (Figure 6.1). Click on the color bars in the world tab to display color pickers for setting the background color. Note that you only see the gold background when you render an image of your scene.

- Horizon color. Color at the horizon.
- Zenith color. Color at the top of the scene.
- Ambient color. Provides an overall lighting effect; an object in the scene will reflect this color regardless of its own material color.
- Sky. Paper, blend, real—these options provide combinations of color gradient across the rendered image.

The examples of sky background combinations in Figure 6.2 have a mist effect added. They are rendered images of a 3D view.

Preview panel showing the horizon color set to gold

Combination of Paper Sky, Blend Sky, and Real Sky

Figure 6.1

Vertical pole object   Wall object with horizontal slats

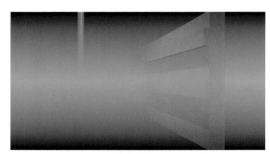

Figure 6.2   Paper Sky + Blend Sky   Paper Sky + Blend Sky + Real Sky

To see the mist effect, "Mist" must be
checked in the "World Settings" tab,
and the "Intensity" value must be set.

Figure 6.3

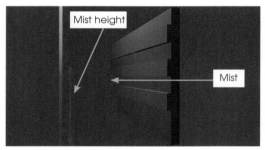

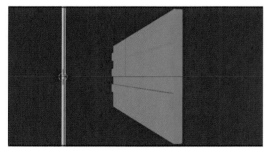

Rendered image   3D window camera view

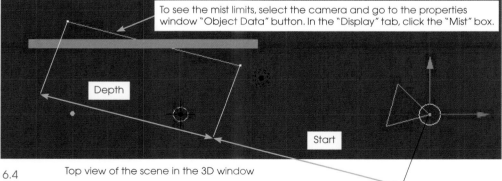

To see the mist limits, select the camera and go to the properties
window "Object Data" button. In the "Display" tab, click the "Mist" box.

Figure 6.4   Top view of the scene in the 3D window

6.2 Mist

Mist settings allow you to introduce a mist or fog effect to your scene (Figure 6.3). To see the mist effect, "Mist" must be checked in the "World" button – "Mist" tab and the "Intensity" value must be set.

- Start. Distance from the camera where the mist starts.
- Depth. Distance over which the mist increases from 0% to 100%.
- Height. Height of the mist (Figure 6.4).

6.3 Stars

The stars tab allows you to introduce stars to your background (Figure 6.5).

Figure 6.5

Check the "Stars" tab.

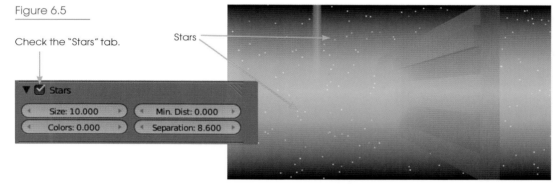

6.4 Texture as Background

Blender's built-in textures can be used to create a background for your scene. The following demonstration will show you how, but you will soon realize that there are many combinations of settings to experiment with. It is a good idea to search the internet and find tutorials showing how to achieve specific effects, but remember that the effects have probably been derived by experimentation.

Begin with the default Blender scene containing the cube object. You can leave the cube selected since the texture we will be applying will affect the scene background and not the cube. Remember that textures do not display in the 3D window; you have to render an image to see them. To make life a little simpler, divide the screen as shown in Figure 6.6.

By default, the properties window displays with the "Render" buttons active. In your setup, make one copy of the properties with the "World" buttons active and the other with the "Texture" buttons active. The "Texture" buttons should be in world texture mode. This setup will allow you to see a preview of your background texture without rendering an image in the 3D window every time you change a setting. The preview only gives an indication of the render and you will have to render an image to see the true result; note the difference in the diagram.

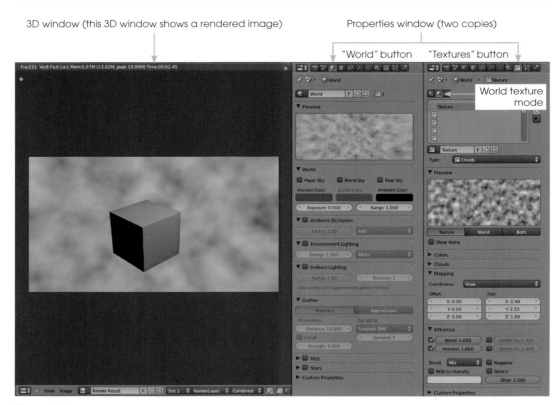

3D window (this 3D window shows a rendered image)

Properties window (two copies)

"World" button   "Textures" button

World texture mode

Figure 6.6

Now, how do we get the background? In the properties window – "Textures" buttons, click on "New" to display the buttons tabs. By default, the texture type "Clouds" opens. You see the clouds texture in the preview panel, but it is a black-and-white image. There is no display in the properties window "World" buttons, and if you render an image in the 3D window (F12), there is only the dull gray background. At this stage, you haven't told Blender what to influence with the texture.

In the properties window – "Textures" buttons (in world texture mode) – "Influence" tab, check (tick) the "Horizon" button (which controls the amount the texture affects the color of the horizon). You will now see the texture as a background in the "World" buttons preview tab. The clouds are pink because of the color in the color bar in the "Influence" tab. Click on the color bar and select a nice pale blue color and the clouds in the preview should look more realistic. A render in the 3D window will give you a precise image of your scene background (Figure 6.7).

The rendered image is not the same as the preview, so you have to adjust the values in the properties window to get the desired effect. In the properties window – world texture mode – "Mapping" tab, adjust the "Offset" and "Size" settings and change "Coordinates"

Figure 6.7

Figure 6.8

in the drop down menu. In the "Influence" tab, try changing the "Blend: Mix" to something else.

In the properties window – "World" button – "World" tab, checking the different "Sky" settings and choosing different colors from the color bars in the horizon, zenith, and ambient settings produce different effects. In the 3D window, select the lamp. In the properties window, try different lamp settings. In the "Lamp" tab, change the lamp type (Point, Sun, Spot, Hemi, and Area). Adjust the "Energy" value and change the light color by clicking on the color bar to reveal a color picker. Render an image at each change to see the different results. Don't forget to try out all the different texture types.

As previously stated, there are many combinations. You just have to experiment and record your settings. When you find something you like that suits your purpose, save it in a .blend file for future use; in this way, you can create your own library.

6.5 Image as Background

You can use any image stored on your computer as a background. Deselect objects in the scene and click the "World" texture type button. In the properties window – "Textures" button, click "New" to add a texture. Select the texture type "Image or Movie" in the "Image" tab. Click "Open" then navigate and select your image. In the "Textures" button – "Influence" tab, click "Horizon." The image will display as the background to your scene when you render (Figure 6.8).

The image renders as a background to the scene.

Learning Unit 7

World Editor – Background Image

Learning Unit 4

Background Image

Note: Altering values in the "Mapping" tab adjusts how the image displays in a render of the scene.

6.6 Image as Template

An image can be displayed in a scene as a template to aid in modeling. With the mouse cursor in the 3D window, press the N key on the keyboard and follow the steps in Figure 6.9.

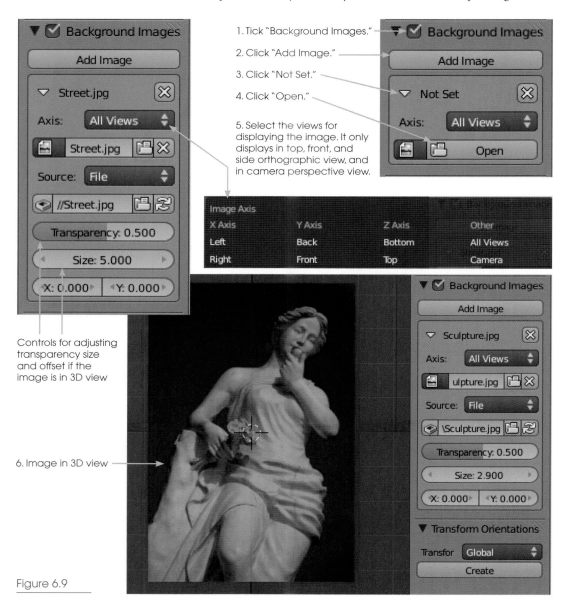

1. Tick "Background Images."

2. Click "Add Image."

3. Click "Not Set."

4. Click "Open."

5. Select the views for displaying the image. It only displays in top, front, and side orthographic view, and in camera perspective view.

Controls for adjusting transparency size and offset if the image is in 3D view

6. Image in 3D view

Figure 6.9

7

Lighting and Cameras

7.1 Lighting

7.1.1 Lighting Types and Settings

The default scene in Blender starts with a cube object, a camera, and a lamp. What the camera sees is what will render as a picture or movie depending on the settings you make. To get a simple rendered view, press the F12 key. This will open a window that displays the rendered output of what the camera is focused on. If the picture shows the cube object as a black silhouette, you do not have a lamp or the lamp settings or placement is incorrect. To exit the render window, press the Esc key.

In most cases, you will need more than one lamp in order to properly illuminate your scene. Most scenes usually require three to four lamps, but be careful not to use too many. Instead of adding lamps, experiment with the distance and energy settings.

7.1.2 Lamp Settings

To create or add a lamp to the scene, position the 3D cursor in a desired location and press Shift + the A key and select "Lamp" from the drop down menu. You can choose your type of lamp (Point, Sun, Spot, Hemi, and Area) and that lamp will be placed in the scene. With the lamp selected, go to the properties window – "Object Data" button to display the setting options (Figure 7.1). The options displayed vary depending on what type of lamp you select. The diagrammatic representation of the lamp in the 3D window also varies depending on the type (Figure 7.2).

Learning
Unit 7

Blender Lighting
– Point Lamp,
Blender Lighting
– Sun Lamp,
Blender Lighting
– Sun Lamp – Sky
and Atmosphere,
Blender Lighting
– Hemi Lamp,
Blender Lighting
– Area Lamp,
Blender Lighting
– Spot Lamp,
Blender Lighting
– Ambient
Occlusion

Figure 7.1

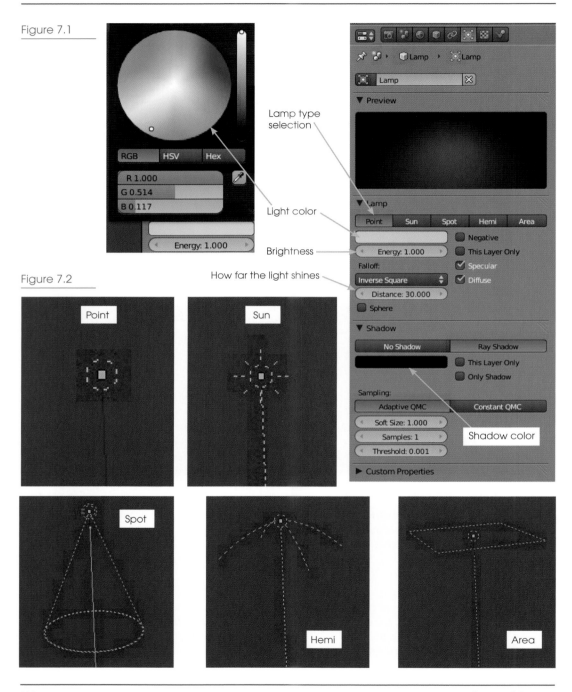

Lamp type
selection

Light color

Brightness

How far the light shines

Figure 7.2

Point

Sun

Spot

Hemi

Area

Shadow color

If you decide that the lamp you have selected is not correct for what you want to achieve, you can change the type in the properties window. Click on the different lamp types in the "Lamp" tab.

Spot lamps or spotlights are particularly useful in creating great effects. They can be scaled, rotated, and positioned to cast shadows and they can also be used with a halo effect to provide a simulation of a light shining through a fog (Figure 7.3). For this and other lamps, experiment with the settings and record your results.

Figure 7.3

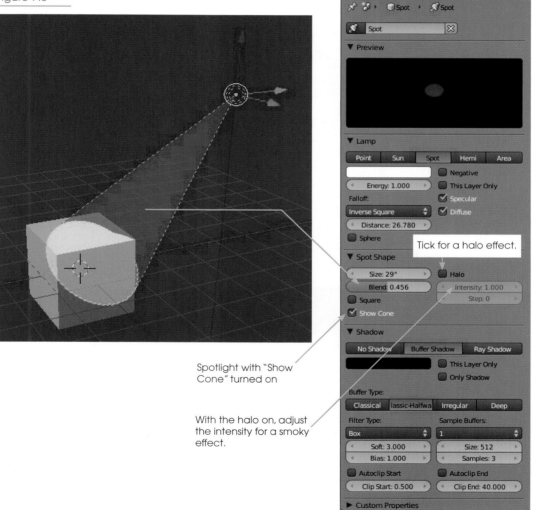

Tick for a halo effect.

Spotlight with "Show Cone" turned on

With the halo on, adjust the intensity for a smoky effect.

Figure 7.4

7.2 Cameras

By default, your scene already has one camera and that is usually all you need, but on occasion you may wish to add more cameras. You can add more cameras by pressing Shift + the A key and selecting "Camera." The new camera will be located where your 3D cursor is positioned and you will have to orientate the camera. To change which camera is active, you need to select that camera and press Ctrl + number pad 0. Figure 7.4 shows the properties window – "Camera" button.

7.2.1 Settings Options

- Perspective or Orthographic. Used to change the camera from showing a true-life perspective view to an orthographic view.
- Focal Length. Sets up a lens length much like a real camera; 35mm is a good, safe setting, but wide and tight angle settings work for different needs.
- Shift. Pushes the camera's view in a direction, without changing perspective.
- Clipping Start. How close an object can get to the camera and still be seen (Figure 7.5).
- Clipping End. How far away objects can be seen by the camera; in very large scenes, this needs to be set higher or things "disappear" from view (Figure 7.5).
- Depth of Field. Used with nodes to blur foreground and background objects; working with nodes will be discussed in Chapter 18.

Figure 7.5

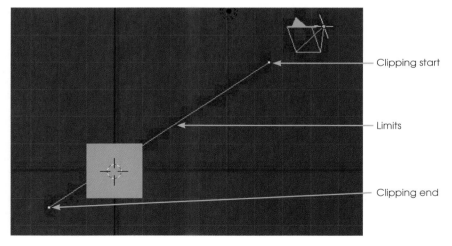

- Limits. Draws a line in the scene to help you visualize the camera's range (Figure 7.5).
- Mist. Gives you a visual display of how far the camera sees if you are adding mist.
- Title Safe. Displays the inner dashed box to help with placement of objects and text.
- Name. Displays the name of the active camera in camera view (number pad 0).
- Size. How big to draw the camera on the screen; you can also control the size with scale.
- Passepartout. Shades the area on the screen outside of the camera's view (Figure 7.6).
- Alpha. Controls the darkness of the shaded area with the slider.

Figure 7.6

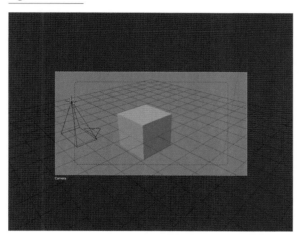

8

Rendering and Ray Tracing

8.1 Render Settings

Rendering is the conversion of the data of the camera view in your Blender scene file into an image file or a movie file. The "Render" tab in the properties window is where you tell the program what you want as an output from your scene (Figure 8.1). Do you want a JPEG picture image or a movie? What size do you want the output to be? Do you want a high quality output or a draft style format? Do you want shadows or ray tracing effects? How about motion blur? If you're doing a movie, how many frames per second do you want the movie to run? Lastly, where do you want to save the file? All of these issues are addressed with the "Render" buttons. Obviously, the higher the quality of the output, the slower it will render and the larger the file size will be when it is finished.

There are many options that need to be addressed in order to save your work as an image or movie. Some of these feature will be discussed in more detail in later chapters. For now, we are just interested in saving basic images in JPEG (.jpg) format and movies in the Windows movie (.mpg) format. Be aware that other options exist and more are added every few releases.

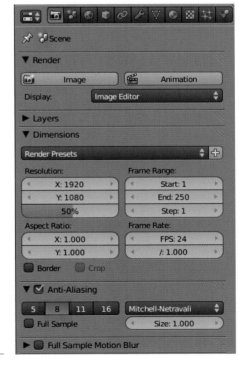

Figure 8.1

Learning Unit 5

Rendering to an Image File

Learning Unit 7

Render Slots

- Render (Figure 8.1)
  - Image. Renders an image the same as pressing F12.
  - Animation. Renders a movie or simple files of your animation; this can take considerable time depending on the animation size.
- Display. Drop down menu for render display options (Figure 8.1).
- Dimensions (Figure 8.1)
  - Render presets drop down menu. Preset rendering sizes for different output formats.
  - Resolution. Manual input of x and y values for rendering size instead of using presets.
  - Aspect ratio. Slider for setting the size of the render display in the 3D window.
  - Frame range. Set the start and end frame for each rendering and the number of steps.
  - Frame rate. Animation playback rate (25 FPS for PAL output, 30 FPS for NTSC output).
- Antialiasing. Output quality settings; they are normally set at 8 to give a nice output without loss of render time (Figure 8.1).
- Shading. Settings that can be turned off to exclude features from the render; the "Alpha Sky" drop down menu gives options for the render background (Figure 8.2).
- Output. The output bar allows you to set where you wish your render to be saved (the default location is the "tmp" folder); the file type drop down menu provides options for the type of file to be rendered and the default file type is PNG (Figure 8.2).

Figure 8.2

8.2 Rendering a JPEG Image

To render a simple JPEG image, set all the options previously discussed. In fact, the default settings will do just fine except for the output file type in the "Output" tab of the properties window—change the default PNG to JPEG. With your scene created in the 3D window, press F12 or the "Render Image" button. With the default settings, the render window will display. Press F3 to open the save window, type in a file name for the image, and press Enter then "Save As Blender File" (Figure 8.3). In the save window you can navigate to a different folder for saving other than the one in the "Output" tab of the properties window.

8. Rendering and Ray Tracing

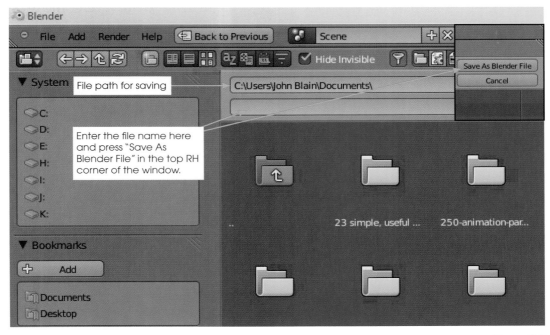

Figure 8.3

Note: If you forgot to change PNG to JPEG, it will not suffice to add a .jpeg extension to the file name. If you entered "FileName.jpg" it will be saved as "FileName.jpg.png" and remain a PNG file type.

8.3 Creating a Video Clip

After you have created your scene with an animation sequence you will be ready to make a movie file. A movie, whether it is a full-length three-hour feature or a short thirty-second television advertisement, is made up of a sequence of clips (movie files) spliced together to tell a story. The following steps are the basics for creating such a file.

1. In the "Output" tab, select the file format from the format selection drop down menu. File formats for television are NTSC for the US or PAL for Europe and Australia. You can also select AVI for playing on your computer.

2. In the "Dimensions" tab, change the file type from the default PNG to MPEG.

3. Also in the "Output" tab, set the path name to the location for saving the file.

4. Make sure "Anti-Aliasing" is ticked and that "8" is selected.

5. Check that the start and end frames of the animation are selected in the "Dimensions" tab.

6. Also in the "Dimensions" tab, check the frame rate is correct: 30 for NTSC or 25 for PAL.

7. In the "Shading" tab make, sure "Shadows" and "Ray Tracing" are ticked.

8. Finally, press the "Animation" button in the "Render" tab.

The video clip (movie file) will take some time to compile depending on the length of the animation. Each frame of the animation has to be rendered and saved. Depending on the complexity of the scene, a frame can take from a few seconds to several minutes to render. To begin, it is best to keep everything very basic and simple. If you get to the stage where you have created a wonderful movie, you can send the animation files to a render farm on the Internet to have them rendered—it saves you time but it costs you money.

8.4 Ray Tracing

Ray tracing is used to produce mirrored and reflective surfaces. It is also used to create transparency and refraction (bending of images through transparent surfaces like a magnifying glass or lens). Ray tracing can create stunning effects but can incur a high cost in render time, so use it sparingly. Don't attempt to ray trace everything—you can get some great shadow and texture effects with spotlight and material settings.

Figure 8.4

8. Rendering and Ray Tracing

The image in Figure 8.4 has been rendered by positioning a sphere above a plane in the 3D window. The plane has a material and an image texture assigned to it. With the sphere selected, subdivided in edit mode, and set smooth, values have been set in the properties window – "Material" button, as shown in Figure 8.5. Note that the camera in the scene has been positioned close to the horizontal midplane and close to the plane and sphere.

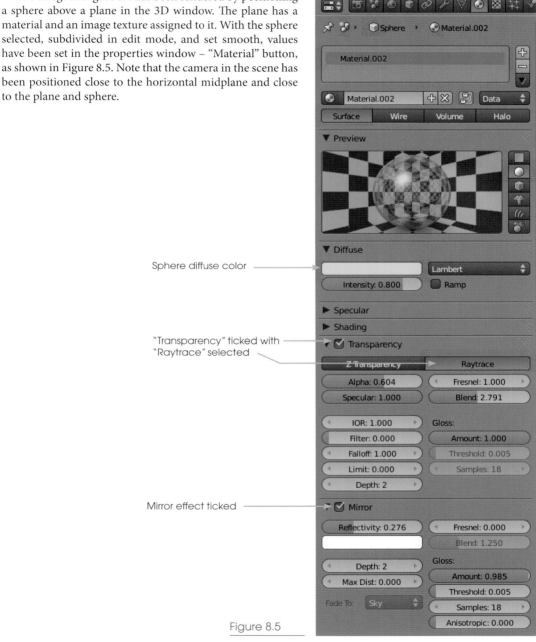

Sphere diffuse color

"Transparency" ticked with "Raytrace" selected

Mirror effect ticked

Figure 8.5

9

Animation Basics

9.1 Introduction to Animation

In this chapter, I will explain how to make objects move about in the scene. This is a big section in Blender with many features. Many of the features will become easier to understand with practice, which will then allow you to progress beyond the basics. This is a highly developed section and new features are being added all the time so it is likely that before this manual is published, new features will be available. We will therefore only attempt the basics.

Before you start, make sure you understand Chapter 8 and the section on rendering. Next, consider what an animation is. Blender uses a certain method of making something appear to move on a computer screen, which may later be transformed into a movie file. This is accomplished by creating a series of still images, each one slightly different from the next, which, when displayed one after the other in quick succession, create the illusion of movement. Each still image is a single frame of the animation. Each frame (image) is rendered, which means the data you enter in the Blender program is correlated and turned into the digital image; this is usually in a JPEG format. Finally, all the images are compiled into one movie file.

After you set up your scene with the object that you wish to animate (the actor), consider what the actor is required to do and how long it should take to do it. Also consider what format you will use in the final render. The render format determines how many frames per second the animation should run at (NTSC for the US at 30 fps, PAL for Australia at 25 fps).

One of the problems that beginner animators experience is trying to make the motions occur in an appropriate time. Remember to look at the frames per second and relate it to time. For example, if you want a movement to take 3 seconds and you are running at 25 frames per second, then the animation has to occur in 75 frames.

In Blender 2.50+, the animation method could be considered in two stages. The first stage is to set up what you want your actor to do in a given time, such as move, change size, or rotate. The second stage is to set up how your actor behaves during the process of moving, changing size, or rotating. The first stage is accomplished by inserting key frames in the animation. Key frames are exactly what the name implies; that is, they are the key (or important) frames within a series of frames. Think of a 10-second animation that, when running at 25 frames per second, would consist of 250 frames. If you want your actor to go from point A to point B and then to point C within the 250-frame animation, you first insert a key frame at point A. This is giving Blender data that says at the frame nominated, locate the actor at position A. Then at the next frame nominated, locate the actor at position B, and so forth for position C. These are the key frames for the animation. Blender will work out all the in-between frames. The key frames also include the data for scaling and rotating the actor as well as other features. This may be stating the obvious, but it is important to understand the concept.

9.2 Moving, Rotating, and Scaling

Moving, rotating, and scaling (along with other features) are accomplished by applying modifiers to the actor. Moving, rotating, and scaling are the three basic modifiers to use in an object animation. When you create key frames in Blender with these modifiers that tell Blender where and how to display the actor at specific frames in the animation, Blender will figure out all the data for the location, scale, and rotation at the in-between frames.

Determining the in-between data is called interpolation. By default, Blender uses Bezier type interpolation, which gives a nice acceleration and deceleration between key frames. Remember, we are considering the movement of an object. When an object moves from point A to point B in a given time, it is said to move at a certain velocity (speed). In theory, the speed could be represented as a straight line graph, but in practice an object at rest (motionless) has to attain the velocity first. The rate at which it attains the velocity is called acceleration. Blender's Bezier interpolation draws curves at the beginning and end of the straight line graph (acceleration and deceleration). You have the options to choose "Constant" or "Linear" type interpolation if appropriate. Selection of interpolation types will be discussed later in this chapter.

Using the term Bezier to describe interpolation is an anomaly. Bezier actually describes a type of line (the line on a graph described in the previous paragraph). A Bezier line or curve in Blender is a line that has control points on it that allow the shape of the line to be altered or edited. In Blender, the control points are located at the position of the key frames. Interpolation is done according to a mathematical formula that determines the shape of the line. When the data for the frames in the animation is drawn as a line on a graph, the line conforms to that mathematical formula. The shape of the line drawn is much like a sine curve, therefore the interpolation could be considered as being type sine.

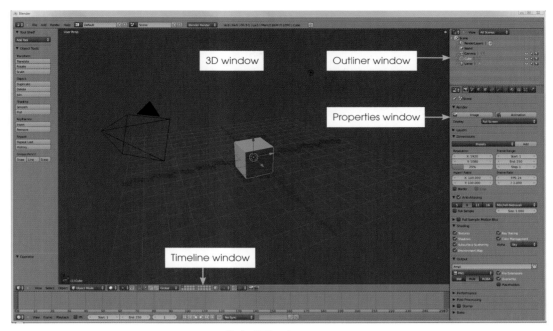

Default Blender scene

Figure 9.1

For the moment, we will accept the default Bezier-type interpolation and demonstrate the insertion of key frames and the creation of a simple animation. We will use the default Blender screen with the 3D window containing the default cube object as the actor. The default screen also displays the outliner window and the properties window at the RHS of the screen and the timeline window across the bottom (Figure 9.1).

To set up our animation, first change the 3D window to top view with orthographic projection (with the cursor in the 3D window press number pad 7 – number pad 5). This just keeps the view simple so we can see where we are going (Figure 9.2). The first step in an animation is to decide what you want your actor to do in a given time. In this case, the actor is the cube object. How long it takes your actor to do something will depend on how many frames per second your animation is run and this is determined by what format your final render will be in.

Let's set our animation to run at 25 frames per second, which would be adequate for PAL format (go to the properties window – "Render" button – "Dimensions" tab – "Frame rate"). Note that the frame range settings are "Start: 1" and "End: 250" (Figure 9.3); this says that our animation will begin at frame 1 and end at frame 250. Running at the rate of 25 frames per second will give an animation time of 10 seconds. If you think about it, 10 seconds is quite a long time for a single action to take place in a video clip.

To make things relatively simple, we will only make our actor (the cube) move in a straight line across the screen along the x-axis and at the same time increase in size.

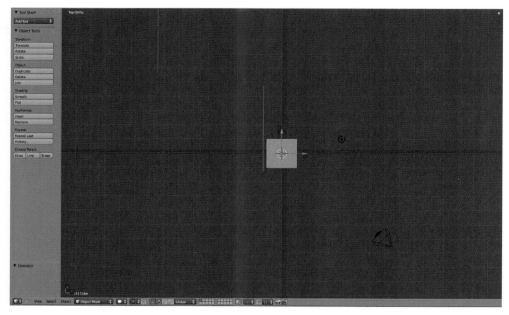

Figure 9.2

Properties window ——

"Render" button ——

Frames per second ——

Figure 9.3

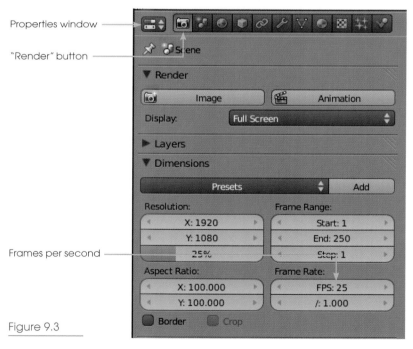

Make sure the cube is selected in the 3D window. We will now insert key frames, only two to start with, just to keep it simple. The default scene is set at frame 1. In the lower LH corner of the window, you will see "(1) Cube" in white lettering (Figure 9.4). This indicates that you have the cube selected at frame 1. If you had ten objects in the scene, all of which were actors with maybe some hidden, it's nice to know what's selected.

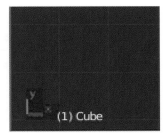

Figure 9.4

Before we insert a key frame, change to frame 25. Go to the timeline window at the bottom of the screen. In the header you will see buttons labeled "Start: 1," "End: 250," and "1." This shows the start frame and end frame that was set by default for the animation and the current frame of the animation. Above the header you will see a scale ranging from 0 to 250 (the total length of the animation in frames). Next to the 0 you will see a vertical green line showing that you are at frame 1. Click on the green line with the LMB and drag the line across to frame 25 (Figure 9.5). Note the number change next to the cube at the lower LH side of the window and in the header bar of the timeline window. Other ways to change the frame are to click on the little arrows on either side of the "1" in the timeline header, click on the button labeled "1" and drag the cursor to the right, or click on the "1," hit delete, and retype the required frame number. *There is always more than one way to skin a cat.*

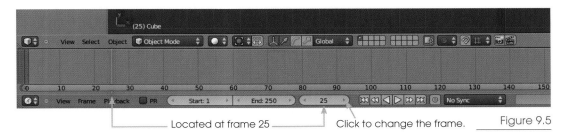

Located at frame 25   Click to change the frame.   Figure 9.5

Now that you are at frame 25 with the cursor in the 3D window, press the I key. In the selection list that displays, select "LocRotScale," which covers moving, rotating, and changing the size of the object (Figure 9.6). You have just inserted a key frame. At this stage, the only way to see this is to click on the green line in the timeline window and drag it away from frame 25. By doing this, you will see a vertical yellow line at frame 25, which indicates a key frame (Figure 9.7).

So far, we have only inserted one key frame and our actor hasn't done anything yet. Going from frame 1 to frame 25 at 25 frames per second equals 1 second. Clicking and dragging the green line in the timeline is called scrubbing the animation, which is actually manually playing the animation; but since we haven't told our actor to do anything yet, nothing happens.

Continue by changing to frame 75 (drag the green line). In the 3D window, grab and move the cube 4 blender units to the right and scale it up to twice its original size. With the cursor in the 3D window, press the I key and select "LocRotScale" again to insert a second key frame. If you move the green line in the timeline window, you will see another yellow key frame line (Figure 9.8). If you continue

Selection list

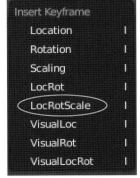

Figure 9.6

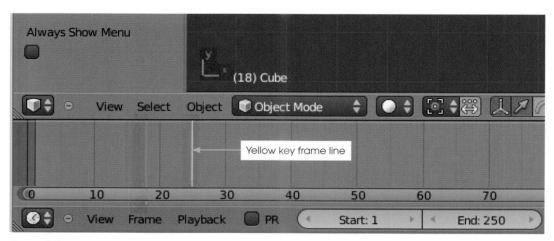

Figure 9.7

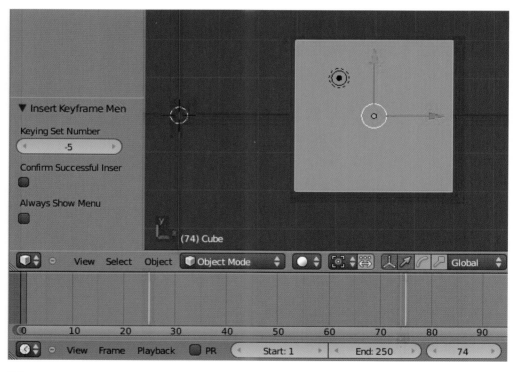

Figure 9.8

9. Animation Basics

moving the green line between frames 25 and 75, you will see the cube move and change in size—you are scrubbing or manually playing the animation. Note that the action only takes place between frames 25 and 75, the location of our key frames; no action takes place on either side of the key frames.

9.3 Viewing Your Animation

To actually play a preview of the animation, move the green line in the timeline to frame 1 then press Alt + the A key with the cursor in the 3D window. Say "one thousand" to yourself slowly (counting one second, while the green line in the timeline moves across to frame 25) and you will see the cube move and increase in size. At frame 75, it stops moving and changing size. The green line in the timeline continues on to frame 250 then jumps back to frame 1 and the preview of the animation plays again. Press Esc to stop playing. Another way to skin this cat is to press the play button in the timeline window (Figure 9.9). This button is much like the play button on any video or audio player.

You can add more key frames to your animation to move, scale, and rotate your actor around the screen. For the most part, location and size keys work flawlessly but care needs to be taken with rotation keys. If you try to rotate an object too far in one set of keys, the object may not rotate in the direction you want it to and it may rotate oddly. Try small angular movements between keys while rotating. There are ways to control this better and tools to simplify the process, which will all be discussed later. Besides rotation, the movement of your actor may not be exactly as planned. Blender automatically defaults to trying to create a smooth flow through the key frames.

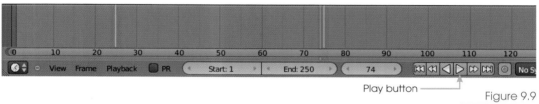

Play button

Figure 9.9

9.4 The Graph Editor Window

The graph editor window shows a graphical display of the animation, and the graphs can be edited to refine and control the actions. Split the 3D window vertically and change one part to the graph editor window. Two panels open: on the RHS is the graphical display panel and to the LHS is the dope sheet (Figure 9.10).

Examine the dope sheet panel (Figure 9.11). In the 3D window, we entered key frames and chose "LocRotScale" as the type. The dope sheet shows a file tree with headings for "Cube," "CubeAction," and "LocRotScale." At the LHS of each line there is a small white triangle that, when clicked with the LMB, opens or closes the directory. Click the LMB on the triangle next to "LocRotScale" to display the list of channels (graphs) in the graphical display. Next to the triangle you should see an eye icon. Clicking the eye icon next to "LocRotScale" activates all of the channels. Click again to close the channels. Each line is a channel for an action in the animation. For instance, the top line "X Location" is the channel for the movement of the cube along the *x*-axis. Clicking the LMB on each of the eye icons

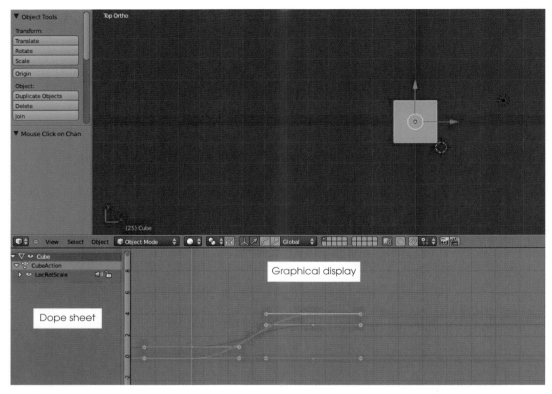

Figure 9.10

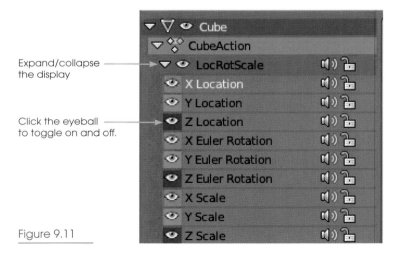

Expand/collapse the display

Click the eyeball to toggle on and off.

Figure 9.11

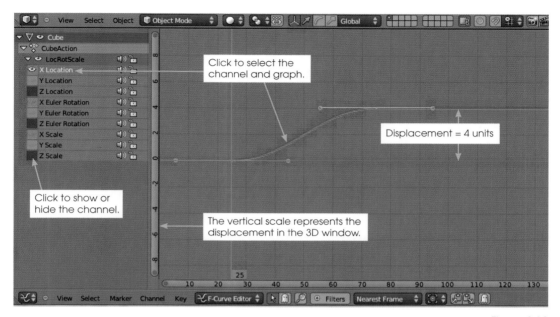

Figure 9.12

will toggle the display on or off. Click all the eye icons except the "X Location" channel. If the name "X Location" turns black and the channel in the graphical display disappears, click the LMB on the name. With only the eye icon for "X Location" active, only the channel for the location of the cube along the *x*-axis is shown (Figure 9.12).

Now note the vertical and horizontal green lines in the graphical display; these are cursors. The vertical green line is the same as the cursor in the timeline window. The horizontal green line cursor provides a visual location for the vertical scale at the LHS. This scale represents the value for the action. For instance, with the "X Location" channel displayed, the values represent the displacement along the *x*-axis of the 3D window. Examine the "X Location" channel in the graphical display. The red line has two short yellow lines attached to it. Each yellow line has a dot at the center and a dot at each end; these yellow lines are called handles. We are looking at a Bezier curve and the yellow lines are called control handles—the control handles are used to change the shape of the curve. I mentioned this type of curve before, and will come back to this topic later.

As previously stated, the location of the vertical green line of the cursor represents the frame number of the animation. You will see it aligns with the frame numbers across the bottom of the window, and at the lower end of the line, a green box holds the frame number. You can click on this line and scrub through the animation the same way as you can in the timeline window. Like all windows in Blender, with the cursor located in that panel, pressing the number pad + and - keys will scale the panel up or down.

Let's get back to the red line ("X Location" channel). The red line shows that from frame 1 to frame 25, there is no displacement of the actor from the midpoint. From frame 25 to frame 75, the actor moves from the midpoint of the 3D window to 4 Blender units along the *x*-axis. From frame 75 to frame 250, the actor remains displaced from the midpoint by 4 Blender units. This is the movement observed when we play the animation. If you now open the eyeball for any one of the "Scale" channels in the dope sheet, you will see a yellow, turquoise, or purple line representing the fact that the actor changes from 1 Blender unit in size to 2 Blender units in size between frame 25 and frame 75. The three lines represent the *x*, *y*, and *z* axes, respectively.

9.5 Editing the Curve

So far we have introduced key frames to set up how we want our actor to behave during the animation and we have seen how that action is graphically represented. We will now see how we can alter the behavior of our actor by altering the shape of the curve representing that action. Remember the type of curve being considered is a Bezier curve, which is designed to be edited.

Go back to the red line. With the cursor in the graphical display, press the A key twice to make sure you have the line selected. If the line shows solid red with the two yellow handles, you are in edit mode; if not, press the Tab key. If you are not in edit mode, the line will be a broken red line without handles.

If you have pressed the A key with the cursor in the graphical editor to deselect a curve and then pressed the A key again to select, the graph appears as a faint red line. Clicking the RMB to select any of the control points turns the line bright red. Clicking on a channel in the dope sheet will accomplish the same thing. It is important to have the line selected bright red before additional control points can be added.

Select the red line with the RMB in edit mode and press the A key to deselect the line; you will have a faint red line with black dots at the location of the handles. Select the handle at frame 75 (click the RMB on the center dot of the handle); the handle will be yellow and the line will be bright red. Hold the RMB and move the handle up 1 unit. Now, click on the right-hand dot on the end of the handle with the RMB, and the left-hand half of the handle fades. Then, click on the right-hand dot on the end of the handle with the RMB and, while holding the mouse button pressed, drag the end of the handle down and to the left. The shape of the curve arches up (Figure 9.13).

Now if you scrub through your animation between frame 25 and frame 75, you will see the actor move along the *x*-axis from zero displacement at frame 25 to something more than 4 Blender units, then return to 4 Blender units at

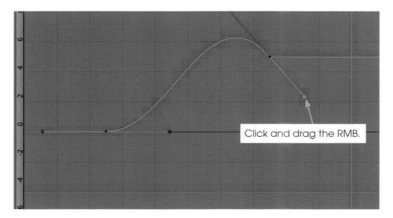

Click and drag the RMB.

Figure 9.13

9. Animation Basics

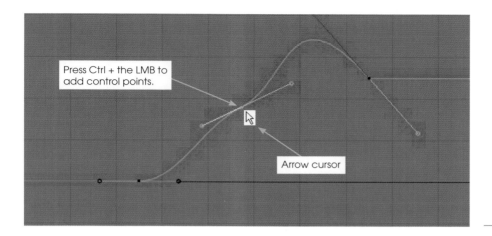

Press Ctrl + the LMB to add control points.

Arrow cursor

Figure 9.14

frame 75. The movement of the actor is being dictated by the shape of the curve. The shape of the curve can thus be altered by moving the ends of the control handles or by selecting the center point of the control handle.

Another feature of the Bezier curve is that control handles may be added anywhere on the curve. In the graphical editor with your "X Location" graph (red line) selected, place your arrow cursor on the line between frame 25 and frame 75, hold the Ctrl key, and click on the line with the LMB (Figure 9.14). Another control handle is created; this is actually another key frame. You can enter a new key frame this way anywhere on the red line in the animation, which is yet another way to skin the cat.

9.6 Other Types of Curves

I had previously made note that, by default, Blender selects the Bezier type interpolation to insert frames between key frames. At this point, it should also be noted that there are two other options. In the graph editor window, select all the channels in the dope sheet panel by clicking open the eyeballs. All the graphs will display in the graphical editor panel. Now press the A key twice to make sure they are all selected.

Go to the graph editor window header – "Key" button – "Interpolation Mode" and you will see the option to select "Constant," "Linear," or "Bezier." Clicking on "Constant" or "Linear" will change the type of graphs and therefore change the action of the actor. "Constant" results in a dramatic quick change from one state to the other at a given frame while "Linear" produces a change following a straight line graph between points (Figure 9.15). The choice of these types of graphs and motions depends on how you want your actor to behave in the animation. Both of the alternatives to Bezier give the option to grab and move points and to add additional points on the graph, but Bezier is by far the most flexible of the three.

Blender interpolates to add frames between the key frames according to which of the previous graph options were selected. Blender can also figure out what to do with the frames of the animation before the first key frame and after the last key frame, which

Figure 9.15

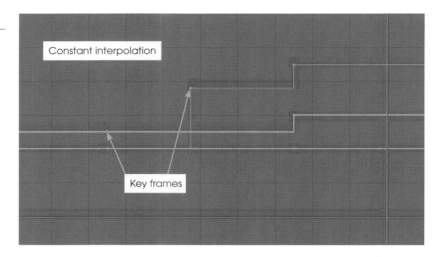

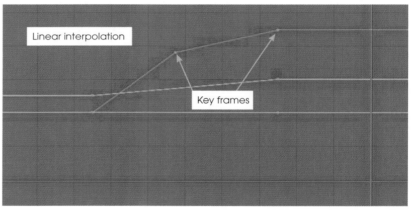

is called extrapolation. There are two extrapolation options in Blender: "Constant" and "Linear." By default, Blender selects "Constant."

Constant extrapolation can be seen with the "X Location" channel selected in the dope sheet. With key frames at frame 25 and frame 75, Blender has interpolated the in-between frames according to the default Bezier method. That is, Blender has inserted frames that comply with a Bezier curve. On either side of the key frames, you can see horizontal lines that dictate no further change in status. This is constant extrapolation. If you go to the graph editor window header – "Channel" button – "Extrapolation Mode" and select "Linear Extrapolation," notice what happens to the curve. Blender takes a look at frames 25 and 26 and from the data plots a straight line coming up at an angle. Blender also looks at frames 74 and 75 and plots a straight line curve leaving the curve. The action of the actor before and after the two key frames will follow these straight line curves.

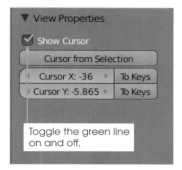

Toggle the green line on and off.

Figure 9.16

Figure 9.17

9.7 Modifying Curves

So far we have discussed creating graphical curves and how to change or modify them, thus changing how our actor behaves in the scene. Blender has more options for more subtle control of animation.

In the dope sheet, display all the channels and select them all. With your arrow cursor in the dope sheet, press the A key until all the channels are highlighted in white. Click on all the eyeballs until they are open. Now press the N key to display a panel with a "View Properties" tab (Figure 9.16). This panel will only provide the option to show or hide the cursor (the green horizontal line). In the dope sheet, close all the eyeballs except for the "X Location" channel. In the graphical editor, click the A key twice to ensure all channels are selected; since only the "X Location" eyeball is open, only that graph will display. Click on the "X Location" channel in the dope sheet.

The new panel will now display four tabs: "View Properties," "Active F-Curve," "Active Keyframe," and "Modifiers" (Figure 9.17). The "Active F-Curve" tab shows that the "X Location" curve is selected and that it is displayed in an "Auto XYZ to RGB" color. This color may be changed by clicking on the drop down menu under "Display Color." It could be advantageous to change the color of a curve if it is required to distinguish the curve from another one.

At this point, we are interested in modifying our curve, not changing its color. Note the "Modifiers" tab with its "Add Modifier" button. Clicking on this button produces a drop down menu with eight options. We will not attempt to demonstrate all of these options at this time, but several are of particular interest. We have the "X Location" channel curve selected in the graph editor panel. Now click on "Add Modifier" and select "Cycles" (Figure 9.18). The graph changes rather dramatically. The curve between frame 25 and frame 75 is the same, but instead of straight lines on either side, Blender has duplicated this curve. By selecting "Cycles," we have made the movement of the curve cycle in 25-frame increments on either side of the 25-to-75 frame block.

We are starting to get into the complexity of Blender and its multiple options. Look at the little "Cycles" panel that has displayed under the "Add Modifier" button. Note the "Before" and "After" options. Each of these have drop

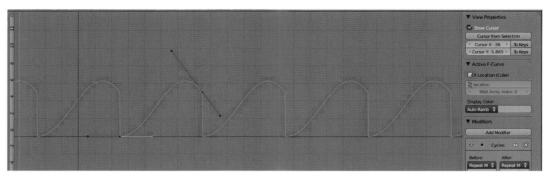

Figure 9.18

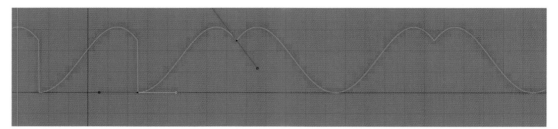

Figure 9.19

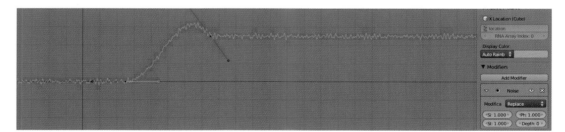

Figure 9.20

down menu buttons that give options for how the cycles are to be repeated before and after the frame block. Click on the "After" button and select "Repeat Mirrored" (Figure 9.19).

Let's have another demonstration. Click on the "X" at the top right hand corner of the "Cycles" panel to delete the modifier. Click on "Add Modifier" again and this time select "Noise" (Figure 9.20). We now have our original graph with the jitters, and if you scrub your animation, you will see that's exactly what you get in the movement of the actor. Of course, it doesn't stop there; the "Noise" modifier contains a drop down to select sub options and buttons to alter values for the options. You now have plenty to play with.

For another demonstration, delete the "Noise" modifier and select the "Built In Function" modifier. This produces a straight sinusoidal graph. Check out the drop down menu in this modifier panel for the selection of graphs based on various mathematical functions. All selections have buttons to control values that are introduced, which provides more stuff to play with.

To get more experienced, try adding multiple modifiers to your curve. Just click on the "Add Modifier" button without deleting what you already have.

9.8 Automatic Key Framing

Previously, key frames have been inserted in our animation by having our cursor in the 3D window, moving the timeline to a particular frame, changing the status of our object, and then pressing the I key and selecting a key frame option. Besides this method, after the frame has been selected and the object status changed, we can press the "Insert Keyframe" button in the toolbar at the LHS of the 3D window (the T key toggles between hiding and showing this panel).

There is another method that makes life a lot easier when multiple key frames are required. In the timeline window header, you will see a red button next to the play control buttons. Clicking on this button toggles automatic key framing on and off (Figure 9.21). With auto on, whenever you move, scale, or rotate your actor object in the 3D window, a key frame will be inserted at whatever frame you have selected. Remember to turn this off after you're done using it.

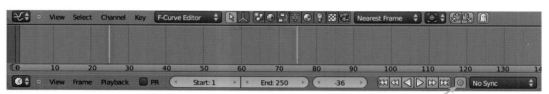

Toggle automatic key framing on and off.

Figure 9.21

9.9 Animating Other Features

Having an understanding of animation basics allows us to look at some of the other things that can be animated in Blender besides the movement, rotation, and size of an object. It is also possible to animate among other things such as materials, textures, lamps, and world settings.

The following is a list of some of the features that can be animated:

- Material animation options
  - Material RGB values. Color can be animated to change.
  - Alpha. The transparency of an object can be animated.
  - Halo size. A halo can grow or shrink in an animation. Setting a halo to zero will make it disappear.
  - Texture offset. Texture applied to an object can be animated. It can move across the face or change in size.

- Lamp animation options
  - Lamp RGB values. The color of light can be animated to change.
  - Energy. The intensity of light can vary.
  - Spotlight size. The angle of the beam can be animated to change.
  - Texture. Texture can be applied to a lamp and animated.
- World animation options
  - Zenith RGB. Color of the zenith (top) can be animated. This is great for sunsets or sunrises.
  - Horizon RGB. Color of the horizon (bottom) can be animated.
  - Mist. Fog can be animated for interesting effects.
  - Stars. Stars can be made to move.
  - Texture offset and size: Texture applied to a world can be made to move.

The list above contains only some of the features that can be animated in Blender. To give you an idea how this is possible, we will take a closer look at the following two examples.

9.9.1 Example 1: Color

Let's start with the color of an object. Open up a new scene in Blender (the default scene with the cube object will do). Go to the properties window and click on the "Material" button. When you open the default scene in Blender, the cube object in the scene is selected. Make sure it is selected before clicking on the "Material" button—after all, we are concerned with the material of the cube object.

The properties window with the "Material" button activated shows a whole bunch of tabs for controlling how the surface of the object displays in the 3D window. To begin, note the "Preview" tab showing a dull gray sphere and below that the "Diffuse" tab with a button showing the same dull gray color.

Look at the timeline window across the bottom of the screen. The green line shows at frame 1 of a 250-frame animation (there is a scale ranging from 0 to 250 along the bottom of the window above the header). We are again going to insert key frames on the timeline so that we can make the color of our cube object change from gray to red over 50 frames of the animation. You could change the starting color of the cube by clicking on the diffuse color button with the LMB to display a color picker, and click anywhere in the colored circle to change the color, but let's just leave things alone for the time being and stick with dull old gray.

Instead of clicking with the LMB on the diffuse color button, click with the RMB and in the menu that displays click on "Insert Keyframes." You have inserted a key frame at frame 1 on the timeline. Change to frame 50 (scrub the green line in the timeline window). Now click with the LMB on the diffuse color button and in the color picker that displays, click on the red part of the colored circle. This changes the color of the cube to red. Click on the diffuse color button again, this time with the RMB and then click on "Insert Keyframes" to insert a key frame at frame 50. Now when you scrub the timeline, you will see the color of the cube change from gray to red over the 50 frames. Hitting Alt + the A key will play this animation. If you open the graphical editor window, you will see the graphical representation of this animation.

9.9.2 Example 2: Spotlight Size

To show how the spotlight may be animated, we first need to put a spotlight into the Blender scene. Let's start again with the default Blender scene with the cube. Change the 3D window to show the front side view and deselect the cube with the A key. With the cursor in the 3D window, hit number pad 1, hit Shift + the A key, then select "Add" – "Lamp" – "Spot." You will see some orange lines appear in the 3D window. Hit the G key (grab) then the Z key and move the mouse up. The G key lets you grab the spotlight so you can move it and the Z key confines the movement to the z-axis. You could also have clicked with the LMB on the blue arrow of the 3D manipulator widget and moved the spotlight up the z-axis. You will see that you have actually moved a cone in the screen. Hit the S key and move the cursor towards the apex of the cone to scale the spotlight down a bit. The light is at the apex of the cone and the circle at the bottom represents the circle of light it would generate.

Now go to the properties window and press the "Object Data" button to display all the buttons that control the properties of the spotlight. Look for the "Spot Shape" tab and you'll notice the button with "Size: 45" in it, which indicates that the angle of the cone is 45 degrees. The timeline window is again across the bottom of the screen and the green line indicates that we are at frame number 1.

Right click on the "Spot Shape Size" button and select "Insert Keyframes" from the menu that displays. The "Size" button will turn yellow indicating that you have inserted a key frame in the timeline. Scrub the green line in the timeline to frame 50. The "Size" button turns green because there is no key frame at frame 50 yet. Left click on the "Size" button and, while holding the mouse button, move the mouse to the left, decreasing the value of the cone angle. The angle of the cone in the 3D window will decrease accordingly. Right click on the "Size" button and select "Insert Keyframes" again, and the button turns yellow. We now have a key frame at frame 50. Scrub the green line in the timeline window between frames 1 and 50 to see the angle of the cone change. You have animated the spotlight size.

Note: Many properties can be animated this way by inserting key frames and changing property values. You have lots of experimenting to do.

9.10 Keying Sets

You can add multiple properties to a group called a keying set, which allows you to animate a whole bunch of stuff at one time. You do this by first defining a keying set. We will again look at our cube actor in the default Blender window. Let's say you want to have the cube move along the x-axis and change color at the same time. Not too difficult—just add a bunch of key frames. But consider if you had a lot of property changes. Adding all those key frames one by one could become tedious. It would be nice if you could do the property changes then hit a button to add all the key frames in one go. Let's do it.

With the cube selected in the 3D window, go to the properties window. We will consider the movement part of the exercise first. Click on the "Object" button in the header and find the "Transform" tab and the "Location" buttons. You will see the values X: 0.000, Y: 0.000, and Z: 0.000. This shows that the cube is at the center of the 3D window in all planes. So, we are concerned with the movement on the *x*-axis. Right click on "X: 0.000" and in the panel that displays, click "Add Single to Keying Set." If you look at the timeline window header, you will see a button labeled "ButtonsKeyingSet" and two little key icons next to it. One of them has a red line across it. Note in the timeline that you are at frame 1. You have just entered the information into a keying set, telling Blender that at frame 1 the cube is located on the *x*-axis at position 0.000.

Now let's consider the color part of the exercise. In the properties window, click on the "Material" button. Right click on the "Diffuse color" button then click on "Add All to Keying Set." Make sure you click on "Add All" not "Add Single"—now the information for the color has been added to the keying set.

In the timeline window header, click on the first of the little key icons (not the one with the red line). You have entered a key frame for the location and color of the cube. You can see this in the graph editor window by opening up all the headings in the dope sheet.

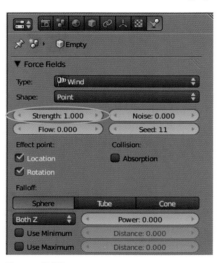

Figure 9.22

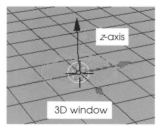

Figure 9.23

Now move to frame 40 or wherever you wish on the timeline. Change the value for the "Transform" – "Location" – "X axis" in the properties window "Object" tab. Right click the new value and click "Add Single to Keying Set." Do the same thing for the "Material" – "Diffuse color" value, but make sure you click on "Add All to Keying Set." Now click on the first of the key icons again to add the new key frame at frame 40. Scrub the timeline to see the cube move and change color.

9.11 Wind Strength Animation

Wind force can be applied to particles and cloth. The wind strength can be animated to provide a realistic reaction to account for varying wind strength. In the 3D window, add an "Empty." Split the 3D window in two and make one half the graph editor window. With the empty selected in the 3D window, go to the properties window "Physics" button. In the "Force Field" tab, click on the "Type" panel to display the drop down selection panel and select "Wind" (Figure 9.22). The wind force is displayed in the 3D window as a stack of circles along the positive *z*-axis (Figure 9.23).

In the physics "Force Field" tab, the "Strength" value refers to the wind strength. Increasing the value causes the circles in the 3D window to move apart, showing the increase. Starting with "Strength = 1.000" at frame 1 on the timeline, right click in the "Strength" panel and select "Insert Keyframe" in the drop down menu that displays (Figure 9.24). A key frame is added in the graph editor window. Click on the vertical green line and drag it along to frame 41. You will see your first key shown as the orange dot at frame 1 (Figure 9.25). With the green line at frame 41, alter the "Strength" value to 7.000 and right click in the "Strength" panel again. Select "Insert Keyframe" and a second key is added in the graph editor win-

Figure 9.24

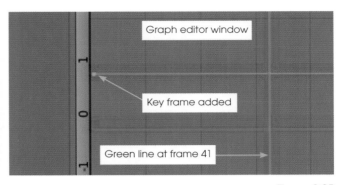

Figure 9.25

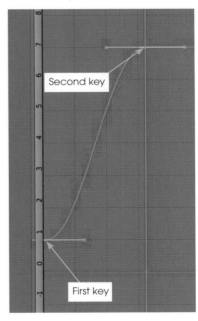

Graph editor window

Figure 9.26

dow (Figure 9.26). By moving (scrubbing) the green line in the graph editor window back to frame 1, you will see the wind strength alter in the 3D window. Move the green line back to frame 1. With your cursor in the 3D window, press Alt + the A key and you will see the wind strength animated.

This method shows you the manual insertion of key frames. To make life easier, there is an automatic insertion of key frames method. Go to frame 41 (you can start where you like but let's build on what we already have). In the timeline window at the bottom of the screen, click on the red button next to where it says "No Sync" (Figure 9.27). Move the green line along the timeline and change the "Strength" value. A third key frame is added in the graph editor window. Repeat this a few times, increasing and decreasing the strength value (Figure 9.28). By scrubbing through the animation, you see the wind strength animated in the 3D window. Move the green line back to frame 1 and press Alt + the A key and play the animation.

With the wind strength animated, you can direct it as particles or soft body objects, which influences how it behaves in an animation.

Figure 9.27

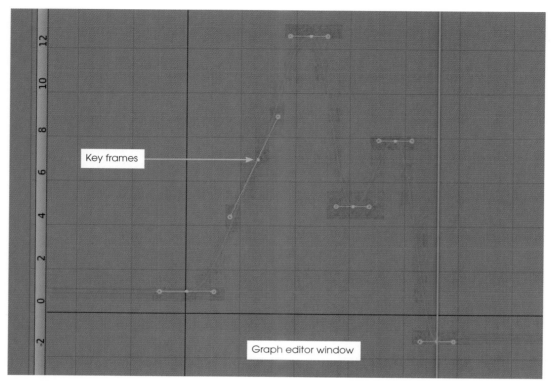

Figure 9.28

9.12 Animation Following Curves

Animating the movement of objects in a scene by inserting key frames can be very tedious when the movement is complex. To animate the movement of an object that twists and turns in the scene over many frames, you have to insert many key frames. Editing the movement at a later stage after executing this method can be difficult, but there is an easier way.

Actually, there are at least two ways, both of which involve having an object follow a predetermined path. One method requires you to set a child/parent relationship between the object and the path; the other method requires that you place a "Follow Path" constraint on the object.

9.12.1 Following a Path: The Child/Parent Relationship Method

Open Blender with the default scene containing the cube object. The scene will be displayed in user perspective view. Change to top orthographic view (number pad 7 for top perspective view then number pad 5 for top orthographic view). By default, the cube is selected in object mode. Deselect the cube by pressing the A key.

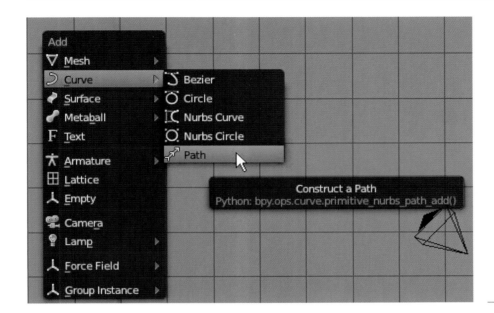

Figure 9.29

We want the cube to move in the scene following a predetermined path. The path will be a curve path (Shift + the A Key – "Add" – "Curve" – "Path") (Figure 9.29). You can use any of the "Curve" options for your path, but for the time being we will use the "Path" option since it is the simplest.

Adding a curve path places a straight line on your screen in object mode. Do not be confused. In Blender, this particular straight line is considered to be a curve and it is also a path. Scale the line to make it five times as long (S key + number pad 5 and click the LMB). If the line runs off the edge of the window, press the number pad - key to zoom out of the scene. The number pad + key will zoom in.

To start, we will make the cube move along the straight line of the curve path. This isn't very exciting, but it will show you the principles of the operation. Deselect the path with the A key and select the cube (click the RMB with the mouse cursor on the cube). Hold the Shift key and click the RMB on the curve path. The cube and the path will both be selected at the same time. Make sure the cube is selected first followed by the path; it's as if you are pointing to the cube and saying "Cube, follow the path."

We will now apply a specific child/parent relationship. In a normal case, selecting the cube then shift selecting the path and applying an "Object" child/parent relationship would simply make the cube the child of the path. If the path moved, the cube would follow. However, we want the cube to move along the path. With both the cube and the path selected, press Ctrl + the P key and select "Follow Path" from the options displayed (Figure 9.30). Remember that in the selection process, the cube must be selected first, followed by the path.

Deselect both the cube and the path with the A key and select only the cube. Move the cube along the *y*-axis of the scene (the G key + the Y key and move the mouse). You will see

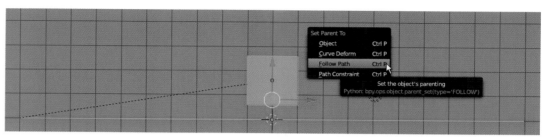

Figure 9.30

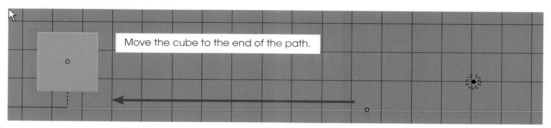

Move the cube to the end of the path.

Figure 9.31

Properties window   "Object Data" button

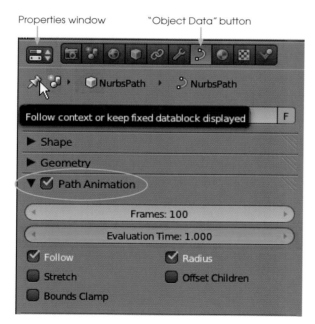

Figure 9.32

a dotted line drawn from the cube to one end of the path. The line indicates that the child/parent relationship is in place. Move the cube to the end of the path where the dotted line is attached (Figure 9.31). Press Alt + the A key on the keyboard or click on the "Play" arrow in the timeline window—either method will play an animation showing the cube moving along the path.

Blender has created a 100-frame animation. With the path selected, the details of the animation can be seen in the properties window – "Object Data" button – "Path Animation" tab (Figure 9.32). You can also see a graphical display in the graph editor window (Figure 9.33).

Note: In the graph editor window, the movement of the cube is drawn as a red line inclined rather steeply. Since the line is straight, it shows that the cube moves with constant velocity (speed) along the path.

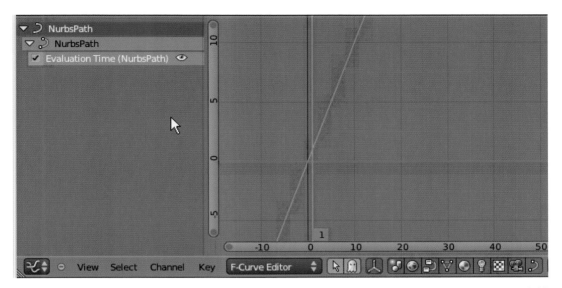

Figure 9.33

The scale along the bottom of the window shows frames of the animation and the vertical scale on the LHS shows displacement (how far the object moves). The displacement from one frame to the next is always the same, hence constant velocity. There is no acceleration or deceleration, as would be the case if you had used key frames.

Now, if you decide that you want to move in something other than a straight line, the speed, acceleration, and direction of movement may have to be modified. The direction of movement is modified by altering the shape of the path in the 3D window. The variation in velocity and acceleration are altered in the graph editor window. We will first alter the direction of movement by reshaping the curve path.

In the 3D window, select the path by right clicking on it, and then tab to put the path into edit mode. Remember, in the beginning of this section we scaled the path to make it longer while it was in object mode. You can do the same thing in edit mode. Just press the S key and drag the mouse or, if you know how many times longer you want the path to be, press the S key followed by a number key (use the number key at the top of the keyboard not a number pad key).

Note that increasing the length of the path does not increase the length of the animation. You still have 100 frames in the animation; therefore, when running the animation at 25 frames per second, your object will move along the path in 4 seconds. If you made the path twice as long, the object would move on the screen twice as fast. Another way to change the speed is to alter the number of frames in the animation in the properties window – "Object Data" button – "Path Animation" tab. If you increase the number of

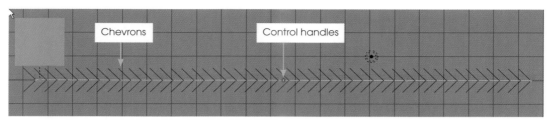

Figure 9.34

frames to 200, it will take the object twice as long to move along the same path length. Controlling the speed of the object can also be done in the graph editor window, but we will come back to that in a moment.

Note: With the path selected in edit mode, there are black chevrons along the path and several orange dots (Figure 9.34). The chevrons indicate the direction of motion and velocity. In this case, they are evenly spaced, indicating constant velocity. The orange dots are control handles for shaping the path—there is one at each end and others in between the ends. By default, when you enter edit mode, all the control points are selected. Press the A key to deselect them, then right click on one point to select it alone.

If you have the manipulation widget turned on, the widget will be located at the selected control point. If you click on the widget handles (with the widget in translate manipulator mode) and drag the mouse, the control point will be moved and the shape of the path will be altered (Figure 9.35). You can select any of the control points and reshape the path in this way. Selecting an end control point and pressing the E key, then dragging the mouse will extrude the end of the path. You can go into front side view or end view and reshape the path in three dimensions, creating any shape you wish.

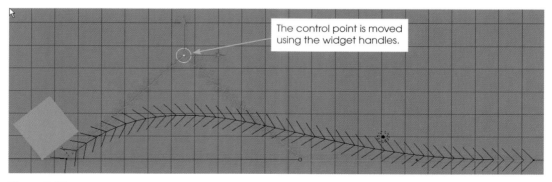

Figure 9.35

After reshaping the path, press Alt + the A key to see the cube move along the path. For the cube to follow the path with its axis aligned to the path, you must have "Follow" ticked in the properties window – "Path Animation" tab. Shaping the path gets the cube moving around in the scene, but it moves along the path at a constant speed. In real life, if the cube came to a sharp corner without slowing down, it undoubtedly would suffer an accident. To create a realistic movement, we need to vary the speed.

Varying the speed is performed in the graph editor window. It helps at this stage if you have both the graph editor window and the 3D window displayed at the same time. Divide the 3D window in two horizontally and change one half to the graph editor window. You will probably have to zoom in on the graph editor window and pan the window into position. At this point, all we have is the red line showing a constant velocity and unfortunately the line is uneditable. The horizontal and vertical green lines are cursor lines; the vertical line is a cursor for positioning along the horizontal timeline measured in frames of the animation, and the horizontal line positions on the vertical displacement scale measured in Blender units.

On the LHS of the graph editor, you will see the dope sheet panel. With the path selected in the 3D window, the dope sheet shows information associated with the path. Click on the lower white arrow at the LHS of the panel and a channel will display labeled "Evaluation Time." Clicking on the eyeball at the LHS of the channel toggles the display of the red line on and off. Clicking on the little speaker icon at the RHS of the channel toggles between selection and deselection of the channel.

The channel in the dope sheet panel is a graphical representation of information associated with the display in the "Evaluation Time" button in the properties widow – "Object Data" button – "Path Animation" tab (the green bar). The same information is displayed as the red line in the graph editor window.

So what is this "Evaluation Time" business? Let's evaluate what we have at this stage. In the 3D window, we have a cube object parented to a curve path. Blender has set the cube to traverse the path in 100 frames of the animation—this happens to be the first 100 frames of the animation. In the timeline window at the bottom of the screen, the total animation is set at 250 frames starting at frame number 1 and ending at frame 250 (Figure 9.36). Playing the animation shows the cube moving along the path starting at frame 1 and reaching the end of the path at frame 100. The animation continues to play on to frame 250.

Figure 9.36

In the properties window – "Object Data" button – "Path Animation" tab (with the path selected in the 3D window) "Frames: 100" is the number of frames to traverse the path. "Evaluation Time: 1.000" is where the cube is located on the path at frame 1. Increasing the

Figure 9.37

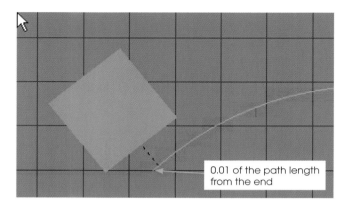

0.01 of the path length
from the end

"Evaluation Time" value moves the cube along the path, and increasing the value to 100 places the cube at the end of the path.

Note: At frame 1, the cube is not located exactly at the end of the path. It is in fact positioned 0.01 of the path length from the end (Figure 9.37). The animation starts at frame 1, not from 0. This is evident where the dotted line between the cube and the path is attached. Obviously you can't have zero frames or you wouldn't have an animation.

You may deduce that the "Evaluation Time" is saying, "This is what our cube is doing at this position." We are only considering location here, but if the cube were animated to change scale, rotate, or change color, its state would be evaluated at whatever position was selected. The "Evaluation Time" value is a percentage of the path length. However, we were considering how to change the velocity of the cube as it moved along the path—let's get back to it.

We have established that the "Evaluation Time" data cannot be modified. We will therefore remove it. With the "Evaluation Time" channel selected (highlighted in white) in the dope sheet panel of the graph editor, place the mouse cursor in the panel and press the X key. The channel and the red line are deleted (Figure 9.38). If the animation is played, the cube does not move; the cube remains parented to the path but there is no longer an animation associated with it.

We will now set up a new animation. In the timeline window make sure the cursor (green line) is located at frame 1 and that the cube is at the start of the path in the 3D window. With the path selected in the 3D window, go to the properties window – "Object Data" button – "Path Animation" tab and set the "Evaluation Time" button value to 0.000. Right click on the "Evaluation Time" button and select "Insert Keyframe" from the drop down menu that displays (Figure 9.39). (Right click on the button a second time if the "Insert Keyframe" fails to display the first time. The first time I click on the button, I get an option to align the tabs in the window.)

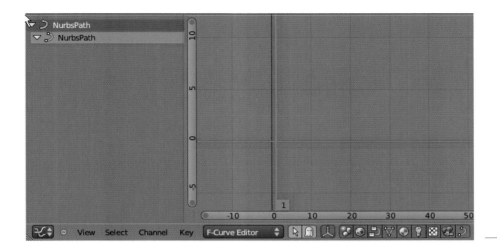

Figure 9.38

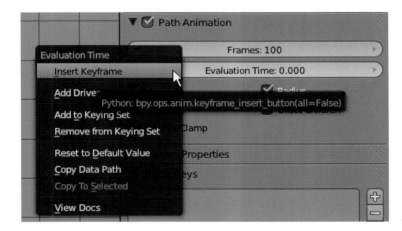

Figure 9.39

The "Evaluation Time" button becomes shaded yellow and an "Evaluation Time" channel is entered in the dope sheet panel (Figure 9.40). A horizontal red line is drawn in the graph editor window with a dot under the vertical green line (cursor); the red line is an animation curve and the dot is a key frame at frame 1.

In the timeline window, move the cursor to frame 150. We will make the cube move along the path in 150 frames. Change the "Evaluation Time" value to 100 to place the cube at the end of the path—we now have the cube at the end of the path at frame 150 (Figure 9.41). Right click on the "Evaluation Time" button and insert another key frame. Zoom in on the graph editor window and you will see a second key frame entered above the first at frame 150. The key frames now have handles attached showing that the animation curve is a

Figure 9.40

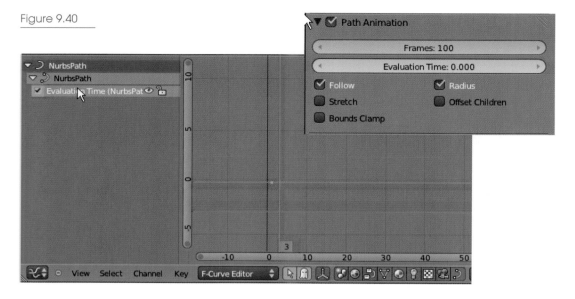

Figure 9.41

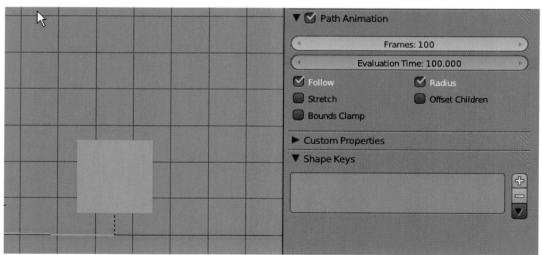

Bezier-type curve, which means it is editable (Figure 9.42). In the timeline window, return to frame 1 and press Alt + the A Key or press the "Play" button to play the animation (Figure 9.43). When the cube moves along the path, there is acceleration at the start and deceleration at the end.

9. Animation Basics

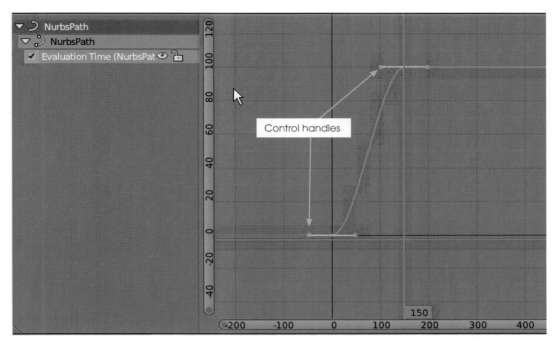

Figure 9.42

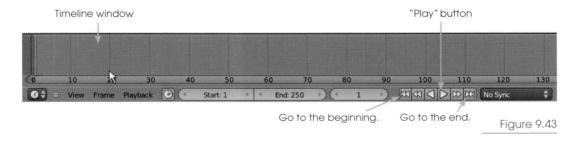

Figure 9.43

Let's play with the movement of the cube as it traverses the path. To alter the movement of the cube, we will edit the animation curve in the graph editor window. To start, we will make the cube take longer to traverse the length of the path in the 3D window. With the mouse cursor in the graph editor window, press the A key to deselect the animation curve then right click on the key frame handle at frame 150 (the upper handle). Press the G key and move the mouse, dragging the handle to the right to frame 400 (Figure 9.44). We have told the cube to move along the path in 400 frames instead of 150 frames. Play the animation to see the cube crawl along.

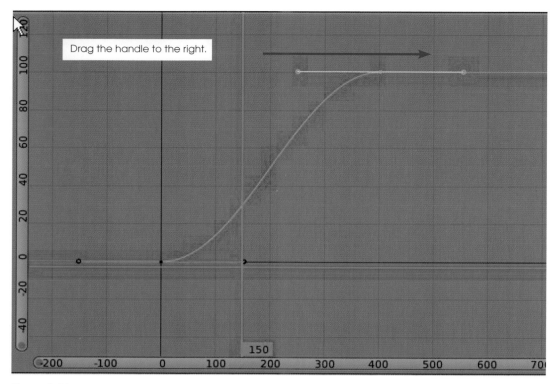

Drag the handle to the right.

150

-200   -100   0   100   200   300   400   500   600   70(

Figure 9.44

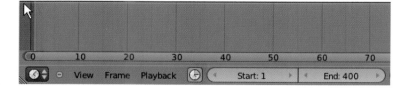

0   10   20   30   40   50   60   70

View   Frame   Playback   Start: 1   End: 400

Figure 9.45

Whoops, the cube doesn't reach the end of the path! In the timeline window, the end frame of the animation is still set at 250, so the animation replays after 250 frames and the cube never reaches the end of the path. In the timeline window, change the "End" value to 400 and replay (Figure 9.45). Now we're right!

Since the animation curve in the graph editor window is a Bezier-type curve, we can add handles to it to further refine movement. Press Ctrl and click the LMB on the curve to add a handle. Add another handle and then press the G key (grab) and position the handles approximately as shown in Figure 9.46. When the animation is replayed, the cube moves along the path then reverses before continuing on to the end. If the animation curve were horizontal between the two intermediate handles, the cube would simply stop for a rest

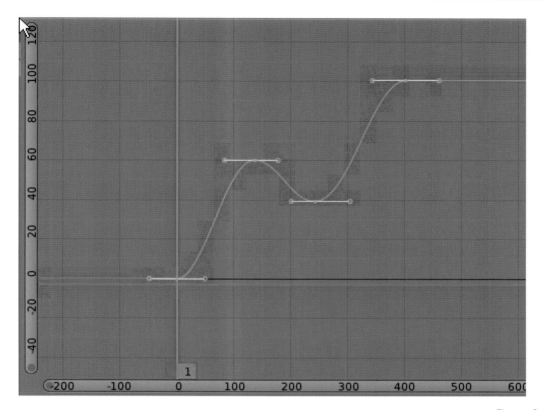

Figure 9.46

along the way. By playing with the animation curve in the graph editor and changing the shape of the path in the 3D window, you have full control over the movement of the cube in the 3D window.

9.12.2 Following a Path: The Follow Path Constraint Method

The foregoing tutorial involving the child/parent relationship is akin to following the long and winding road. Now we can take the shortcut, but remember that shortcuts miss out on the detail of the journey.

We will now have the same cube object follow the same path but immediately have an editable Bezier curve instated in the graph editor window. Start with the default scene with the default cube object and leave the 3D window in user perspective view (the default view when Blender opens). Deselect the cube and add a curve path as previously described. Scale the length of the path five times. With the path selected, tab into edit mode and use the handles on the curve to shape the path as shown in Figure 9.47. Deselect the path and select the cube.

Figure 9.47

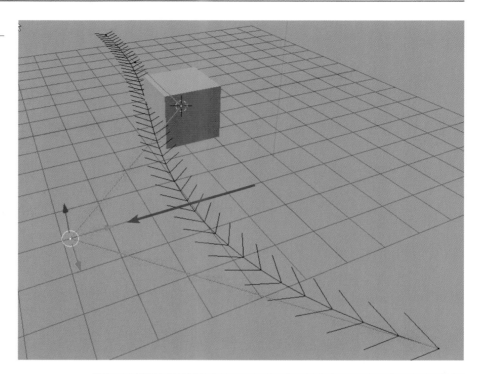

Figure 9.48

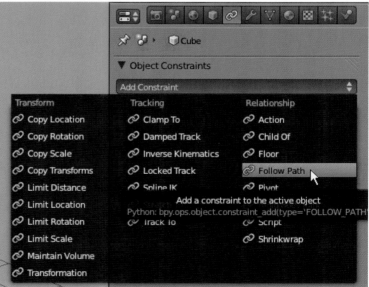

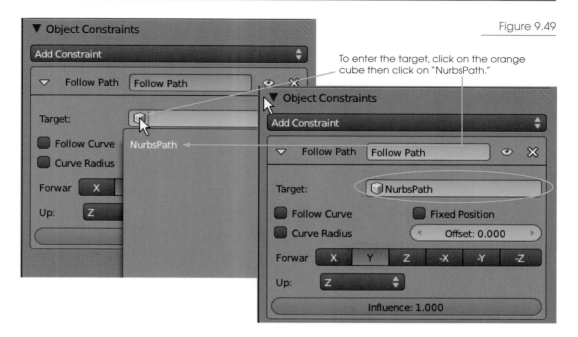

Figure 9.49

To enter the target, click on the orange cube then click on "NurbsPath."

In the properties window "Object Constraints" button, click on "Add Constraint" and select "Follow Path" from the selection menu (Figure 9.48). In the "Object Constraints" tab that opens, enter the target as "NurbsPath" and tick "Follow Curve" (Figure 9.49). The cube is now positioned at the start of the path.

Deselect the cube and select the path. In the properties window – "Object Data" button – "Path Animation" tab, note that "Frames: 100" and "Evaluation Time: 0.000" (Figure 9.50). This says that there is a 100-frame animation with 0.000 as the start position. Right click on the "Evaluation Time" button and select "Insert Keyframe." Note that in the timeline window, the "Start: 1" and "End: 250" values indicate the animation duration (i.e., 250 frames).

Click on the "Go to End" button in the timeline window to locate the timeline cursor at frame 250 (recall Figure 9.43). In the "Path Animation" tab, change the "Evaluation Time" value to 100, which positions the cube at the

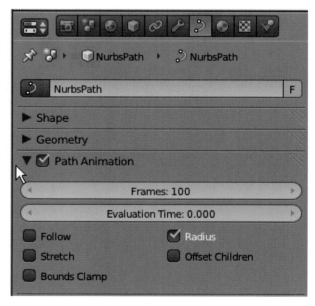

Figure 9.50

9.12. Animation Following Curves

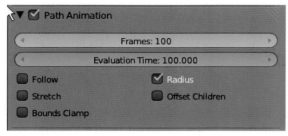

Figure 9.51

end of the path in the 3D window (Figure 9.51). Right click on the "Evaluation Time" button and select "Insert Keyframe" again. In the timeline window, click on the "Return to Start" button to go to the start of the animation and click "Play" to see the cube move in the 3D window following the path (Figure 9.52).

In the graph editor window, you now have an animation curve that is the editable Bezier type as discussed in the previous method.

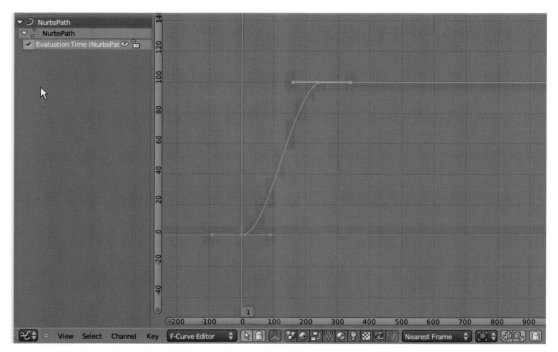

Figure 9.52

10

3D Text

10.1 Introduction to 3D Text

Learning Unit 8
Text Objects

3D text can be a very important element to add to a scene. Think of all the television advertisements that contain text and how it is animated. There are two ways of adding text to a scene in Blender: one way is to use the built-in text generator and the other is to use an external program. Text made in Blender can be easily edited in the properties window. Text made in an external program like Elefont may give you additional options and different fonts.

10.2 Creating 3D Text in Blender

To create text in Blender, put your scene in top view with orthographic projection (number pad 7 then number pad 5). Text is entered into the scene in the top view. Locate the cursor at the point in the scene where you want your text to go. Press Shift + the A key and select "Add Text" (Figure 10.1). The word "Text" displays in the 3D window in object mode. Tab into edit mode—the word "Text" now has a typing cursor at the end of it (Figure 10.2). You can now backspace to delete letters and type in your own words just like in a text editor. Don't worry about the font style or size at this stage. When you have typed in the words you want, tab back into object mode; this is where you shape and color the text (Figure 10.3).

Figure 10.1

Figure 10.2

Object mode

Edit mode

Typing cursor

The word "Text" has been deleted
and "Edit Mode" typed in its place.

Tab to edit mode.

Figure 10.3

Tip: Make sure your 3D window background is a darkish color. Since the default text color is the default gray, it is difficult to see against a light background.

Before you do any shaping or coloring, you can move, rotate, and scale the text just like any object in Blender. Changing the text into something interesting is done in the properties window. Select the text in the 3D window then go to the properties window – "Object Data" button.

10.3 The Object Data Button

Width, extrude, and bevel depth sliders control exactly what they say.

- The width slider controls the text width.
- The extrude slider extrudes the text to a 3D shape.
- The bevel depth slider controls the bevel size.

Experiment with the settings to modify the shape of the text (Figure 10.4).

The default font style is entered as "Bfont." You can change this to whatever font styles you have on your system. If you are using a Windows operating system, you can find the font styles in the Windows "Fonts" folder (C:/Windows/Fonts). To change the font style, click on the "Search Folder" icon and in the search window navigate to your fonts folder and select a different font. Blender will accept any of the Windows fonts, but some may be distorted

Figure 10.4

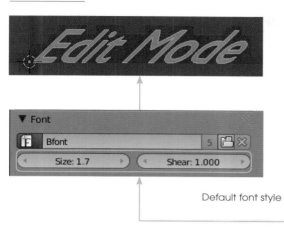

Default font style

when they are extruded into 3D shapes. To select a different font type, enter the default font in object mode in the 3D window and go to the properties window – "Object Data" button. Click in the folder icon as shown in Figure 10.5 to open the file browser window. Navigate to the font style you require and select a font. Press the "Open Fonts" button at the top RHS of the window. The selected font will be applied in the 3D window. Depending on the font selected, you may have to zoom in to see it. As you can see in Figure 10.5, you can assign different font styles such as regular, bold, and italic.

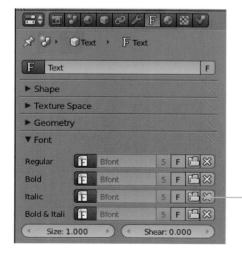

Folder icon to open the file browser to select a font type

Figure 10.5

"Search Folder" icon

Note that the font selected is only applied to the text object selected in the 3D window. The text is treated as an object, therefore the font style (values) you have assigned are for the selected object only. Entering a second text object will require that you assign a different set of data.

In the "Fonts" tab, the underline position and thickness values only operate when "Underline" is ticked under "Character." Underlining occurs as you type your text in edit mode.

10.4 Creating Text on a Curve

Text in Blender can be made to follow the shape of a curved path. Begin by adding text to your scene as previously described; when it is in object mode, deselect it with the A key. Add a curved path to the scene by pressing Shift + the A key – "Curve" – "Path." Note that by default the path is named "NurbsPath." The curve path is added to the scene in object mode and appears as a straight line (Figure 10.6). You can scale it to make it longer and reposition it in object mode, but you will have to tab to edit mode to extrude or shape it into a curve (Figure 10.7). With the curve shaped however you'd like, tab back to object mode and deselect it.

Select the text object and in the properties window – "Object Data" button – "Font" tab, find the "Text on Curve" panel. Click on the little cube icon and in the drop down menu that displays select "NurbsPath" (Figure 10.8). The text is shaped to follow the profile of the curve.

Figure 10.6

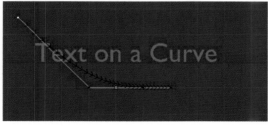

Figure 10.7

Edit mode   Object mode

Click on the cube icon.

Figure 10.8

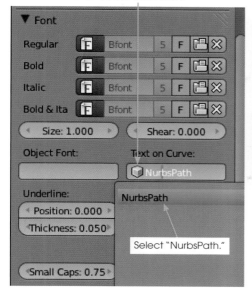

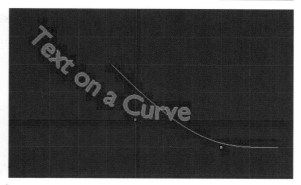

10.5 Converting Text to a Mesh Object

There is only limited functionality in the text "Object Data" button – "Geometry" tab for modifying the text shape. Unless you have extruded the text, it remains a 2D plane object. Entering edit mode only allows you to retype a text change. To perform editing, which actually changes the shape of the text, you have to convert to a mesh object. To do this, select the text in object mode then press Alt + the C key and select "Mesh from Curve/Meta/Surf/Text" in the drop down menu that displays (Figure 10.9). Tab to edit mode and you will see that the text is now a mesh object with vertices that can be moved, rotated, and scaled (Figure 10.10).

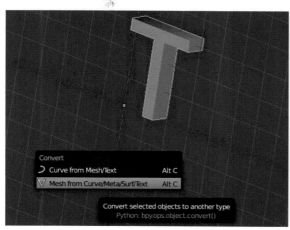

Figure 10.9

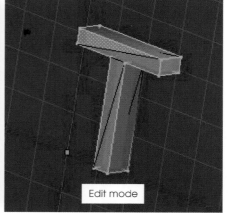

Figure 10.10

10.6 Converting Text to a Curve

If you would like to perform some fancy editing of a single letter, you can convert the letter into a curve. The outline of the letter becomes a curve with handles, which allow you to manipulate the shape into anything you wish. Add text, then in edit mode delete and retype your letter. Scale it up, rotate, and move it where you like then tab to object mode. Press Alt + the C key and select "Curve from Mesh/Text" (Figure 10.11). Now in edit mode you will see the outline of your letter as a curve with manipulating handles (Figure 10.12).

Figure 10.11

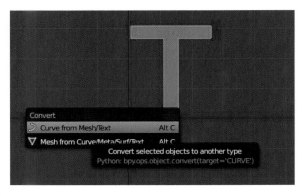

Figure 10.12

Edit mode   Object mode

10.7 Elefont 3D Text

Text can be created in an external 3D text editor and imported into Blender. A popular program to use is the freeware program Elefont available at www.armanisoft.ch. This is a simple-to-use program that saves the file in a .dxf format. Any program that exports 3D text as .dxf or VRML (.wrl) will work. The Elefont interface is shown in Figure 10.13.

After you have created your text in Elefont, save the .dxf file and make note of where you saved it. Open Blender and go into top view in the 3D window. In the information window header, click on "File" then "Open." The Blender file browser window will open. Navigate to the folder where you saved your file.

Figure 10.13

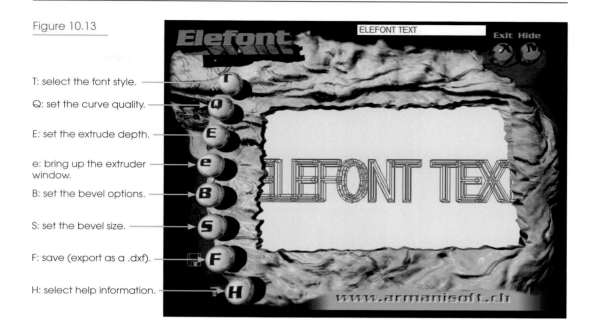

T: select the font style.

Q: set the curve quality.

E: set the extrude depth.

e: bring up the extruder window.

B: set the bevel options.

S: set the bevel size.

F: save (export as a .dxf).

H: select help information.

Note: By default, Blender does not display all files in the browser window. Go to the header at the top of the window and click on "Enable Filtering" (Figure 10.14). This will display all the files in any folder.

Click on your .dxf file and then click on "Open Blender File" (at the upper LHS of the window). Your text will be displayed in the Blender 3D window but note that each letter is a separate object. Since each letter is a separate object, you can apply a different material color to each letter. To join all the letters into a single object, shift select all the letters then

Click on "Enable Filtering." Figure 10.14

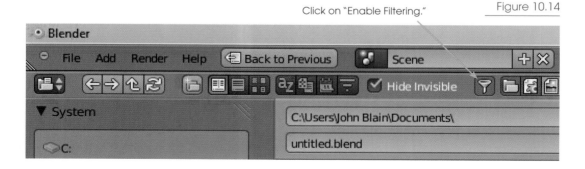

Figure 10.15

The letters are joined in object mode.

Figure 10.16

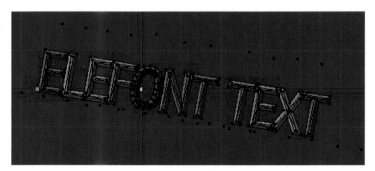

Edit mode showing the mesh object

press "Join" in the tool shelf (or press Ctrl + the J key) (Figure 10.15). Tab to edit mode to see the mesh object (Figure 10.16). The text can now be edited as a single object and made to follow the profile of a curve by adding a modifier to the text object—modifiers will be discussed in Chapter 12.

NURBS and Meta Shapes

11.1   Using NURBS
11.2   Creating a Lofted Tunnel
11.3   Meta Shapes

Figure 11.1

11.1 Using NURBS

When you press Shift + the A key and select "Add," you will notice other object types besides meshes, cameras, and lights that can be created. One other type of object that can be created is a surface (NURBS). NURBS stands for Non-Uniform Rational B-Spline, which means it's a type of editable curve or surface that can be converted to a mesh object. If you look at the "Surface" menu, you will see a variety of shapes that can be created. These shapes can be used as they are or converted to meshes so you can work with vertices. To get you started and give you an idea of how this is achieved, follow the procedure outlined below.

Start a new scene in Blender and delete the default cube. Place the scene in top view (number pad 7) and add a NURBS circle (Shift + the A key – "Add" – "Surface" – "NURBS Circle"). The NURBS circle will be displayed in the scene in object mode (Figure 11.1).

Tab to edit mode and you will see the circle surrounded by manipulation handles, which by default are all selected (Figure 11.2). Deselect the handles using the A key and right click on a handle to select it. If you have the manipulation widget turned on, you can use it to move the handle and deform the circle (Figure 11.3). Alternatively, you can press the G key and drag the mouse.

Tab into object mode to see the deformed circle (Figure 11.4). The deformation may be what you want or you may wish to further refine the shape.

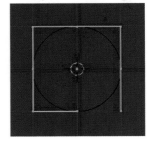

Figure 11.2

Figure 11.3

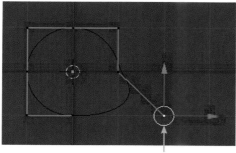

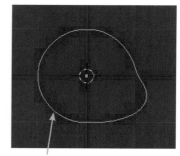

Figure 11.3

Manipulation widget

Deformed circle

Figure 11.4

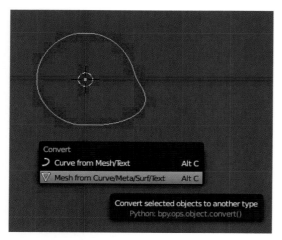

Figure 11.5

You can do this by converting the NURBS shape into a mesh object. With the shape selected in object mode, press Alt + the C key and select "Mesh from Curve/Meta/Surf/Text" in the drop down menu (Figure 11.5). We are converting "Surf" into a mesh object. Obviously this same command is applicable to converting "Curve," "Meta," and "Text" into a mesh object.

Tab to edit mode and you will see the shape now has vertices applied that you can select and manipulate to further modify the shape (Figure 11.6). The A key will deselect the vertices you have just moved and pressing the A key again will select all the vertices.

Tab to object mode then press Alt + the C key; this time select "Curve from Mesh/Text" (Figure 11.7). This option creates a mesh curve object from the mesh object. Tab back to edit mode and you now have a curve

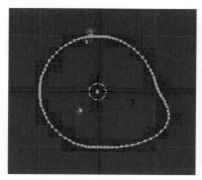

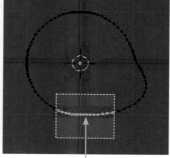

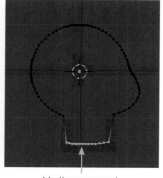

Figure 11.6

Vertices selected

Vertices moved

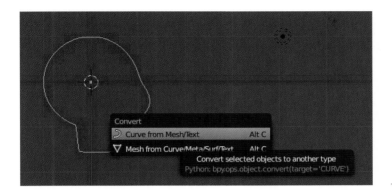

Figure 11.7

circle object. You can use the "Geometry" values in the properties window – "Object Data" button to manipulate the object's shape or select vertices and move them (Figure 11.8). Since this is a curve circle, it can be used as a path in animation.

This procedure shows that by converting one type of object to another, you have different options for shape manipulation.

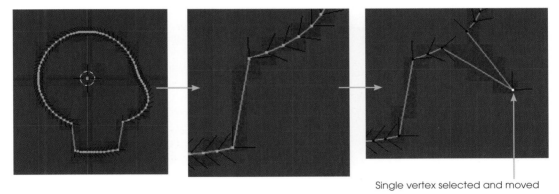

Single vertex selected and moved

Figure 11.8

11.2 Creating a Lofted Tunnel

This process will take several profiles of a NURBS circle, which are all manipulated to different profiles, and connect them together to form a hollow object (tunnel).

First, create a NURBS circle as described in Section 11.1. The circle is entered in the scene in object mode, so you need to tab into edit mode. Select the points and shape the circle a bit. After shaping, go back into object mode and change your view so you are looking down on the circle (number pad 7). Use Shift + the D key to duplicate the circle several times and position them accordingly, then rotate your view so you can shift select each circle. In edit mode, edit the shapes. After shaping the circles, exit edit mode and select all the circles by RMB clicking on them while holding Shift. Join the circles together, pressing

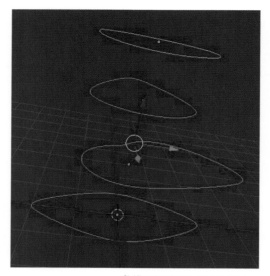

Figure 11.9 — Shift select the circles and join them together.

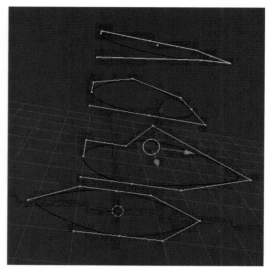

All the vertices are selected. — Figure 11.10

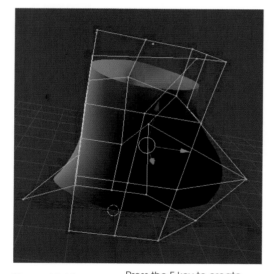

Figure 11.11 — Press the F key to create the lofted shape.

"Join" in the tool shelf (Figure 11.9). For the final step, press Tab for edit mode, press the A key to select all the vertices (Figure 11.10), then press the F key to create a lofted shape (Figure 11.11).

11.3 Meta Shapes

There are several meta shapes you can use in Blender (Figure 11.12). Meta shapes are added to a scene in object mode like any other shapes: press Shift + the A key – "Add" – "Metaball" and select either ball, capsule, plane, ellipsoid, or cube. Be sure to deselect one shape before adding another, otherwise the two shapes will be automatically joined. When meta shapes get close to one another, they begin to pull and flow together like droplets of liquid (Figure 11.13). The shapes can be animated and textured, and reflection and transparency can be applied to create some stunning effects.

12

Modifiers

"Object Modifiers" button

Properties window

Modifiers

Figure 12.1

12.1 Introduction to Modifiers

A modifier in Blender is the application of a process or algorithm upon an object. In other words, once you have created an object in the scene you can apply a neat set of data that will change the shape or way the objects behave. The modifiers are designed to take some of the hard work out of shaping an object. Be warned, though, that applying some of Blender's modifiers is not straightforward and has to be performed in conjunction with other processes. Without some instruction on how to apply the modifiers, a lot of trial and error can be involved. To save you all that trouble, the following chapter on modifiers is offered as a guide. You will still have to experiment and record your findings to become proficient in the application of modifiers.

Modifiers are found in the properties window – "Object Modifiers" button (Figure 12.1). The "Object Modifiers" button is only displayed when an object to which a modifier can be applied is in the 3D window. Some objects cannot have modifiers applied. Note that if there are objects in the 3D window to which modifiers may be applied (not necessarily selected), clicking the "Add Modifier" button and selecting a modifier will apply a modifier to the last object that was selected. This occurs even though that object is not selected at the time.

Figure 12.2

Drop down
selection menu

Displayed modifiers panel

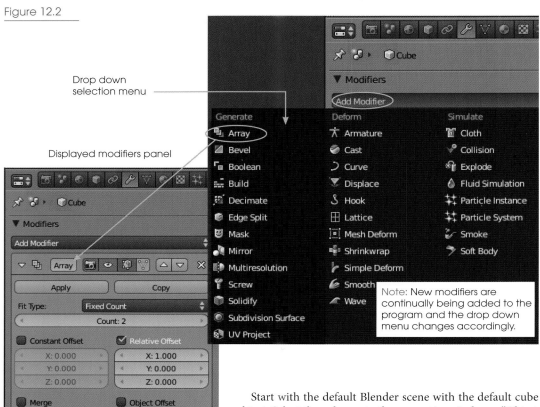

Note: New modifiers are
continually being added to the
program and the drop down
menu changes accordingly.

Start with the default Blender scene with the default cube object. Select the cube, go to the properties window – "Object Modifiers" button, and click on "Add Modifier" to display the modifier drop down selection menu (Figure 12.2). Adjust the values to produce the desired effect then apply the modifier. Applying the modifier permanently sets the action.

12.2 Modifier Stacks

Before explaining the individual modifiers, I should note that in some cases it is appropriate to apply more than one modifier to an object. When this is done the modifiers are placed in a stack in order of priority. The priority can be changed by moving a modifier up or down in the stack. Also note that although modifiers are generally applied in object mode, some may be used in edit mode. Figure 12.3 shows an array modifier and a bevel modifier applied.

The following pages will give a basic insight into how some of the modifiers are employed. The full listing of modifiers available are shown in the modifier selection drop down menu in Figure 12.4. The circled modifiers will also be covered in later chapters related to armatures (Chapter 15), particle systems (Chapter 13), and fluid simulation (Chapter 17).

Click to enable the modifier settings to be applied in edit mode.

Click to move the modifier up in the stack.

Click to move the modifier down in the stack.

Figure 12.3

Figure 12.4

12.3 Modifiers for Generating

12.3.1 Array Modifiers

The array modifier creates an array of copies of the base object, with each copy offset in a number of possible ways. Figure 12.5 shows a UV sphere object with an array modifier applied to it with "Count: 3" (the base object plus two copies equals an array of 3) and x and y offsets ("X: 1.500" and "Y: 1.000"). There are three types of offset functions available: relative, constant, and object. Note that Figure 12.5 is using the relative offset function. With "Count: 2" and an offset along the x-axis of "X: 1," the difference between relative and constant is shown in Figure 12.6. The object offset function is shown in Figure 12.7 and is combined with a second array modifier.

Learning Unit 6

Array Modifier

Figure 12.5

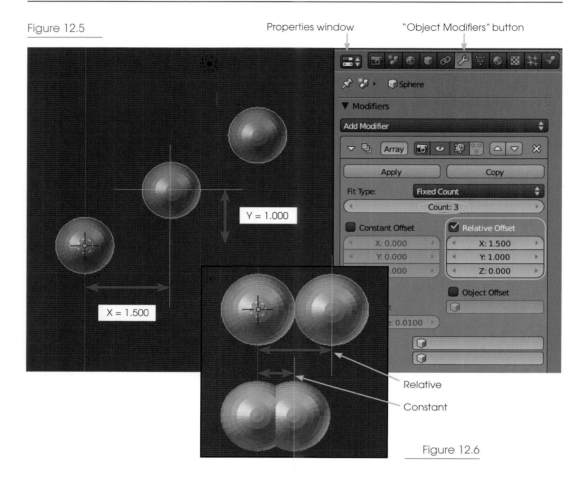

Properties window   "Object Modifiers" button

Figure 12.6

12.3.2 Object Offset Using Array Modifiers

Learning
Unit 6

Multiple
Modifiers

In Figure 12.7, the vertices of the sphere object have been moved +3 Blender units along the *x*-axis (tab to edit mode and drag the vertices to the right). This leaves the center of the sphere at the center of the scene coinciding with the 3D cursor. Relocating the sphere's vertices is merely done for clarity to move the final result away from the cube. An array modifier is applied to the sphere; the "Count" value is 2 and there is a "Constant Offset: X" value of 6.000 (Figure 12.8). This creates an array with two spheres, with the second sphere displaced +6 Blender units from the first.

A second array modifier is added, but this time the modifier is applied to the array that was created by the first modifier. This second array modifier also has a "Count" value of 2, which produces an array consisting of the first array plus an instance of the first array. The second array modifier uses an "Object Offset: Cube," which tells the modifier to use the lo-

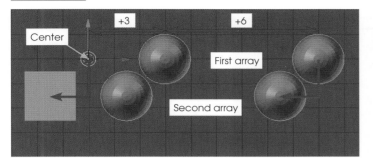

cation coordinates of the cube in the scene as the displacement values for the second array. The cube is located at $x = -1.5$ and $y = -1.5$. Accordingly, the second array of spheres is displaced from the first array by these values.

12.3.3 Bevel Modifiers

The bevel modifier simply adds a bevel to the corners of an object; the size of the bevel is controlled by the "Width" button (Figure 12.9).

Figure 12.9

Learning Unit 6

Bevel Modifier

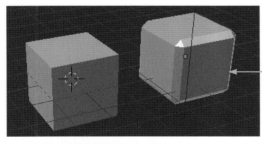

Default cube with a bevel modifier applied

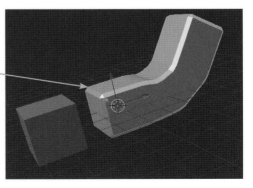

Extruded cube with a bevel modifier applied

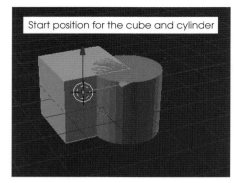
Start position for the cube and cylinder

Figure 12.10

12.3.4 Boolean Modifiers

Boolean modifiers are used to create shapes by using a difference, intersection, or union operation between objects. To demonstrate this, we will use the default cube and a cylinder object. Be warned that, unless you have a super fast computer, some calculations can take several seconds.

Start with the cube and cylinder and position them as shown in Figure 12.10 (this will be the same setup for all three operation types). Begin with the Boolean type "Intersect." To make sure the procedure works, set the vertices count for the cylinder to 16 (add the cylinder, then change the number of vertices in the tool shelf).

Learning Unit 6
Boolean Modifier

Intersect. Intersecting objects creates an object that is the shape of the overlap of two objects. The cube will be the object that is modified, so you must first select the cube. Click the properties window – "Object Modifiers" button – "Add Modifier" and select type "Boolean." The operation type by default is "Intersect." In the "Object" panel click on the little cube icon and select "Cylinder" in the drop down menu (Figure 12.11). Note that this panel always shows a little cube icon despite the shape of the actual object being selected.

In the "Display" tab click on "Apply" and the modifier panel disappears. In the 3D window move the selected object to reveal the new object, which is now the shape of the overlap (Figure 12.12). The cylinder object remains in the scene.

Boolean modifiers

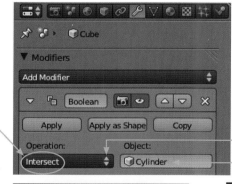

Figure 12.11

Click the cube icon and add the cylinder.

3D window after applying the modifier

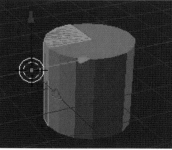

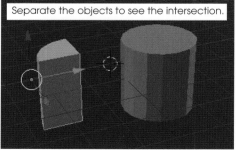
Separate the objects to see the intersection.

Figure 12.12

Union. Uniting objects creates a shape that is a union of the two objects. Add a Boolean modifier to the cube and select operation type "Union." In the "Object" panel click the little cube icon again and select "Cylinder." Click "Apply" and move the selected object in the 3D window; the two objects are now fused together (Figure 12.13).

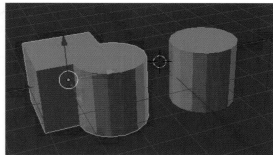

Figure 12.13

Difference. Differentiating objects creates a shape that is the difference of the two objects. In other words, it subtracts the overlap of the objects from the object being modified. Follow the same procedure as the foregoing examples, but this time select the operation type "Difference" and see the result (Figure 12.14).

12.3.5 Build Modifiers

The build modifier creates the effect of something building linearly over a period of time. For example, text can be animated to build across the screen. Any object can have a build modifier, but to see a nice effect, a high vertex count is required.

Add some text to the scene, select the text in the 3D window, and add a build modifier (Figure 12.15). As soon as you add the modifier, the text disappears from the screen (Figure 12.16). Press Alt + the A key to see the animation of the text building (Figure 12.17).

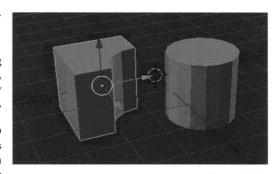

Figure 12.14

Text in the 3D window selected in object mode

Figure 12.15

Text with the build modifier added

Part of the text is showing.

Figure 12.16

Text building while playing the animation

Build direction

Figure 12.17

12.3.6 Decimate Modifiers

The decimate modifier allows a reduction in vertex count without too much alteration to the object's shape. Select the default cylinder in object mode and click "Add Modifier" – "Decimate" (Figure 12.18). Change the ratio from 1 to 0.600—notice that there isn't much change to the appearance of the cylinder in object mode. Tab to edit mode to see the reduction in the number of vertices.

Figure 12.18

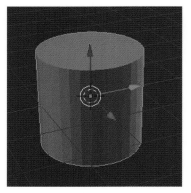

Default cylinder before the
modifier is applied

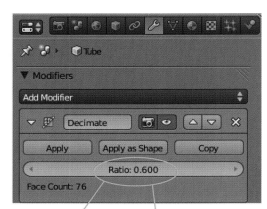

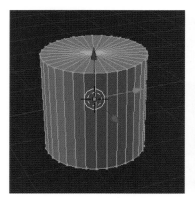

Default cylinder in edit mode
showing the vertices before the
modifier is applied

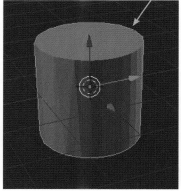

Default cylinder after the modifier is
applied with a ratio of 0.600; not too
much has changed

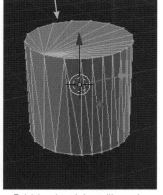

Tabbing back to edit mode
shows the reduction in the
number of vertices.

12.3.7 Edge Split Modifiers

The edge split modifier allows you to split an object apart by selecting vertices, edges, or faces. As an example start with the default scene with the default cube object. In object mode with the cube selected, add an edge split modifier and click "Apply" (Figure 12.19). Tab to edit mode, select a face, and drag the mouse to pull the face away from the cube; the face remains part of the object even though it is separated (Figure 12.20). Selecting an edge will open a face like the lid on a box (Figure 12.21). Selecting a vertex will allow a corner to be moved (Figure 12.22). Selecting all with the A key and then pressing Ctrl + the V key – "Remove Doubles" will rejoin the faces.

Figure 12.19

Face select mode

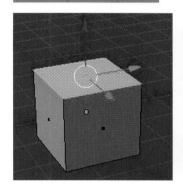

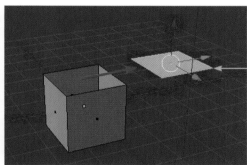

Drag the mouse to pull the selected face away from the cube.

Figure 12.20

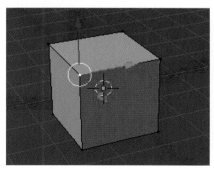

Edge select mode

Figure 12.21

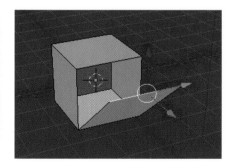

Figure 12.22

Selecting a
vertex will allow
a corner to be
moved. Selecting
different vertices
will produce some
interesting results.

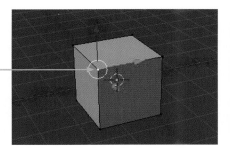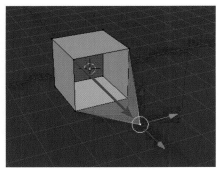

Vertex select mode

12.3.8 Mask Modifiers

The mask modifier allows portions of a mesh that are defined by vertex groups to be the only part of the mesh that is visible or the only part that displays. Select a few cube vertices in edit mode after subdividing and click "Add Group" in the "Object Data" tab (Figure 12.23). The vertices are assigned to the vertex group named "Group." Click "Assign."

Switch to the "Object Modifiers" button and select the mask modifier. The mode should be "Vertex Group" and the vertex group should be "Group." Tick the "Invert" box and tab to object mode—only the group with the modifier applied to it is visible (Figure 12.24). By using the modifier, visibility can be controlled without removing any vertices from the cube.

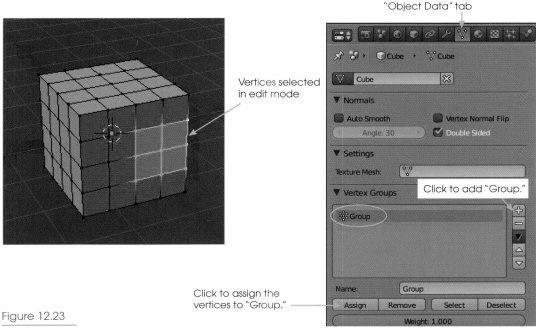

"Object Data" tab

Vertices selected
in edit mode

Click to add "Group."

Click to assign the
vertices to "Group."

Figure 12.23

Figure 12.24

"Object Modifiers" button

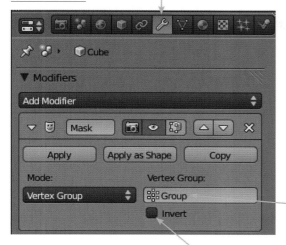

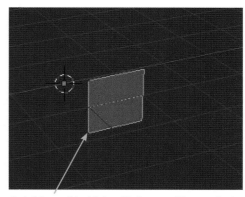

Only "Group" is visible with the modifier applied.

"Group" is invisible when "Invert" is ticked.

12.3.9 Mirror Modifiers

The mirror modifier allows the construction or deformation of a mesh on one side of a center point to be duplicated (mirrored) on the opposite side. Start with a plane in edit mode in top view and subdivide the object into four parts by clicking "Subdivide" on the object tools panel (Figure 12.25). Shift select the vertices on one side of the plane and delete them. Add a mirror modifier in the "Object Modifiers" tab, and you'll see the deleted half of the plane mirrored (Figure 12.26). Grab a vertex and deform it; notice that the other half of the plane mirrors the deformity (Figure 12.27).

Learning
Unit 8

Mirror Modifier

The plane in edit mode

The plane subdivided

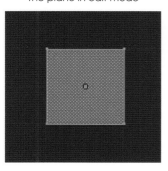

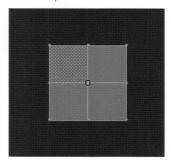

Figure 12.25

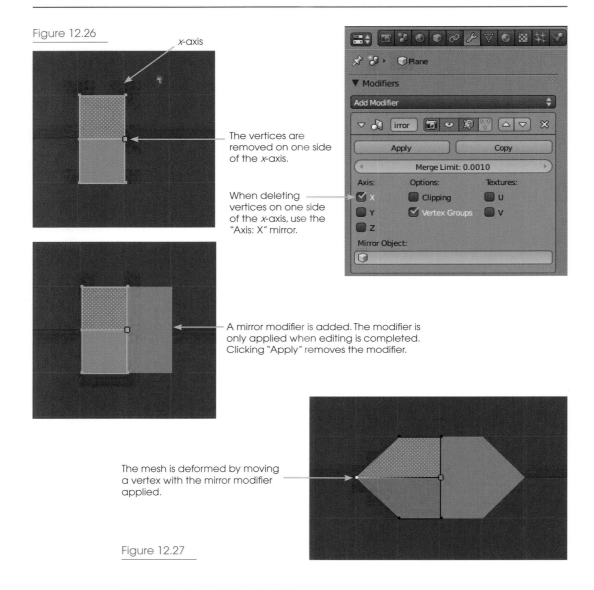

Figure 12.26

x-axis

The vertices are removed on one side of the *x*-axis.

When deleting vertices on one side of the *x*-axis, use the "Axis: X" mirror.

A mirror modifier is added. The modifier is only applied when editing is completed. Clicking "Apply" removes the modifier.

The mesh is deformed by moving a vertex with the mirror modifier applied.

Figure 12.27

12.3.10 Multiresolution Modifiers

The multiresolution modifier is much like the subdivision surface modifier. Figure 12.28 is taken from the Blender documentation and perhaps beginners should put it aside for future study. The insert is placed here to make you aware of the modifier's existence.

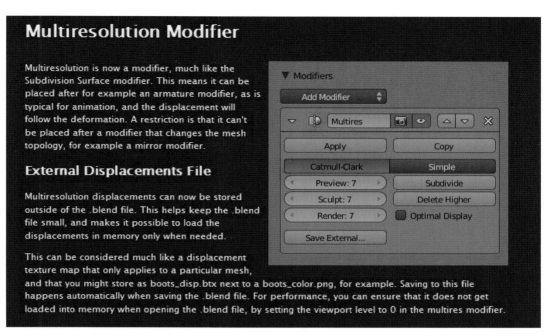

Multiresolution Modifier

Multiresolution is now a modifier, much like the Subdivision Surface modifier. This means it can be placed after for example an armature modifier, as is typical for animation, and the displacement will follow the deformation. A restriction is that it can't be placed after a modifier that changes the mesh topology, for example a mirror modifier.

External Displacements File

Multiresolution displacements can now be stored outside of the .blend file. This helps keep the .blend file small, and makes it possible to load the displacements in memory only when needed.

This can be considered much like a displacement texture map that only applies to a particular mesh, and that you might store as boots_disp.btx next to a boots_color.png, for example. Saving to this file happens automatically when saving the .blend file. For performance, you can ensure that it does not get loaded into memory when opening the .blend file, by setting the viewport level to 0 in the multires modifier.

Figure 12.28

12.3.11 Screw Modifiers

The screw modifier allows a shape to be generated by revolving a profile around an axis. To demonstrate this, we will construct a spring. All operations are conducted in the default 3D window user perspective view. Follow the steps in the exact order listed below.

1. Delete the default cube object and add a circle. Scale the circle down by 0.500.
2. Tab to edit mode and move the circle along the x-axis to move vertices away from the object center (press the N key to display the "Transform" panel and change the median to "X: −6.000") (Figure 12.29).
3. Tab to object mode (Figure 12.30).
4. Add a screw modifier to the circle (Figure 12.31).
5. Change the settings in the modifier panel in Figure 12.32 to the ones below:
   – Axis: Y (revolve about the y-axis)
   – Steps: 100 (produces a smooth surface)
   – Screw: 10 (offsets the revolution)
   – Angle: 1000 (number of revolutions)

The circle in edit mode

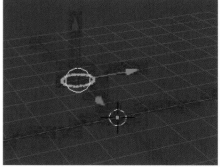

Figure 12.29

Figure 12.30

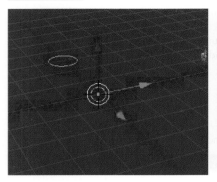

The circle in object mode

Figure 12.31

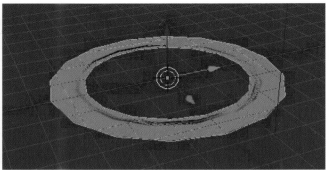

The circle revolved about the default *z*-axis
with a screw modifier applied

Figure 12.32

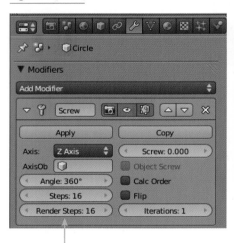

Change the default
values shown here to
those listed in step 5.

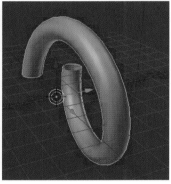

Revolved about the *y*-axis

Screw: 10

Angle: 1000

12.3.12 Solidify Modifiers

The solidify modifier provides a tool for creating solid objects from thin-walled objects. To demonstrate this, begin with a simple plane object selected in the 3D window. Add a solidify modifier in the properties window—look closely at the plane and you will observe that it now has a thickness (Figure 12.33). Note that the solidify modifier by default has two values: "Thick: 0.0100" (thickness) and "Offs: −1.0000" (offset).

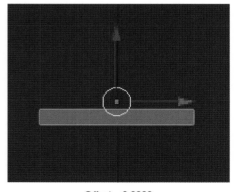

Figure 12.33

To get a better idea of what these values mean, increase them to "Thick: 0.2000" and "Offs: −2.0000." Change the 3D window to front view (number pad 1); you will see the thickness increased and that it is offset below the midplane of the scene (Figure 12.34).

Figure 12.34

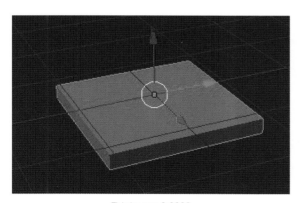

Thickness: 0.2000

Offset: −2.0000

Figure 12.35

Figure 12.36

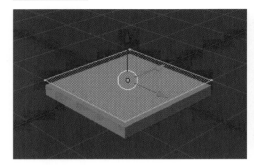

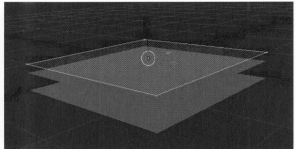

Tab to edit mode and see that the original vertices of the plane object remain on the mid-plane of the scene (Figure 12.35). Tab back to object mode and change the 3D window to user perspective view. In the "Object Modifiers" panel untick "Fill Rim"—instead of a single thick plane, there are now two thin planes (Figure 12.36). Tick "Fill Rim" again in the modifier tab and then add a subdivision surface modifier below the solidify modifier; the thick plane will look like a flattened octagonal shape. This shape can be modified by changing the "Inner," "Outer," and "Rim Crease" values in the solidify modifier panel. Changing all three values to 1.000 produces the thick plane object.

With the inner, outer, and rim crease values set back to 0.000, note the value "View: 1" under "Subdivisions" in the subdivision surface modifier panel. If you change this to "View: 0" you have the thick plane again. Changing the view value from 0 to 1, then to 2, then to 3, and then to 4 changes the thick plane progressively into a smooth flat disc.

For a practical demonstration of the solidify modifier, create a new scene with a cylinder object instead of the default cube. Delete the upper end cap of the cylinder by deleting the single vertex in the center of the cap while in edit mode. You now have a thin-walled container. Add a solidify modifier and increase the thickness value to produce a thicker wall. Play with the offset value to change the size. Add a subdivision surface modifier and alter the view value to modify the shape. With the subdivision surface modifier added you can use the inner, outer, and rim crease values to control the shape.

12.3.13 Subdivision Surface Modifiers

The subdivision surface modifier is used when the "Smooth" button in the shading section of the tools shelf does not quite do the job, and you don't want to subdivide your mesh by adding more vertices. The following example shows a useful method.

Start with the default cube and switch to front view (number pad 1) and tab to edit mode. Extrude one face of the cube and tab back to object mode in user perspective view (Figure 12.37). Add a subdivision surface modifier using the default settings (Figure 12.38). Under "Subdivisions," change the "View" value to 4. Tab to edit mode and see that the original number of vertices has changed (Figure 12.39).

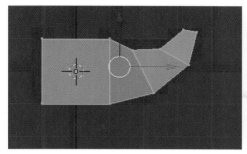

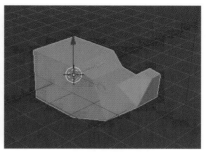

Figure 12.37

Default cube with one face extruded, rotated, and scaled

Tab back to object mode.

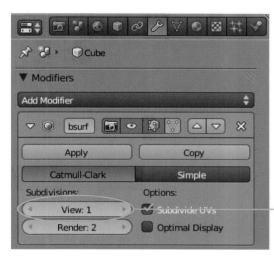

Default settings in the subdivision surface modifier panel

Figure 12.38

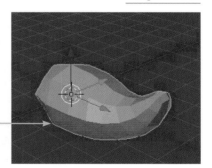

Figure 12.39

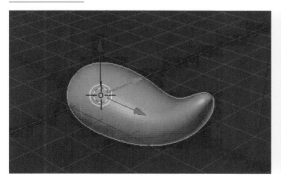

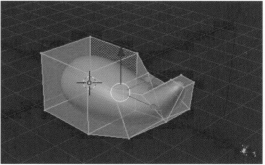

"View" value changed to 4

Tab to edit mode.

12.3.14 UV Project Modifiers

The UV project modifier allows projection of an image onto the surface of an object. Before the modifier can be applied, the scene must contain certain items and certain settings are required. To demonstrate the very basics of the process we will project an image onto one face of the cube in the default Blender scene.

Before we begin, we must have the following items:

- an object on which to project the image (default cube),
- an image to be projected (know the location of an image you'd like to use on your computer),
- a camera to see what is being projected and to allow for rendering, and
- a projector to do the projecting.

Start with the default Blender scene and go to top view (number pad 7) in top orthographic projection (number pad 5). The scene already contains a cube object, camera, and lamp. For this exercise the lamp isn't necessary since the image we will be projecting will be self-illuminating. We will leave the lamp in place anyway.

The first thing to do is to add a projector. Any object can be used as a projector and it is common to use an empty or a camera for this purpose. Since we already have a camera, it is very simple to duplicate it by pressing Shift + the D key. When the camera is duplicated,

Figure 12.40

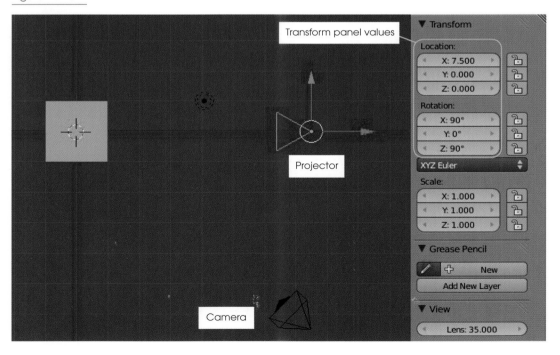

Blender automatically names it "Camera.001." Go to the properties window – "Object" button and rename the new camera "Projector" by clicking on the name, deleting it, retyping it, and pressing "Enter." In the 3D window move the projector and position it as shown in Figure 12.40. You may position the projector anywhere you like but this demonstration will be easier to follow if you copy the example exactly. To precisely position the projector, use the "Transform" panel and enter the values as shown. This will put the projector squarely pointing at the cube on the *x*- and *y*-axis.

Deselect the projector and change the 3D window to camera view (number pad 0). To perform image projection, the object being projected on must have a material with some unique settings. In the 3D window (while still in camera view), select the cube and go to the properties window – "Material" tab. The default cube in the default scene comes preloaded with a material, which is the dull gray color that you see. If you have added a new cube object, you will have to add a new material.

With a material added, change the following settings in the "Material" tab as shown in Figure 12.41:

- In the "Diffuse" tab, set "Intensity: 1.000."
- In the "Shading" tab, tick "Shadeless" and set "Ambient: 0.000."
- In the "Transparency" tab, tick "Transparency" and check that "Alpha: 1.000" is set.
- In the "Options" tab, tick "Face Textures" and leave "Traceable" ticked.

We now have to tell Blender what image we want projected and give some coordinates to project to. Split the 3D window in two and make one half a UV/image editor window. In the 3D window with the cube selected, change the viewpoint shading to "Textured" (Figure 12.42). Tab to edit mode and change to face select mode (Figure 12.43). Press the A key to deselect all the faces then right click on one face of the cube to select just the one face. With the cursor in the 3D window, press the U key and select "Project From View" (Figure 12.44). You will see the face you have selected appear in the UV/image editor window.

Figure 12.41

Figure 12.42

Figure 12.43

Face select mode

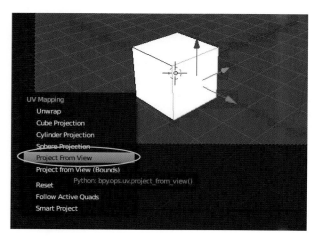

The selected face appears in the UV/image editor window.

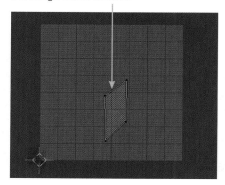

Figure 12.44

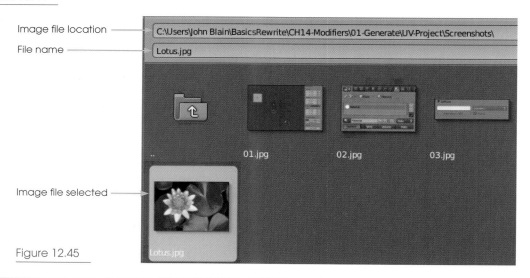

Image file location — C:\Users\John Blain\BasicsRewrite\CH14-Modifiers\01-Generate\UV-Project\Screenshots\

File name — Lotus.jpg

01.jpg   02.jpg   03.jpg

Image file selected —

Lotus.jpg

Figure 12.45

In the UV/image editor window, load your image by clicking "Image" in the header then selecting "Open." This opens a file browser window where you can navigate to the folder containing your image. Click on the image file and click "Open" on the upper RHS of the screen (Figure 12.45). Your image displays in the UV/image editor window, but you can still see the outline of the face you have selected (Figure 12.46).

If you press the A key to select the face outline and the G key and move the mouse, you will see the image projected on the face in the 3D window move at the same time (Figure 12.47). If you press F12 and render with the cursor in the 3D window, you will see whatever portion of the image that is covered by the face outline in the UV/image editor window rendered onto the selected face of the cube. You can also scale the face outline to capture more or less of the image. This example shows you one method of projection, but that's not where we were heading to begin with. We want to use our projector, but we have given Blender the information about our image and have established some mapping coordinates.

At long last we can add our UV project modifier. The cube remains selected. In the properties window – "Object Modifiers" button, click "Add Modifier" and select "UV Project" to display the modifier panel (Figure 12.48). In the modifier panel click on the panels shown and select your image, the projector, and the UVTex coordinates. Render (press F12) to see the image projected onto the face of the cube. By moving the projector in the 3D window relative to the cube or moving, rotating, or scaling the cube relative to the projector, the portion of the image displayed can be controlled (Figure 12.49).

Outline of the selected face — Figure 12.46

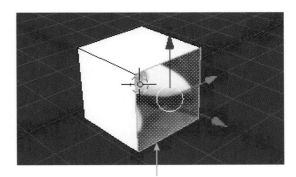

Image on the selected face — Figure 12.47

Click and select your image file.

Click and select "Projector."

Note: If you have used a duplication of the default camera as a projector and haven't renamed it "Projector," then the name of your projector will be "Camera.001."

Click and select "UVTex."

Figure 12.48

Figure 12.49

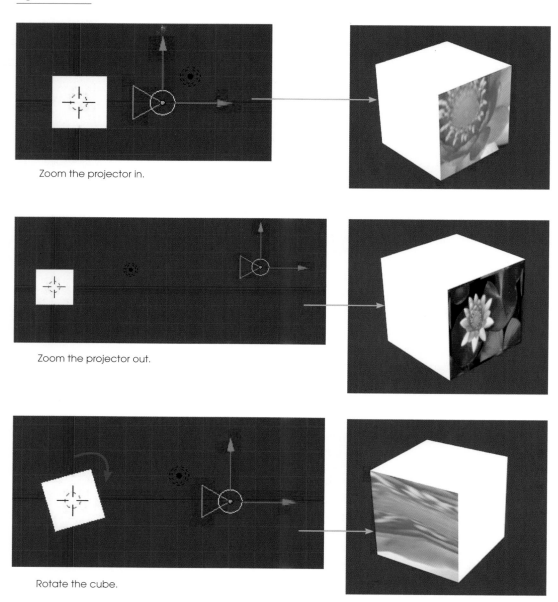

Zoom the projector in.

Zoom the projector out.

Rotate the cube.

12.4 Modifiers for Deforming

12.4.1 Armature Modifiers

Figure 12.50

The armature modifier is the mechanism that links a mesh object to a deforming armature. In Chapter 15, the procedure for automatically assigning an armature to a mesh is described by setting up a child/parent relationship. Setting this relationship automatically adds an armature modifier to the mesh being deformed. Instead of setting up a child/parent relationship, the armature modifier can be manually added and the deforming armature named.

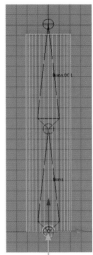

In the default scene, delete the cube and change to front view. Add a single bone armature to the scene (press the Shift key + the A key – "Add" – "Armature" – "Single Bone"). Tab to edit mode, press the E key, and click and hold the LMB, dragging the mouse up to extrude a second bone. Tab back to object mode. In the properties window – "Object Data" button – "Display" tab, check the "Names" button to show the bone names in the 3D window. Deselect the armature by pressing the A key, add a cylinder to the scene, and position it as shown in Figure 12.50. With the cylinder in edit mode, subdivide the mesh once and tab back to object mode.

Armature modifier added with the mesh object selected

Figure 12.51

With the cylinder selected, add an armature modifier and click on the little cube icon in the "Object" panel and select "Armature" from the drop down menu (Figure 12.51). Selecting "Armature" tells the modifier that you will deform the cylinder using the armature object in the 3D window. Deselect the cylinder, select the armature, and change to pose mode in the 3D window header. Pose mode allows you to manipulate the individual bones in the armature, which in turn deforms the mesh object to which the modifier is applied. Click the RMB on "Bone.001" to select it then press the R key and drag the mouse to the right to rotate the bone (Figure 12.52). Observe how the tube deforms.

Figure 12.52

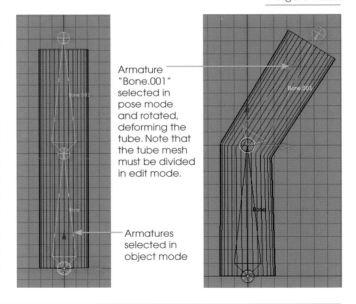

Armature "Bone.001" selected in pose mode and rotated, deforming the tube. Note that the tube mesh must be divided in edit mode.

Armatures selected in object mode

Figure 12.53

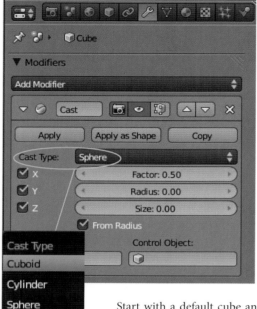

12.4.2 Cast Modifiers

The cast modifier shifts the shape of a mesh, curve, surface, or lattice to any of the predefined shapes included in the modifier (i.e., sphere, cuboid, or cylinder). The modifier panel in Figure 12.53 includes the following buttons:

- X, Y, Z. Untick the boxes to disable the deformation on that axis.
- Factor. The slider controls the deformation; 0 = original, add or subtract to deform.
- Radius. Only deforms the vertices within this distance from the center (0 = infinite).
- Size. Controls the size of the projection shape (0 = automatic).
- Vertex Group. If vertices are assigned to a vertex group, only those vertices will be affected.
- Control Object. If a control object is used, this determines the center of the effect.

Start with a default cube and subdivide it three times in edit mode. Apply a different cast type (sphere, cylinder, and cuboid) in the modifier panel and notice the results (Figure 12.54).

Figure 12.54

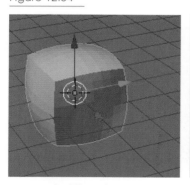

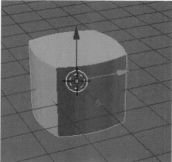

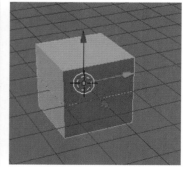

Cast Type: Sphere   Cast Type: Cylinder   Cast Type: Cuboid

Learning Unit 6

Curve Modifier

12.4.3 Curve Modifiers

The curve modifier uses a curve to deform a mesh. Start with the default Blender scene and scale the cube on the *x*-axis (use the S key + the X key) and subdivide it six times in edit

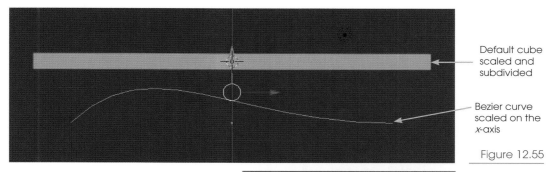

Default cube
scaled and
subdivided

Bezier curve
scaled on the
x-axis

Figure 12.55

mode (Figure 12.55). Add a Bezier curve to the scene and scale up (press the S key and drag the mouse). Deselect the curve and select the cube. Tab to object mode and add a curve modifier to the scaled cube and enter "BezierCurve" as the name of the Bezier curve in the "Object" panel (Figure 12.56). Select the curve in the 3D window and change its shape in edit mode to manipulate the shape of the scaled cube (Figure 12.57).

Figure 12.56

Scaled cube with a curve modifier added

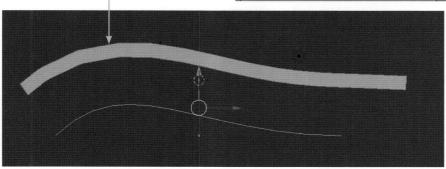

Figure 12.57

12.4.4 Displace Modifiers

The displace modifier uses a texture to displace the vertices of a mesh. If vertices are assigned to a vertex group and the group is entered in the modifier, only the vertices belonging to the group will be affected.

Learning
Unit 8

Displace Modifier

Figure 12.58

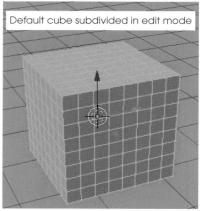

Start with the default Blender scene and with the cube selected in edit mode, subdivide it three times (Figure 12.58). Tab back to object mode and in the properties window – "Object Modifiers" button, click "Add Modifier" and select "Displace" (Figure 12.59). We will use a texture to displace the vertices on the cube's surface. Make sure the cube has a material applied and in the properties window – "Textures" button, change the texture type to "Distorted Noise." Go back to the "Object Modifiers" button and in the "Modifiers" tab click on the "Browse texture to be linked" button. The default texture data slot to which you assigned the distorted

"Textures" tab   Figure 12.59

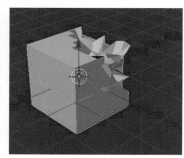

Figure 12.60

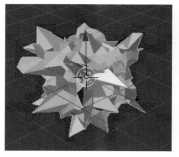

Default cube with a displace modifier added   Only the vertex group is selected.

Figure 12.61

noise texture is named "Tex." Click on "Tex" and switch to object mode; the vertices on the cube's surface have been displaced according to the intensity of the texture mapped to the surface of the cube (Figure 12.60, left). You will have to play around with the values in the "Modifiers" tab to establish their effect.

Start over and this time, after subdividing the surface of the cube, deselect all vertices then create a vertex group. Repeat the process, again selecting "Tex" in the "Modifiers" tab, and this time select "Group" in the "Vertex Groups" slot of the modifier. Now, only the vertices in the vertex group are displaced (Figure 12.60, right).

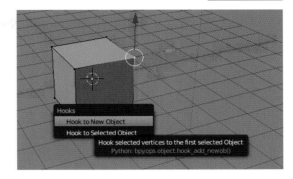

12.4.5 Hook Modifiers

The hook modifier allows you to manipulate or animate selected vertices of a mesh while in object mode. Vertices are assigned (hooked) to an empty object that can be moved in object mode by pulling the selected vertices with it. This can be use for a static mesh deformation or the movement can be animated.

Let's move one corner of a cube. Start with the default scene with the cube object selected. Tab to edit mode and deselect all vertices with the A key, then select one vertex (corner) by pressing it with the RMB. Press Ctrl + the H key and select "Hook to New Object" (Figure 12.61). An empty is added to the scene (orange line under the widget), and by going to the properties window – "Object Modifiers" button, you will see that a hook modifier has been added named "Hook-Empty" (Figure 12.62). Select and move the empty in object mode and you'll see that the cube deforms (Figure 12.63).

Figure 12.62

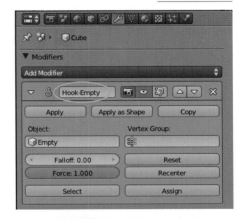

Figure 12.63

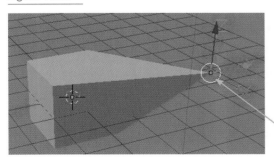

An empy has been added.

In edit mode, you can move the corner of the cube away from the empty. However, when the empty is selected and moved in object mode, the corner follows.

12.4.6 Lattice Modifiers

The lattice modifier is used to deform a mesh object or to control the movement of particles. By using the modifier, it is simple to shape a mesh object that has many vertices. A lattice is a nonrenderable grid of vertices, therefore it does not render in the scene. You can use the same lattice to deform several objects by giving each object a modifier pointing to the lattice.

Let's deform a UV sphere object with a lattice modifier. Delete the default cube, add a UV sphere to the scene, then add a lattice. Change to "Textured" mode in the viewport shading. Before you can see the lattice mesh, you will have to scale the lattice up (press the S key + drag the mouse); the lattice is entered as a simple mesh cube. Select the UV sphere and add a lattice modifier. Enter "Lattice" under the "Object" tab (Figure 12.64). Select the lattice, go to the "Object Data" button in the properties window, and alter the u, v, and w values in the "Lattice" tab to subdivide the lattice mesh (Figure 12.65). In edit mode, select a single lattice vertex and move it to deform the UV sphere mesh (Figure 12.66).

Figure 12.64

Figure 12.65

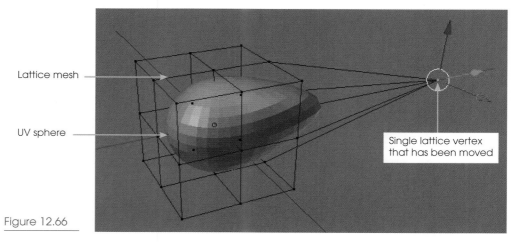

Lattice mesh

UV sphere

Single lattice vertex
that has been moved

Figure 12.66

12.4.7 Mesh Deform Modifiers

The mesh deform modifier can deform one mesh with another cage mesh. This is similar to a lattice modifier but instead of being restricted to the regular grid layout of a lattice, the cage can be modeled to fit around the mesh object being deformed. The cage mesh must form a closed cage around the part of the mesh to be deformed, and only vertices within the cage will be deformed. Typically the cage will have far fewer vertices than the mesh being deformed.

After modeling a UV sphere mesh object, surround it with a simple cage mesh by scaling a cube to fit around the elongated sphere then selecting vertices in edit mode and extruding them. Apply a mesh deform modifier to the scaled UV sphere. Enter the name of the cage mesh and press "Bind" to link the two meshes. The "Bind" operation may take several seconds to calculate depending on the complexity of your model. Wait until "Bind" changes to "Unbind" before selecting vertices on

Click on "Bind" and wait until it changes to "Unbind."

Figure 12.67

the cage (Figure 12.67). By dragging, scaling, and rotating the selected vertices, the original mesh will be deformed (Figure 12.68). The proximity of the cage to the original object has an influence on how the deformation reacts.

Note: The cage mesh will render in the scene; therefore, with the cage surrounding the elongated sphere, all you will see is the cage. You can select the cage and move it away from the sphere, keeping the deformation, but the cage will still render. To see the elongated sphere deformed without the cage, click on "Apply" in the modifier tab. The modifier is applied to the sphere and removed. You can now delete the cage and the elongated sphere remains deformed.

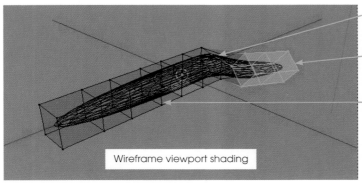

The UV sphere is scaled along the *x*-axis to form an elongated worm shape.

Part of the cage is selected, moved, and rotated to deform the sphere.

The cube is extruded to form a cage.

Wireframe viewport shading

Figure 12.68

Figure 12.69

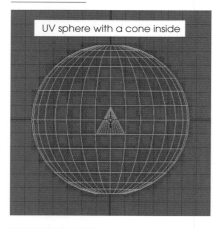

UV sphere with a cone inside

12.4.8 Shrinkwrap Modifiers

The shrinkwrap modifier takes a mesh and shrinks it down, wrapping the mesh around another object. The deformed mesh can then be offset to produce shapes in between the original shape and the deformed shape.

Delete the cube in the default Blender scene and add a UV sphere and a cone mesh object; the cone should be located inside the UV sphere, which is easy to see when both objects are viewed in "Wireframe" mode (Figure 12.69). Add a shrinkwrap modifier to the UV sphere, and enter "Cone" in the "Target" panel (Figure 12.70). Change the "Offset" value; notice how the shape changes when you increase the value to 1.25 and 3.00 (Figure 12.71).

Figure 12.70

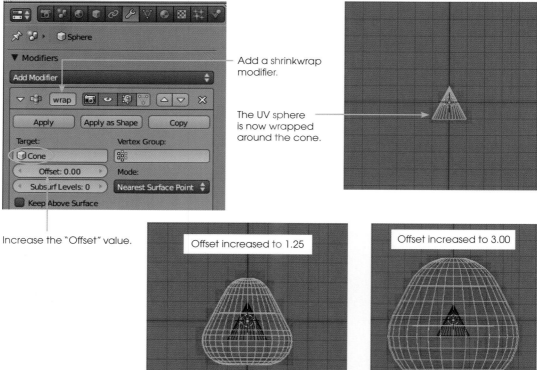

Add a shrinkwrap modifier.

The UV sphere is now wrapped around the cone.

Increase the "Offset" value.

Offset increased to 1.25

Offset increased to 3.00

Figure 12.71

The simple deform modifier deforms a mesh by increasing factor values in the modifier and having a second object with an influence. To see this modifier in action, add a UV sphere in the default scene with a scaled down cube located in the center of the sphere (Figure 12.72). Switch to wireframe mode and add the simple deform modifier to the UV sphere with "Cube" entered as the origin (Figure 12.73). Change the factor value to see the modifier applied; select the cube with the RMB and manipulate it on an axis to deform the sphere (Figure 12.74).

Learning
Unit 6

Simple Deform
Modifier

Figure 12.73

Figure 12.72

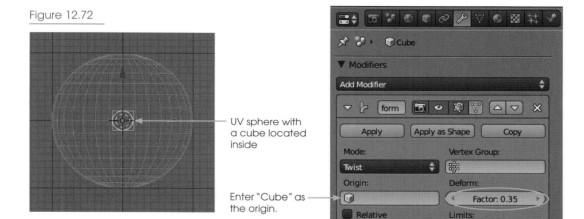

UV sphere with
a cube located
inside

Enter "Cube" as
the origin.

Figure 12.74

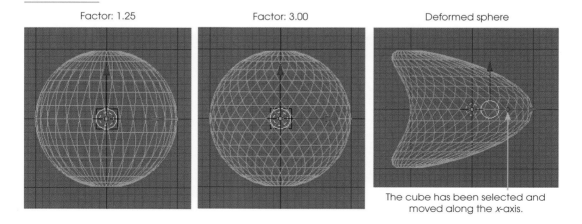

Factor: 1.25   Factor: 3.00   Deformed sphere

The cube has been selected and
moved along the x-axis.

Figure 12.75

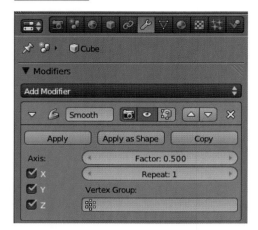

12.4.10 Smooth Modifiers

The smooth modifier smoothes the mesh object by softening the angles between adjacent faces; this shrinks the size of the original object at the same time. The modifier is based on the "Smooth" function in the tools panel. The modifier panel in Figure 12.75 includes the following buttons:

- X, Y, Z. Specifies along which axis the modifier will be applied.
- Factor. Defines the amount of smoothing. Lower or negative values can be used but can deform the mesh object.
- Repeat. Specifies the number of smoothing iterations.
- Vertex Group. Vertex group named to specify which vertices are affected (if no vertex group is specified, the whole object is affected).

Figure 12.76 shows the differences when these values are applied to a monkey object.

Figure 12.76

| Factor: 0.500, Repeat: 1 | Factor: 2.00, Repeat: 1 | Factor: 2.00, Repeat: 2 |

12.4.11 Wave Modifiers

The wave modifier applies a deformation in the form of a wave. To demonstrate, we will apply the modifier to a plane. In the default Blender scene, delete the cube and add a plane. Scale the plane up (the S key + 6), tab into edit mode, and subdivide the plane by clicking "Subdivide" in the tools panel five times. Tab back to object mode.

Go to the properties window – "Object Modifiers" button and click "Add Modifier" to open the drop down selection menu. Select "Wave." In the 3D window, you immediately see the plane deform; it is pulled up in the middle and punched in at the top of the bulge

Wave form control values

(Figure 12.77). The wave modifier has been applied on both the *x*- and *y*-axes. In the "Modifiers" tab you see "X," "Y," and "Cyclic" ticked (Figure 12.78). "X" and "Y" refer to the axis and "Cyclic" means that an animation of the wave will repeat over and over.

With your cursor in the 3D window, press Alt + the A key to see the animation play. Press Esc to stop. Untick the "X" axis in the "Modifiers" tab and play again—a wave along the *y*-axis results. At the bottom of the "Modifiers" tab, change "Speed" to 0.09, "Width" to 1.08, and "Height" to 0.34 (Figure 12.79). Play the animation again. You can change these values to whatever you want; in fact, go ahead and play around with different values to see what happens. It's the only way to get the idea.

Figure 12.79

12.5 Modifiers for Simulating

12.5.1 Cloth and Collision Modifiers

The cloth modifier allows a mesh object to be animated to exhibit the characteristics of a cloth material or fabric. To demonstrate the application of the modifier, follow this brief tutorial.

In a new scene delete the default cube and add a plane object. Scale the plane up four times and in edit mode subdivide four times. A reasonable number of subdivisions are required to produce a good effect. With the plane selected in the 3D view in object mode, go to the properties window – "Object Modifiers" button and add a cloth modifier (Figure 12.80).

Figure 12.80

"Object Modifiers" tab

Refers to the "Physics" button

With your cursor in the 3D window, press Alt + the A key to play an animation. At this stage, the animation will simply show the plane descending and disappearing out of view. Press Esc to end the animation. If you look in the properties window – "Scene" tab, you will see that a gravitational effect is applied (the "Gravity" box is ticked); therefore, the plane descends due to this force.

Look at the "Physics" tab in the properties window (Figure 12.81). Adding a cloth modifier has automatically added data for the physical properties of a cloth. Note that "Cloth Presets" is applied under the "Presets" tab. There is a drop down selection menu here for a variety of material types. Leave the preset as the default setting. Also note that there is no tick in the "Pinning" box, therefore this property is not activated. "Pinning" refers to pinning the cloth in place such as to a notice board or clothesline.

In the 3D window with the plane selected, tab into edit mode, deselect all the vertices, and then select only the two vertices on the rear corners of the mesh. Go to the properties window – "Object Data" button – "Vertex Groups" tab and click on the + sign to add a vertex group. With the two vertices selected press "Assign," which assigns the two vertices to

Figure 12.82

Figure 12.81

"Physics" tab ———

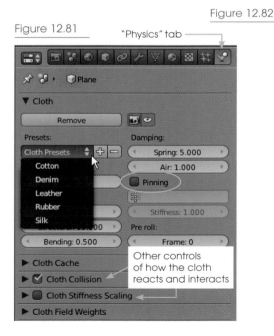

Other controls of how the cloth reacts and interacts

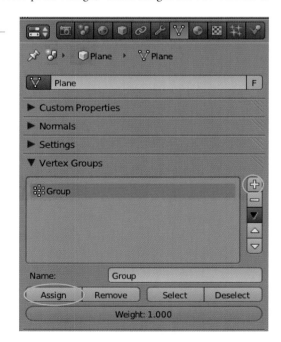

the group (Figure 12.82). Note that Blender has named the vertex group "Group." You can of course change this name if you wish. Tab back to object mode, go to the "Physics" button and tick "Pinning," then click on the vertex group panel just below "Pinning" and click on "Group" to select the vertex group (Figure 12.83). In the 3D window, press Alt + the A key to play the animation again. Observe that the plane (cloth) falls away as if pinned in place and held by its two corners (Figure 12.84). Press Esc to stop the animation.

Figure 12.83

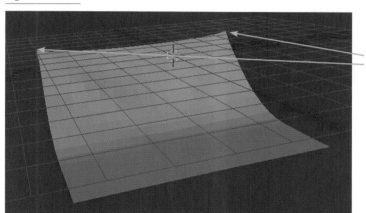

Figure 12.84

The two rear corners appear to be pinned in place, and the rest of the cloth falls away.

The cloth plane can be made to interact with other objects in the scene. Add a UV sphere and position it below the plane as shown in Figure 12.85. With the sphere selected, go to the properties window – "Object Modifiers" button and add a collision modifier. Replay the animation and you will see the cloth plane fall and drape over the sphere (Figure 12.86).

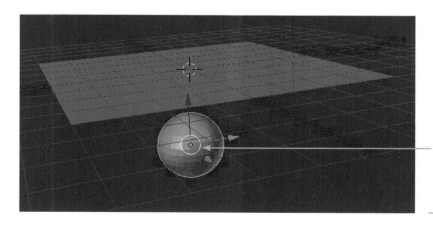

The UV sphere is selected in the 3D view as indicated by the manipulation widget.

Figure 12.85

Figure 12.86

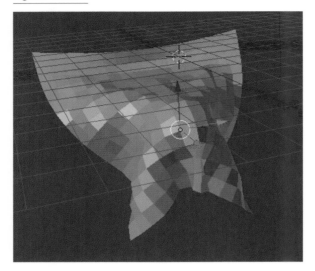

Adding modifiers to objects introduces data in the "Physics" button, which controls how the objects react and interact. It is beyond the scope of this basic demonstration to explain all the settings. Experiment with the settings and record your findings to become proficient in the use of these modifiers.

12.5.2 Explode Modifiers

The explode modifier lets you make a mesh object fly apart or explode. Before you can apply an explode modifier, you must apply an emitter particle system. If you are working methodically through this manual, you haven't learned to apply an emitter particle system yet, so maybe put this on hold until that information is attained. I will write the procedure now since it is such a neat modifier—bookmark this page and make sure you return to it later.

In the 3D window, delete the cube and add a UV sphere. Leave the default number of segments and rings and zoom in on the sphere a bit. With the sphere selected, go to the properties window – "Particles" button and in the panel click on the plus sign to add a particle system (Figure 12.87). In

Figure 12.87   "Particles" tab

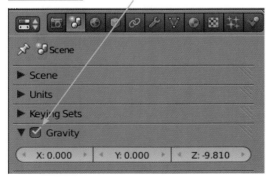

Figure 12.88   Remove the tick.

the "Emission" tab, change the "Amount" value to 100 and the "Lifetime" value to 250. In the properties window – "Scene" button – "Gravity" tab, untick "Gravity" (Figure 12.88). In the properties window – "Object Modifiers" button, click "Add Modifier" (you will see that there is already a particle system modifier applied) and select "Explode." With your cursor in the 3D window, press Alt + the A key to see the sphere fly apart (Figure 12.89).

Figure 12.89

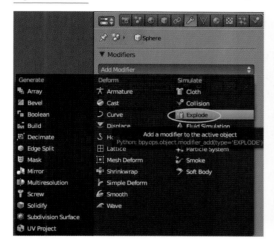

12.5.3 Particle Instance Modifiers

Figure 12.90

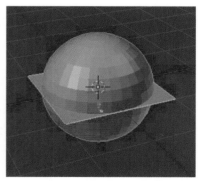

The particle instance modifier allows you to duplicate an object and position the duplicates to mimic the position and number of particles emitted from a particle system. It follows that in order to apply the particle instance modifier to an object, you must have a second object in the scene object with a particle system attached.

As always, an example is a good way to explain this type of application. Before you begin, be familiar with particle systems as described in Chapter 13. In a new scene, delete the default cube and add a plane object. Deselect the plane and add a UV sphere—both the plane and the sphere will be located at the center of the world (Figure 12.90).

Figure 12.91   Remove the tick.

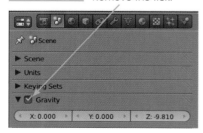

Go to the "Scene" button in the properties window and untick "Gravity" (Figure 12.91). This is done so that particles emitted from an object will not be subject to a gravitational force.

Figure 12.92

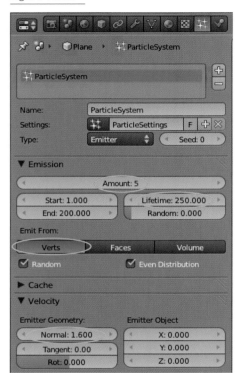

With the plane selected in the 3D window, add a particle system. Use the default system and change the following settings (Figure 12.92):

- "Emission" tab
  - "Amount: 5"
  - "Lifetime: 250.000" (the length of the default animation in frames)
  - Emit from: "Verts" (particles will emit from the vertices)
- "Velocity" tab
  - "Normal: 1.600" (gives the particles a starting velocity)

With the UV sphere selected in the 3D window, add a particle instance modifier. Click in the object panel and select "Plane." In the "Create From:" and "Show Particles When:" columns, tick the boxes as shown in Figure 12.93. We only want to show objects associated with live particles and we want to control the size of the objects by adjusting the size of the particles.

Go back to the plane's particle system and in the "Physics" tab, set "Size: 0.300" (Figure 12.94). This controls the

Figure 12.93

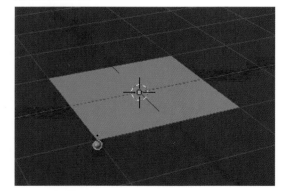

3D view after the modifier settings change

Figure 12.94

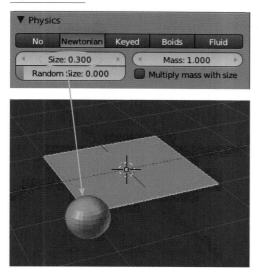

Figure 12.95

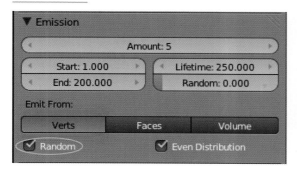

There are five spheres, corresponding to "Amount: 5."

Particle instances generated from the vertices

Figure 12.96

size of the object instances in the 3D window. Press Alt + the A key with the cursor in the 3D window to animate the generation of particles and duplicates of the sphere. You will see that the spheres are being generated from the corners of the plane (vertices) in a random order. In the plane's particle system – "Emission" tab, "Random" is ticked (Figure 12.95).

Allow the 250-frame animation to play then press Esc. You can use the up/down and left/right arrow keys to move through the animation frame by frame to see the sphere duplications; you can also render an image at any stage to see the result (Figure 12.96). You will probably have to reposition the camera to get a good view.

Figure 12.97

The sphere is moved from the center of the scene, but the emitter plane remains at the center.

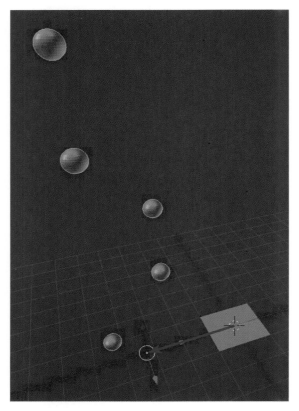

Finally, while at frame 1, select the sphere and drag it away from the center of the scene. Step through the animation again. The spheres are generated, mimicking the position of the plane's vertices (Figure 12.97). If you render an image (press F12), you will see the particles rendered as halos as well as the sphere duplicates.

This example has demonstrated that you can duplicate objects through the use of a particle system and control the effect with the particle system. As always, there are plenty of controls with which you can experiment. You will find detailed tutorials on the internet describing specific applications of the particle instance modifier (see the References section).

12.5.4 Smoke Modifiers

The smoke modifier provides a way to add a smoke simulation to your scene. The following example is a procedure for demonstrating the smoke modifier. This procedure has been compiled from various tutorials existing at the time of writing and only encompasses a very basic example. Experimentation will be required to fully understand the application of this modifier.

Create the domain. Before you can add smoke to your scene, you need to define the area where the smoke simulation takes place. In Blender physics, this area is called a domain. In this case, choose a cube object and scale it in object mode to fit the camera view (Figure 12.98).

Make sure you are in object mode and go to the properties window. At this point, there are two methods of adding a smoke modifier domain to the object:

- Method 1. Select the "Object Modifiers" tab – click "Add Modifier" – select "Smoke" (Figure 12.99). Select the "Physics" button – select the "Smoke" tab – click "Domain."
- Method 2. Select the "Physics" tab – select the "Smoke" tab – click "Domain" (Figure 12.100).

Figure 12.98

Camera view

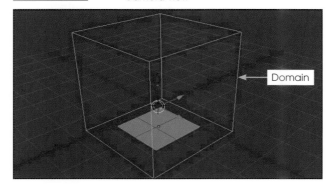

Domain

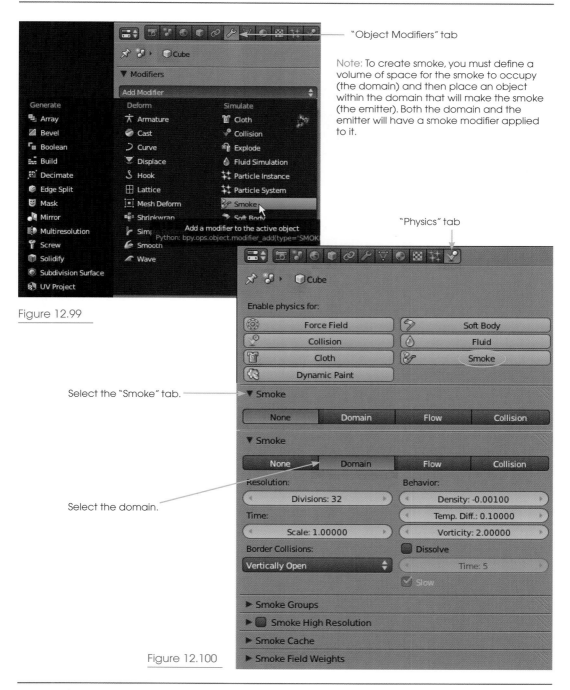

"Object Modifiers" tab

Note: To create smoke, you must define a volume of space for the smoke to occupy (the domain) and then place an object within the domain that will make the smoke (the emitter). Both the domain and the emitter will have a smoke modifier applied to it.

Figure 12.99

"Physics" tab

Select the "Smoke" tab.

Select the domain.

Figure 12.100

In either case, you must select "Domain." The cube in the 3D window changes to an orange outline indicating that a domain has been applied.

Figure 12.101

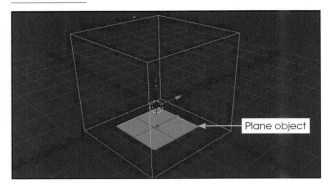

Plane object

Create the flow object. Now that we have defined the volume that will contain smoke, we will add an object from which the smoke will be emitted. Deselect the domain cube, add a plane object, and make sure it's inside the domain cube (Figure 12.101). With the plane selected, go to the properties window – "Physics" button – "Smoke" button to add the smoke modifier. This time choose "Flow" (Figure 12.102). The smoke will not be emitted from the plane itself but from particles that are emitted. Adding smoke in the "Physics" button and selecting "Flow" has

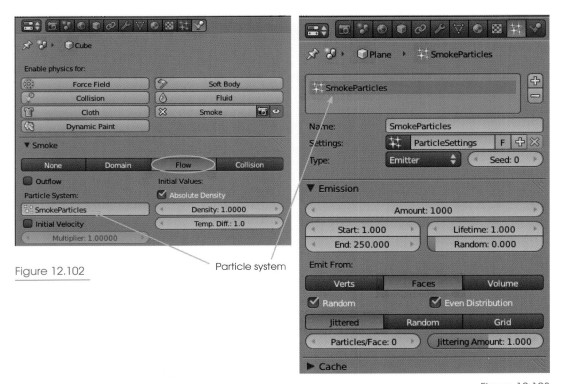

Figure 12.102

Particle system

Figure 12.103

automatically added a particle system to the plane. This can be seen by selecting the "Particles" button in the properties window header (Figure 12.103). The smoke will eventually be seen coming from the plane in a render of the scene. However, you can prevent the plane from rendering by unticking "Emitter" in the "Particles" button – "Render" tab.

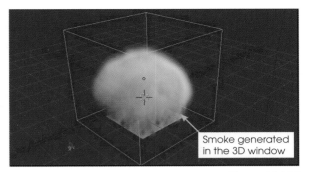

Smoke generated in the 3D window

Figure 12.104

To preview the smoke, press Alt + the A key with your cursor in the 3D window. You will see smoke emit from the plane and rise in the domain (Figure 12.104). The default animation length is 250 frames so let this play to completion and then press Esc to cancel. You can then scrub through the animation in the timeline window to view the smoke at various stages of the animation.

Note: Sometimes scrubbing the animation (dragging the green line in the timeline window) doesn't work in this instance. Using the up/down arrows on the keyboard to step through the animation in 10-frame increments doesn't work either. Using the right arrow to step in single-frame increments starting at frame 1 is the only solution.

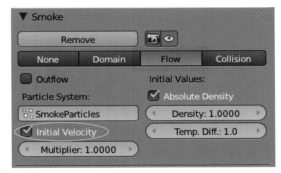

Figure 12.105

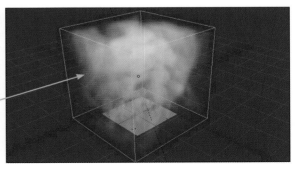

Figure 12.106

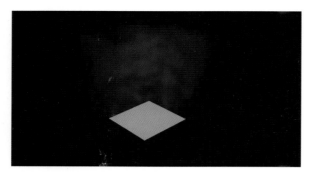

Figure 12.107

In essence, this is the application of the smoke modifier, but of course the effect can be modified. In the first instance in the "Physics" button – "Smoke" tab, ticking "Initial Velocity" activates a multiplier that controls the smoke generation speed (Figure 12.105). There is a marked difference even with the value set at 1. Other changes to the smoke generation may be made by settings in the emitter's particle system. For example, in the "Force Field Settings" tab, selecting "Vortex" from the drop down menu for "Type 1" generates a swirling effect as the smoke is generated (Figure 12.106). Another example is changing the "Normal" value in the "Velocity" tab to something like –3.000 with the emitter plane located towards the top of the domain; this produces a descending smoke effect (Figure 12.107). Experimentation will reveal many other variations.

Rendering. Rendering at this point will result in just rendering an image of the cube domain. This issue can easily be resolved by working on the material and texture of the domain cube. Select the cube and go to the "Material" button. Change the material to "Volume" and set the "Density" value to 0 (Figure 12.108). If you set the density to values larger than 0, the domain cube will be filled with the material.

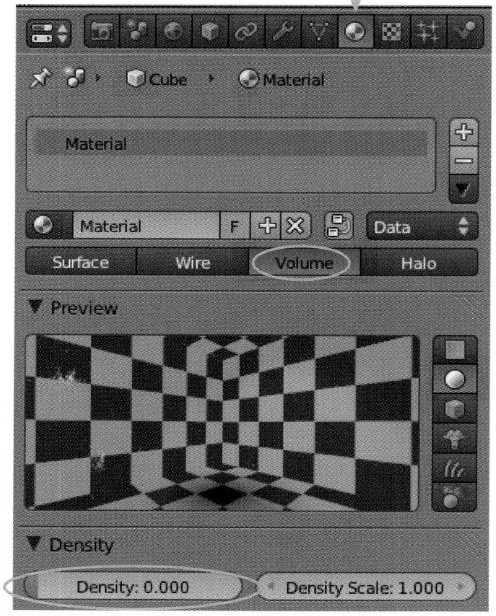

Next, go to the "Textures" button and change the texture type to "Voxel Data" (Figure 12.109). In the "Voxel Data" tab, click in the "Domain Object" panel and select "Cube." In the "Influence" tab, tick "Density" and leave it at 1.000 ("Emission Color" should be automatically checked, too). Now you should be able to render single frames (press F12 and Esc to cancel).

"Material" tab

Figure 12.108

Tip: To see the smoke more clearly, under the "World" tab, choose a very dark color for the horizon. In the 3D window, add a hemi lamp, point it at the smoke, and make the light color something bright and increase the "Energy" value (Figure 12.110).

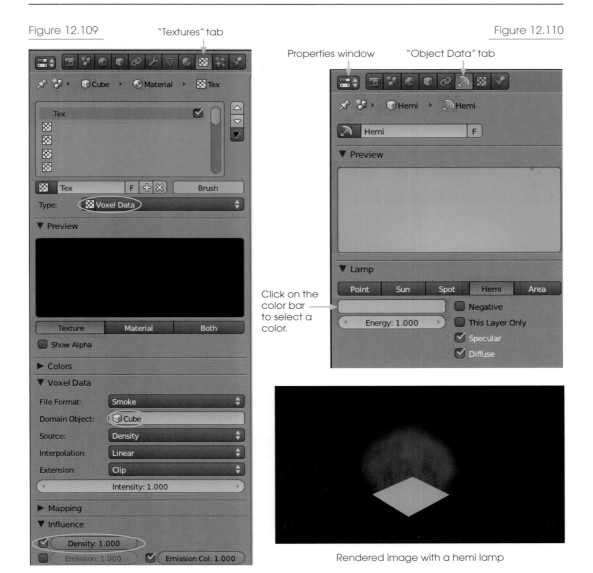

Figure 12.109

"Textures" tab

Figure 12.110

Properties window   "Object Data" tab

Click on the color bar to select a color.

Rendered image with a hemi lamp

12.5.5 Soft Body Modifiers

The soft body modifier in some respects is similar to the cloth modifier in that it allows the animation of a deformation of a mesh object. To demonstrate this modifier, use a UV sphere positioned above a plane. Scale the default plane up four times and, in edit mode, subdivide it four times (Figure 12.111).

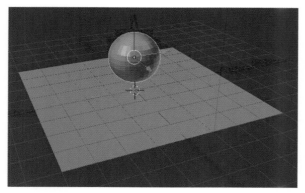

Figure 12.111

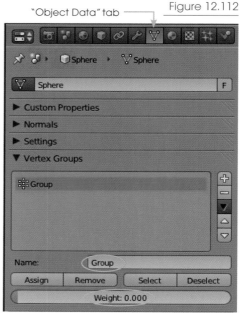

Figure 12.112

"Object Data" tab

In the 3D window, select the UV sphere, tab into edit mode, and with all the vertices selected create a vertex group (properties window – "Object Data" button – "Vertex Groups" tab – click on the + sign – click "Assign"). Set the "Weight" value to 0.000, which means that the vertices will not be anchored and will be able to fall under the influence of the "Gravity" setting in the "Scene" tab (Figure 12.112).

Figure 12.113

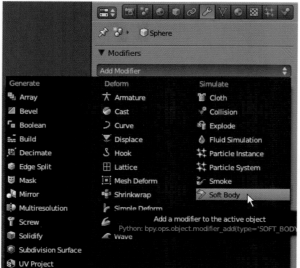

Add a soft body modifier and in the "Physics" tab – "Soft Body Goal" tab – "Vertex Group," enter "Group" (Figure 12.113). Pressing Alt + the A key in the 3D window will play an animation of the sphere falling through the plane. Deselect the sphere, select the plane, and add a collision modifier (Figure 12.114). When the animation is played, the sphere now descends and deforms as it comes in contact with the plane, eventually becoming a flat blob on the surface of the plane (Figure 12.115).

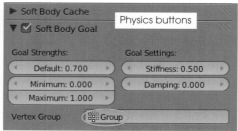

Physics buttons

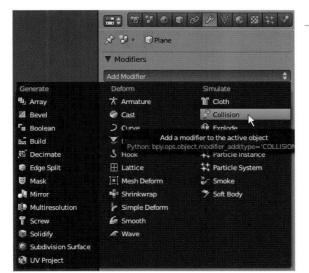

Figure 12.114

Figure 12.115

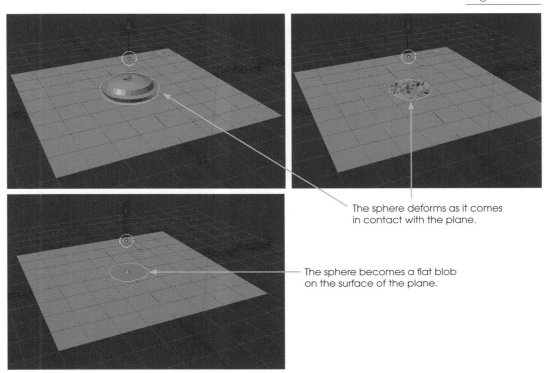

The sphere deforms as it comes in contact with the plane.

The sphere becomes a flat blob on the surface of the plane.

13

Particle Systems

13.1 Overview

This overview is intended as an introduction to the particle systems in Blender. When considering Blender, a particle is a small dot on the computer screen; the dot may be displayed in a variety of ways, but for now think of it as just a dot. In Blender, particles are emitted from an object and can be manipulated to produce varied effects (e.g., to simulate snow, fire, smoke, clouds, sparks, and hair). To produce particles, an object selected in the scene must have a particle system assigned to it. The emission of the particles is played as an animation and then rendered to produce the simulation effect. The best way to see how this is accomplished is to follow a few simple instructions and run a particle system.

Before setting up a particle system, we should establish basic nomenclature so that we're able to understand the instructions in this manual. Let's begin with the default Blender scene; the main windows are outlined in Figure 13.1.

13.1.1 Nomenclature

When referring to the properties window – "Particles" tab, the nomenclature in Figure 13.2 will be observed.

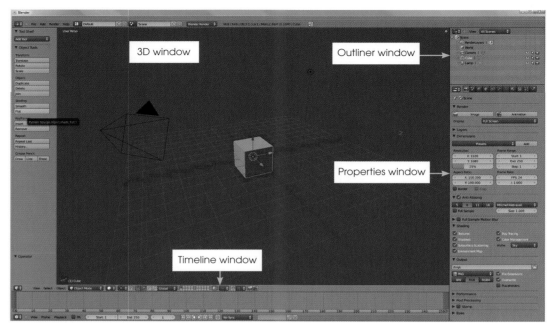

Figure 13.1

13.2 Setting Up a Particle System

Open Blender, delete the default cube object from the scene, and add a new UV sphere. Leave the default values for the sphere as they appear in the properties window. With the sphere selected, go to the properties window and click the "Particles" button. Click on the white + sign next to the empty panel to add a particle system (Figure 13.3). The window will display with an array of tabs and buttons that allow the setup of the system—this may appear daunting at first, but Blender has automatically created a system with default settings (Figure 13.4). The first thing to note is the "Type: Emitter" at the top of the panel. Clicking on the tab where the word "Emitter" is displayed will open a drop down menu with the selection options "Emitter" and "Hair." ("Type: Hair" is a separate system that will be discussed later.)

With the cursor in the 3D window, press Alt + the A key to run an animation showing particles being generated. Note that the timeline window is displayed across the bottom of the screen and will show a green line moving as the animation plays. With the emitter object selected, the animation will play showing particles as small orange squares being emitted from the UV sphere and then falling towards the bottom of the screen (Figure 13.5). If the emitter object is not selected, the particles show as small black dots. The animation will play for 250 frames then repeat itself. Press Esc to stop the animation. Using the up/down arrows on the keyboard or by dragging the green line in the timeline, move the animation forward to

Figure 13.2

Figure 13.3

Properties window   "Particles" button

Panel

Data ID button

Drop down menu

"Emission" tab

Selection box

Value button

Slider

Tab closed

Tab open

Selection buttons

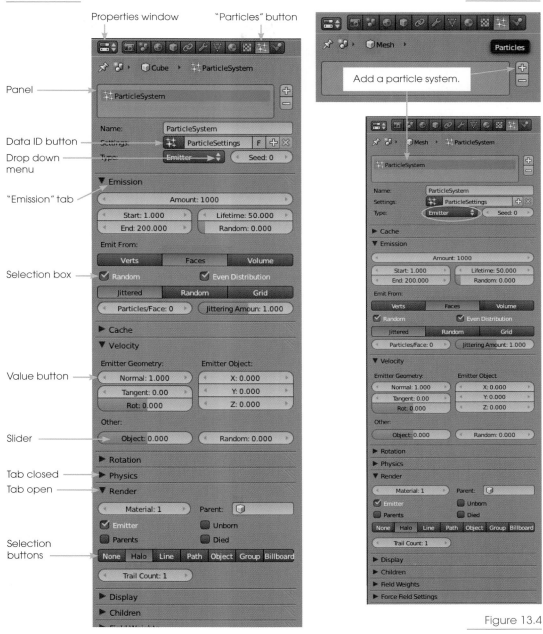

Add a particle system.

Figure 13.4

Figure 13.5

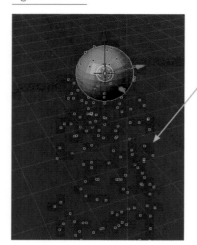

The particles are emitted as orange squares, as seen in the 3D window with the sphere selected.

Figure 13.6

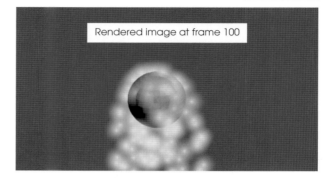

Rendered image at frame 100

frame 100; the particles will now be displayed as they occur at frame 100. Render the scene (press F12) and an image will be rendered showing the UV sphere and the particles as halos (fuzzy balls of light merged together) cascading downwards (Figure 13.6). If the animation were to be rendered as a video, you could play this in action. Press Esc to cancel the image and return to the 3D window.

Note that particles emit their own light, therefore it is not necessary to have a lamp in the scene. If the default lamp is deleted from the scene, the image rendered will show the halos but the emitter object will be black. The reason that the emitter is seen at all is because the render has a default gray background. If the background were black you would not see the emitter.

By default, Blender renders an image at 50% of the 3D window size. If you want to change that, go to the properties window – "Render" button and change the percentage value (drag the slider) in the "Dimensions" tab – "Resolution" button. You can also alter the "X" and "Y" values above the percentage slider to vary the aspect ratio of the image.

In essence, the previous example demonstrated a particle system being applied. It is now time to progress and discover how to manipulate the system. In the previous demonstration, the particles emitted from the sphere cascaded downwards; this was meant to create a realistic scene because a gravitational effect was applied. We will now turn that effect off. Go to the properties window – "Scene" button and remove the tick from the little box in the "Gravity" tab (Figure 13.7). Set the animation in the timeline back to frame 1 and replay the animation (Alt + the A key). This time the particles emitted from the UV sphere disperse in all directions away from the sphere (Figure 13.8). Note that the particles seem to only move for a certain time and disappear before the end of the animation; obviously there is something happening to cause this.

Take a look at the properties window with the "Particles" button activated and look at the "Emission" tab (Figure 13.9). You will see the following values: "Amount: 1000,"

Figure 13.7

"Scene" button

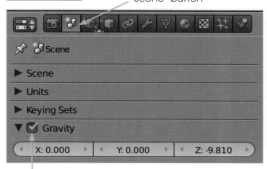

Figure 13.8

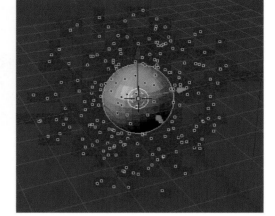

Click to remove the tick and turn gravity off.

"Start: 1.000," "End: 200.000," and "Lifetime: 50.000." These values mean that 1000 particles will be emitted starting at frame 1 and stopping at frame 200, but each particle will only be visible for 50 frames. Therefore, the particles disappear after existing for 50 frames. Also look at the "Velocity" tab and the "Normal: 1.000" value (Figure 13.10). This means that particles are being emitted at a speed of 1 unit per second normal to the surface of the sphere (at 90 degrees to the surface). Increase the "Lifetime" value to 200 and replay the animation. Now particles are displayed for the whole 250-frame animation since particles emitted at frame 200 stay visible until frame 250 (50 frames).

Just to demonstrate another particle emission control feature, change the "Emitter Geometry Normal" value to 0.000 and the "Emitter Object Y" value to 10.000 in the "Velocity"

Figure 13.9

Figure 13.10

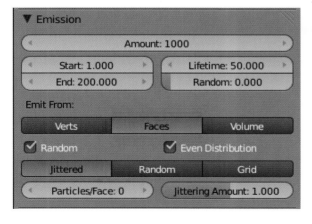

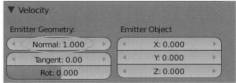

Figure 13.11

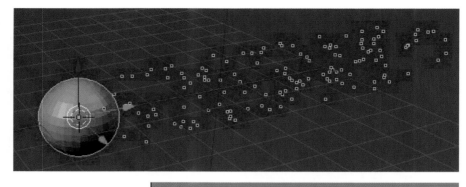

Figure 13.12

Emit From:

Verts | Faces | Volume

tab. Replay the animation and you'll see that all the particles emitted move fairly rapidly along the y-axis of the scene (Figure 13.11). You have just told Blender to emit the particles along the y-axis at 10 units per second instead of emitting them at 1 unit per second at 90 degrees (normal) to the face on the surface of the sphere. Note that "Emit From Faces" in the "Emission" tab is activated (Figure 13.12).

The forgoing example has demonstrated how a particle system is instigated and can be controlled by values in the "Particles" tab. We will leave these buttons alone for the time being and come back later. Let's now look at where and how particles are emitted from an object. In the properties window – "Particles" buttons – "Emission" tab, note the "Emit From" buttons: "Verts" (vertices), "Faces," and "Volume." The default value "Faces" is highlighted in blue. To see the effect of these buttons, start with a new Blender scene and delete the default cube. Add a plane object and remove the 3D manipulator widget (removing the widget

Figure 13.13

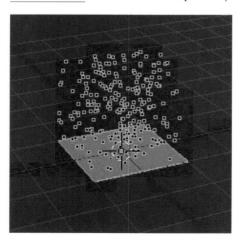

will let us see more clearly what is happening when particles are emitted). Untick the "Gravity" button in the "Scene" tab and add a particle system to the plane. Press Alt + the A key and play the animation showing the particle generation. You will see the particles being generated on the face of the plane object (Figure 13.13). The particles are being generated at an initial velocity of 1 unit per second normal to the face of the plane (at 90 degrees to the surface), which is in accordance with the default values in the "Velocity" tab.

In the "Emission" tab – "Emit From" buttons, select "Verts" and replay the animation. You will now see the emission of particles from the four corners of the plane (Figure 13.14). Selecting "Faces" or "Verts" depends on what you want to see in your final render.

We will now investigate particle generation. Start over with a new Blender scene and delete the default cube object.

Figure 13.14

Figure 13.15

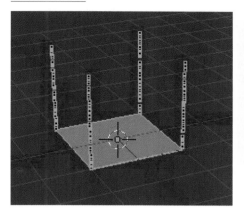

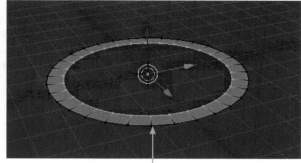

The outer vertices are extruded and scaled down to form the inner ring.

Add a circle object to the scene and scale it up three times (press the S key + 3). Tab into edit mode and with all vertices selected, press the E key (extrude), click the LMB followed by the S key (scale), and move the mouse towards the center of the circle. When you are finished creating the new shape, press the RMB (Figure 13.15). With the E key you have extruded (created a new set of vertices) and the S key has allowed you to scale the set of new vertices. Tab back to object mode and add a particle system. Go to the "Scene" tab, untick "Gravity," and play the animation. You will see particles being generated, but some are moving up and some are moving down (Figure 13.16). Note that the default "Emission" tab – "Emit From" value is "Faces" and the "Velocity" tab – "Emitter Geometry" – "Normal" value is 1.000. We are therefore emitting particles from the faces of the object at 1 unit per second normal to the circle's face. In modeling the circular plane object, some faces have been assigned a negative normal value and some have been assigned a positive normal value, hence the

Figure 13.16

movement of the particles as seen in the animation. The normal values need to be recalculated to align them in the same direction.

To realign the normals, tab into edit mode and select all the vertices. With the cursor in the 3D window, press Ctrl + the N key. "Make Normals Consistent" will display in the side panel at the lower LH corner of the screen. Tab back to object mode and replay the animation. All the particles will move in the same direction but not necessarily upwards. Note that if the normal value is changed to –1.000, the particles will move in the opposite direction; set the normal value to –1.000 so the particles will move up.

Now let's have a close look at what is happening to the particles. If you look at the values in the

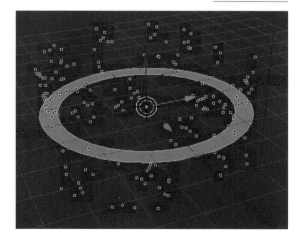

Figure 13.17

"Particles" button – "Emission" tab, you see that 1000 particles are being generated starting at frame 1, ending at frame 200, with a lifetime of 50 frames. You will also see "Random" and "Even Distribution" boxes ticked so the particles are being spread between the faces in a random order as they are generated. "Random" would appear to take precedence over "Even Distribution." Note also that "Jittered" is highlighted in blue—"Jittered" means that particles appear in a random position in any one face on the object. Untick the "Random" box and play the animation. The particles are now generated from one face after the other around the circle plane object. Increase the "Lifetime" value to 200 to make the particles display longer in the animation. Note that if the animation is played without the object selected, the particles will appear as small black dots instead of the little orange squares.

Cycling the animation in the timeline to frame 200 produces a spiral array in the 3D window, which may be rendered as an image (Figure 13.17). You will however have to relocate the camera in the scene to render an image of the complete spiral. By default, Blender renders an image of a particle system that includes the emitter object. To render without the emitter object, go to the "Render" tab in the "Particles" button and untick the "Emitter" box.

The spiral has been generated with a "Normal Velocity" value of 1.000. If this value is deleted and the "Emitter Object Y" value in the "Velocity" tab is set to 1.000, the spiral will generate flat along the y-axis when the animation is replayed (Figure 13.18)—how the array of particles is generated is controlled by the values entered in the "Velocity" tab.

So far, the particles that have been generated have been displayed as dots or little orange squares in the 3D window and have been rendered as halos. In the "Render" tab, you will

Figure 13.18

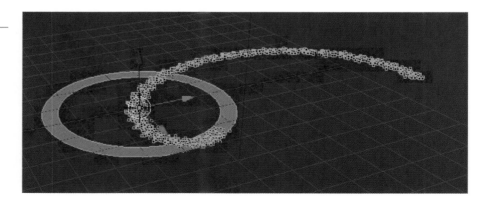

see a selection of render options: None, Halo, Line, Path, Object, Group, and Billboard (Figure 13.19). Select the "Object" option and reduce the number of particles in the "Emission" tab "Amount" to 32. Our plane circular ring object was created from a circle with 32 vertices, therefore it has 32 faces. Reducing the particle amount to 32 gives us approximately one particle per face. This is approximate since at this point the generation of the particles follows an animation curve that accelerates and decelerates. Play the animation again to regenerate the particles, then cycle through the animation and at

Figure 13.19

frame 200 you will see 32 particles; however, they are not evenly spaced along the spiral (Figure 13.20). This is showing the influence of the acceleration change in the generation. We are only concerned with reducing the particle count just now.

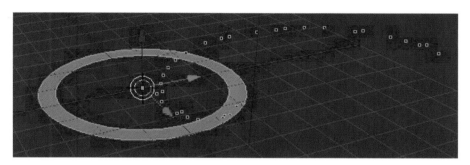

Figure 13.20

Deselect the ring in the 3D window, add a UV sphere object, and note that it is called "Sphere" (see the lower LH corner of the window). Deselect the sphere and reselect the ring. In the "Particles" button – "Render" tab select render type "Object," look for "Dupli Object," and select "Sphere" in the drop down panel that displays. The particles are now displayed in the 3D window as tiny little spheres (Figure 13.21). Go to the "Physics" tab

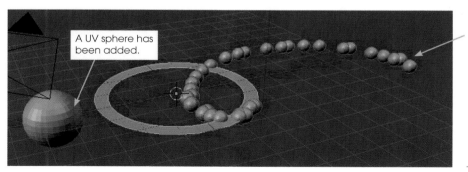

Figure 13.21

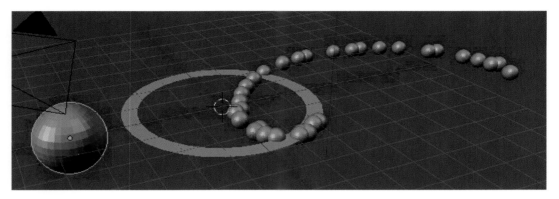

Figure 13.22

and increase the "Size" value to increase the size of the tiny spheres in the 3D window. Render to see an image of the spheres.

Up to now everything created and rendered has been the default dull gray color. Adding a new material color to the sphere will cause the array of spheres to display and render in that material color (Figure 13.22). Adding a material to the ring in the 3D window will cause the particles with a halo value to render in that material color.

This demonstration of particle system applications has only shown the tip of the iceberg. We must now delve into a detailed study of the "Particles" button to ascertain the function of each tab and formulate the logic of the particle systems interface. There are many excellent tutorials available online to complement this study (see the References section), and it is recommended that you attain a full understanding of the buttons to allow for the transition from an operator of the program to a creative artist.

13.3 Particle Settings and Material Influence

We will continue the study of the particle system by examining the particle settings and material influence and seeing how settings are entered to create effects. The possible effects that can be created are endless and only limited by the imagination: particles can be deflected off other objects, blown by the wind, displayed before they are built, and much more. It would be impossible to demonstrate everything and only by experimentation and recording settings for future use will you become proficient. Remember that a particular effect can be saved as a Blender file, which can be imported into a scene in another Blender file. When you create something interesting, it's worth saving and recording for future use. Blender doesn't come prepacked with instant goodies, so the objective for a Blender artist should be to compile an extensive library.

The particle settings are controlled by the "Particles" button, which consists of a series of tabs housing buttons and sliders allowing values to be entered (Figure 13.23). As we have already seen, Blender automatically creates a particle system when the "Add" button is pressed. Now, we must modify that system to produce the particular effect that we require. The system is then saved to a cache to be used.

Properties window

"Assignment" tab: how
particles are assigned

"Cache" tab: saving
the particle system

"Emission" tab: how
particles are generated

"Velocity" tab: how fast
and in what direction

"Rotation" tab: how
particles rotate

"Physics" tab: rules of
animation and interaction

"Render" tab: how
images and video display

"Display" tab: how
particles display onscreen

"Children" tab: particles
generate other particles

"Field Weights" tab: values
affecting force fields

"Force Field
Settings" tab:
modifiers
affecting
particles

"Vertexgroups"
tab: where
particles
originate

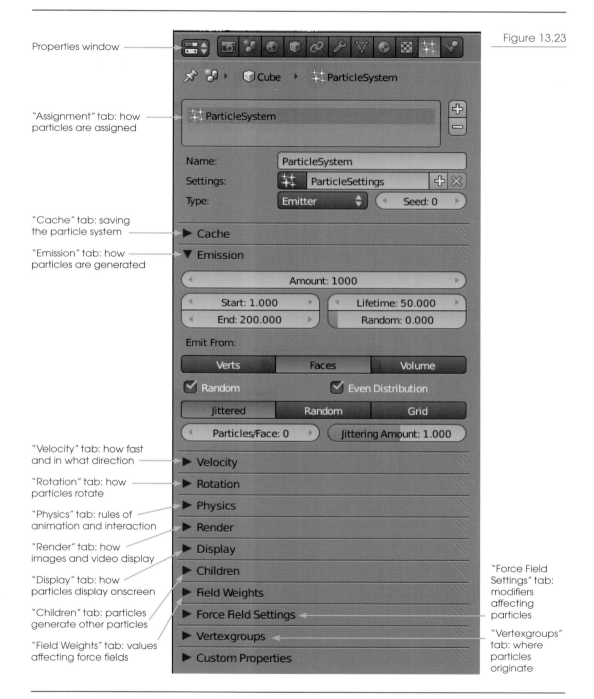

Figure 13.23

13.3. Particle Settings and Material Influence

Note: In Figure 13.23, I have taken the liberty of labeling the first part of the "Particles" button as the "Assignment" tab. This part of the window is always open unlike the remainder of the tabs, which are opened and closed by clicking on the triangles at the upper left-hand corner of each tab. The "Assignment" tab controls what we do with a particle system when we have created a system (modified the default system). We will therefore postpone the discussion of this tab until the very end of this chapter.

13.4 The Particles Panel

The "Particles" panel displays all the options relating to how particles are generated and displayed. To understand how to create specific effects using particles, we must first look at some of the tabs.

Figure 13.24

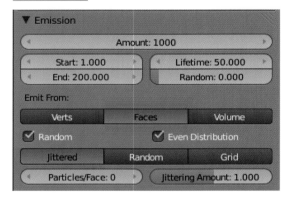

13.4.1 The Emission Tab

The "Emission" tab controls how particles are emitted (Figure 13.24).

- Amount. The number of particles emitted in the animation between the start and the end frame settings.
- Start. The frame number in the animation where particles will start to be emitted.
- End. The frame number in the animation where particle emission will stop.
- Lifetime. How long each particle will be visible (number of frames) in the animation.
- Random. Particles are emitted from faces in a random order.
- Emit From. Particles may be emitted from either vertices, faces, or the volume. "Faces" is selected in Figure 13.24, as indicated by the blue highlight.

The remaining options in the tab control the order of particle generation.

- Random, Even Distribution; Jittered, Random, Grid; Particles/Face, Jittering Amount. These options vary depending on which of the "Emit From" options has been selected. Experimentation and recording of results are required to establish combinations for specific applications.

13.4.2 The Velocity Tab

The "Velocity" tab settings control how fast and in what direction particles are emitted from a mesh object (Figure 13.25).

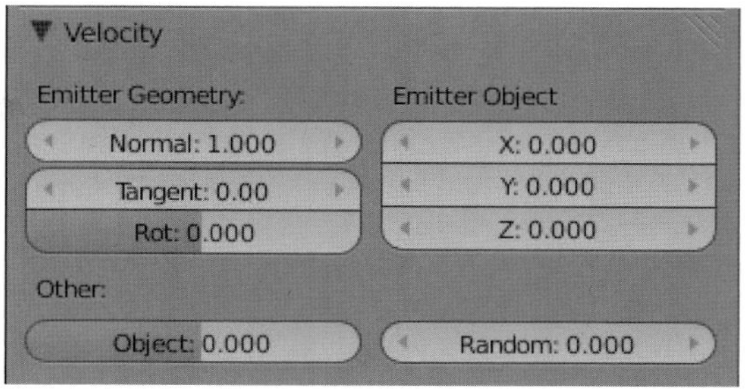

- Emitter Geometry
  - Normal. Velocity of the particles normal (at 90 degrees) to the emitting surface.
  - Tangent. Velocity of the particles parallel to the surface.
  - Rotation. The value rotates the direction of the surface tangent.
- Emitter Object
  - The velocity of particles along the *x*, *y*, and *z* axes in the scene.

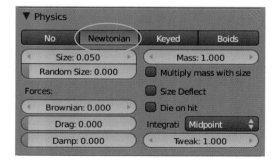

Figure 13.25

Note: All values may be entered as positive or negative, which reverses the direction.

- Other
  - Object. The object gives the particles a starting speed and direction.
  - Random. Gives the starting speed direction a random variation.

Note: The "Other" values are best demonstrated with particles being displayed as objects. See also the "Render" tab.

13.4.3 Physics

Physics determine the way particles move and interact with the world around them. Note the selection bar at the top of the "Physics" tab with "Newtonian" highlighted in blue (Figure 13.26). "Newtonian" is the normal particle physics that we will consider at this time. The other options are:

- No. Particles stick to their emitter for the whole lifetime.
- Keyed. Allows particles to be directed from one emitter to another, setting up a chain of particles moving from one place to the other.

Figure 13.26

- **Boids.** Allows particles to be given rules of behavior, which allow them to represent flocks, swarms, herds, and schools of various kinds of animals.

Just for the moment the only setting we need to concern ourselves with in the "Newtonian" system is the "Size" value, which controls the size of the particles as seen in the 3D window and as rendered in an image or movie.

13.4.4 Display

The "Display" tab controls how particles are seen in the 3D window. The options in this tab are useful when multiple particle systems are in play and it is desirable to distinguish between the particles in the different systems. Let's work with our examples and begin by starting a particle system to recap what we learned previously.

13.5 Starting a Particle System

Open Blender with its default scene containing a mesh cube object. Delete the cube and add a UV sphere, keeping the segments and rings at 32. The number of segments and rings may be altered in the tools panel (the T key toggles between hiding and showing this panel) at the lower left of the screen. With the sphere selected in the 3D window, go to the properties window – "Particles" button and click the white + sign to add a particle system.

Blender has created a complete particle system that we can modify to produce whatever effect we want. Note the timeline window displayed across the bottom of the screen;

Figure 13.27

Figure 13.28

Figure 13.29

"Scene" button

The "Gravity" box is ticked.

Gravity force = –9.810, Earth's gravity

Figure 13.30   Figure 13.31

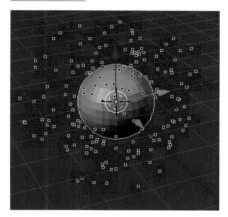

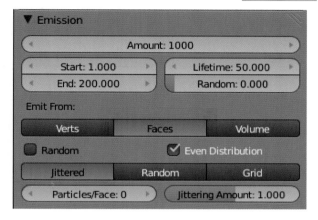

the timeline shows a 250-frame animation window as seen by "Start: 1" and "End: 250" (Figure 13.27). With your cursor in the 3D window and with the UV sphere selected, press Alt + the A key to play the animation of particles being generated. The particles emit from the surface of the sphere in a random order and fall towards the bottom of the screen. The animation plays for 250 frames then repeats. Press Esc to cancel.

Click on the green line and drag it over to frame 41 to see the view in Figure 13.28. The particles behave in this manner since there is a gravitational force being applied. Have a look at the properties window – "Scene" button and note the tick in the "Gravity" box (Figure 13.29). Click on the tick to remove it and play the animation again—this time the particles emit from the sphere and float off into space (Figure 13.30). They still emit in a random order from the faces of the sphere. Look at the "Emission" tab and note the values inserted (Figure 13.31). These values tell us that 1000 particles will be generated in the animation starting at frame 1 and ending at frame 200 during the animation and that the animation is 250 frames in length. There is also a "Lifetime" value that tells us that when a particle is generated, it remains visible for 50 frames. Therefore, a particle generated at frame 200 will remain visible until frame 250.

Note the tick in the box labeled "Random" in the "Particles" button – "Emission" tab. This is providing the random order of generation of the particles. Click on the tick to remove it.

Front view   Figure 13.32

Top view

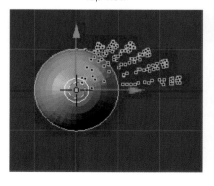

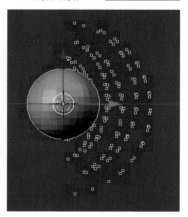

Play the animation again and press Esc to cancel. The 3D window is in user perspective view, therefore it is difficult to see what has been achieved by removing the "Random" tick. Change the view to top view (number pad 7) then to front view (number pad 1) (Figure 13.32). With the timeline advanced to frame 41, you will see an ordered array of particles.

Figure 13.33

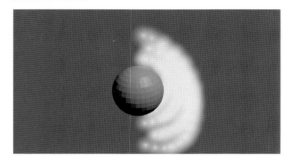

Figure 13.34

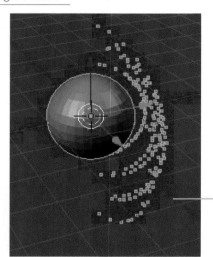

13.6 Material Influence on Particles

Particles emit their own light so it isn't necessary to have lamps in the scene when particles are rendered. To give particles color, you have to add a material to the emitting object. We can render an image at frame 41 of what we have already created by pressing F12 on the keyboard—what we get is a plain gray-and-white picture (Figure 13.33). Press Esc to cancel the image. With the sphere selected in the 3D window, go to the properties window – "Material" button. Press "Add New" and click on the diffuse color bar to display the color picker. Select a color (I've chosen red) then render the image again (Figure 13.34).

We see the emitter object (sphere) and the particles rendered in the same color. To advance this subject a little further, go to the "Particles" button and find the "Render" tab. In the "Render" tab, you will see "Halo" highlighted in blue (Figure 13.35). This is telling Blender to render the particles as halos. Since there are a considerable number of particles visible at frame 41, our

Rendered image

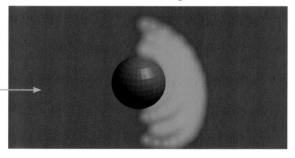

rendered image shows us a colored blob. Note also the tick in the "Emitter" box; this tells Blender to render the emitter object in the image. Click in the box to remove the tick. Go back to the "Material" button and find the "Transparency" tab. Click and add a tick in the "Transparency" box. Reduce the "Alpha" value to 0.050 and render again: now only the particles are rendered and they are transparent (Figure 13.36).

This has demonstrated some of the effects of materials on particles. There are many more combinations to play with. We will have a look at adding halo effects to particles and at the

Figure 13.35

Figure 13.36

Figure 13.37

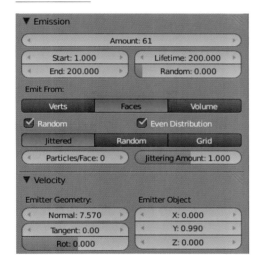

Figure 13.38

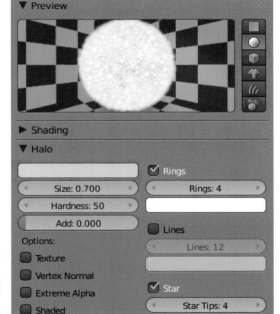

same time introduce a few more tricks to give you the feel for the versatility of the particle system.

Open a new Blender scene, delete the cube, and add a plane object. Leave the "Gravity" box in the "Scene" button ticked to maintain a gravity effect. With the plane selected, go to the properties window – "Particles" button and add a particle system. In the "Emission" tab, change "Amount: 61" and "Lifetime: 200" (Figure 13.37). In the "Velocity" tab, change "Normal: 7.500" and "Emitter Object Y: 0.990." At the bottom of the "Velocity" tab set "Random: 2." We are decreasing the amount of particles so we don't flood the scene, but changing the "Lifetime" value makes the particles visible longer in the animation. We still have gravity working, but with normal velocity at 7.500 the particles will project up before descending. Setting "Emitter Object Y: 0.990" gives the particles a slight horizontal velocity along the *y*-axis, making them move in an arc.

Figure 13.39

3D window at frame 41

Rendered image

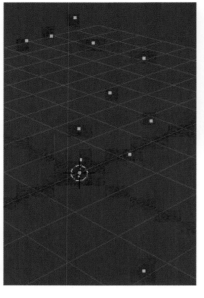

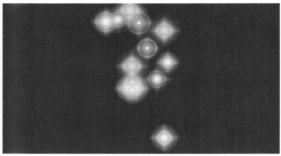

Now let's jazz the particles up a bit. With the plane still selected, go to the "Material" button and add a new material. Just above the "Preview" tab, change to a halo material ("Halo" will become highlighted in blue). Click on the color bar and select a nice bright yellow. Change the halo size to 0.700 and tick "Rings" and "Star" (Figure 13.38). Press Alt + the A key and run the animation. Press Esc to exit, then cycle the animation to frame 41 and render the image (Figure 13.39).

Experiment with rings, lines, stars, and halo size. For example, in the "Material" tab untick "Rings" and "Star tips" to change the particle render back to a plain halo. Set the halo size to 4 so that the image fills the camera view. In the "Halo" tab, decrease the "Alpha" value to 0.100 to give the halo a transparent look; this should produce something that looks like a cloud of smoke. If you place an object in the

Monkey positioned behind the particles

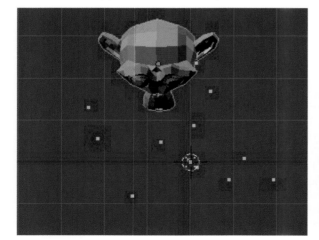

Figure 13.40

Rendered image

scene (in this case, a monkey object) and position it where the particles are at frame 41, the object renders in the smoke cloud (Figure 13.40). There are many combinations, all producing different effects, so make sure you experiment and record your results.

Figure 13.41

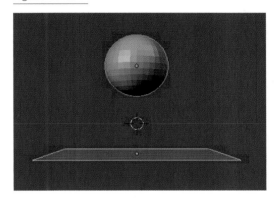

Figure 13.42

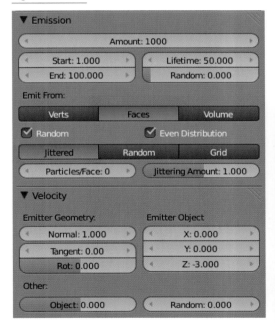

13.7 Particle Interaction

Particles can interact with other objects and be affected by forces like wind. Particles can bounce off other objects and act like sparks or droplets. To show how these features work, set up a scene with a sphere positioned above a plane as shown in Figure 13.41 (the plane is scaled up three times). With the sphere selected, go to the properties window – "Particles" button and add a particle system. In the "Emission" tab, set the "End" value to 100 and in the "Velocity" tab, set the "Emitter Object: Z" value to –3.000 (Figure 13.42). With your cursor in the 3D window, press Alt + the A key to play the animation of the particle generation—you will see the particles fall and pass through the plane, as in Figure 13.43.

Figure 13.43

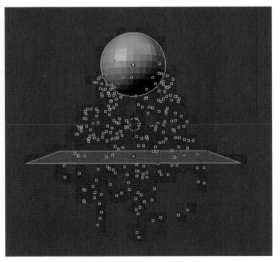

Figure 13.44

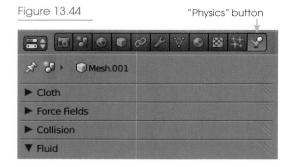

"Physics" button

The next step is to stop the particles from falling through the plane. Select the plane and go to the properties window – "Physics" button (Figure 13.44). Select the "Add" button in the "Collision" tab and press Alt + the A key again to replay the animation (remember you must be at frame 1 before you replay); you will now see the particles bounce up from the surface of the plane (Figure 13.45).

Tip: Shift select the sphere and the plane to see the particles better.

By increasing the "Particle Damping: Factor" value in the "Collision" tab to 1.000, the particles will land on the plane but they will no longer bounce; they will just slide off the surface. By experimenting with other particle and collision settings and by applying materials with halos, line, and stars, you can simulate sparks bouncing with high-quality results.

Figure 13.45

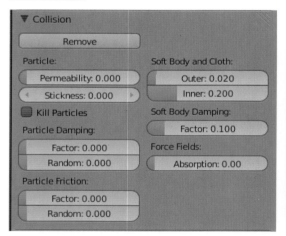

13.8 Wind

Blender allows particles to be influenced by a simulated wind force. To create a wind effect, you have to place an object in the scene and assign a wind force to it. An object called an empty is great for this since it doesn't render. Begin by opening a new scene, deleting the cube, and replacing it with a UV sphere. Add a particle system to the sphere and leave the default settings. Add an empty to the scene, select the empty with the RMB, and position it just below the sphere off to one side, as shown in Figure 13.46.

Figure 13.46

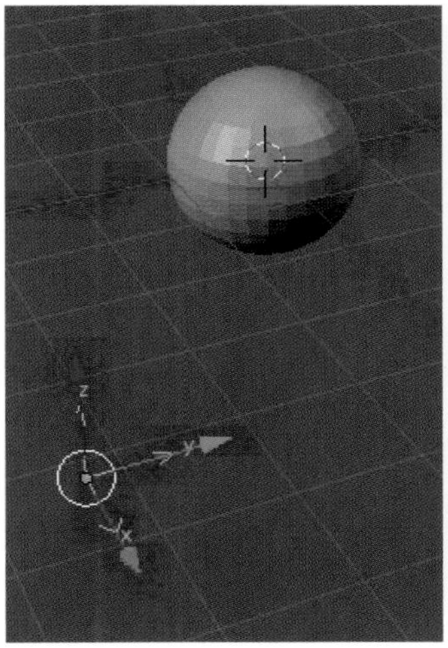

Figure 13.47

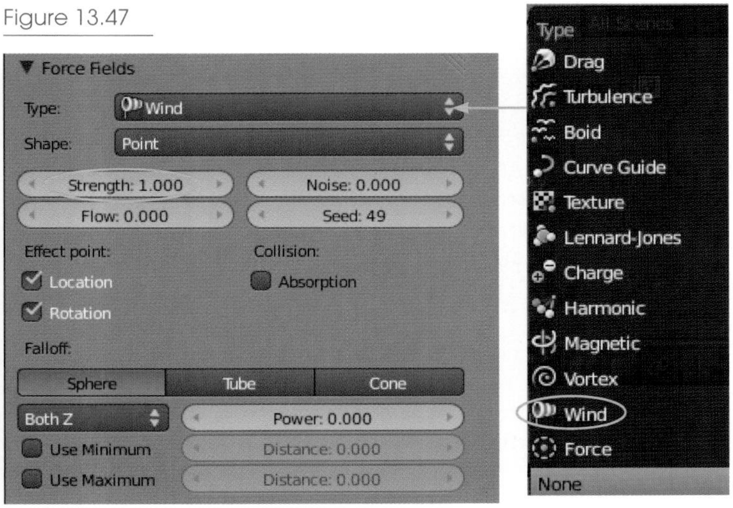

▼ Force Fields

Type: Wind

Shape: Point

Strength: 1.000   Noise: 0.000

Flow: 0.000   Seed: 49

Effect point: Collision:

☑ Location   ☐ Absorption

☑ Rotation

Falloff:

Sphere   Tube   Cone

Both Z   Power: 0.000

☐ Use Minimum   Distance: 0.000

☐ Use Maximum   Distance: 0.000

Type All Scenes

🐟 Drag
🦐 Turbulence
🌀 Boid
🎣 Curve Guide
📷 Texture
🦞 Lennard-Jones
🔋 Charge
🎵 Harmonic
🧲 Magnetic
🌀 Vortex
💨 Wind
💠 Force
None

Figure 13.48

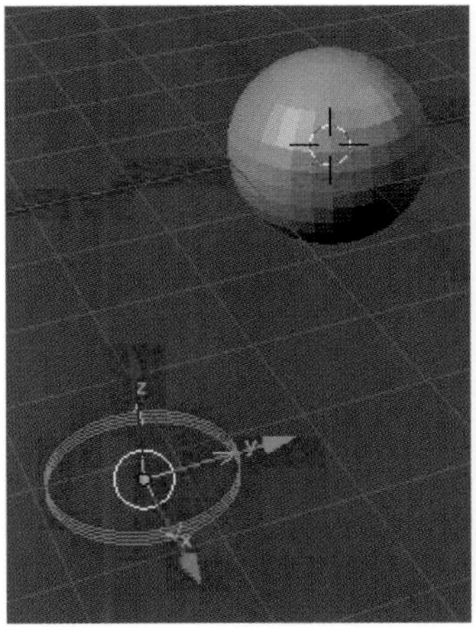

Figure 13.49

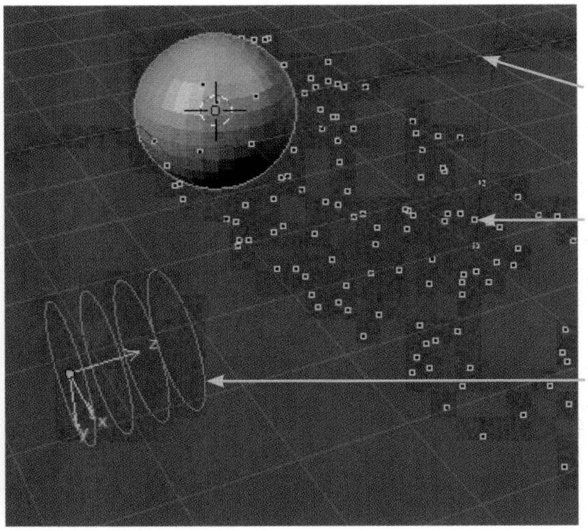

Global y-axis

Particles blown along the global y-axis

Empty wind force rotated about the x-axis with a strength value of 10

The sphere will emit particles that will fall downwards since the "Gravity" box is ticked in the "Scene" tab. With the empty selected in the 3D window, go to the properties window – "Physics" button and click on the "Force Fields" button. Select "Wind" from the "Type" drop down selection menu (Figure 13.47). You will see the wind force field in the 3D window attached to the empty object (Figure 13.48). The wind force is acting along the z-axis of the empty object at a strength of 1.000. We want the wind to blow the particles falling from the sphere along the global y-axis. With the empty selected, rotate it about the x-axis so that the empty local z-axis points in the same direction as the global y-axis. Increase the "Strength" value to 10 and play the animation to see the sphere's particles being blown (Figure 13.49). Wind strength is able to be animated, which creates a realistic wind effect.

13.9 Sample Particle Settings

The following are some sample settings for various uses. Follow the settings carefully otherwise you will not get the results as demonstrated. Settings can be tweaked to produce whatever results you want and only by experimentation will you discover what can be achieved. Remember to record settings for future use when you discover something especially neat.

13.9.1 Snow Effect

In a new scene, delete the cube and add a plane. Scale the plane up five times and subdivide the surface four times. Position the plane at the top of the screen above the camera out of camera view—the plane is there to emit particles, not to be included in the rendered image or movie. Go to the properties window – "Scene" button and set "Gravity Z: –0.210." This is a low value since we want our snow to float down gently. Remember, if there are other objects in the scene that are affected by gravity, they will also float.

Add a particle system to the plane. In the "Emission" tab, set "Lifetime: 200" and in the "Velocity" tab set "Normal: 0.010" and "Random: 0.320." We want the particles to display for a fair amount of time, not go careering off at a hundred miles an hour. In the "Material" button, add a material (white is appropriate) and set it as "Halo." Set the halo size to 0.050 to make small snowflakes. Run the animation to generate particles then advance the animation to about frame 230 and render an image (Figure 13.50).

Figure 13.50

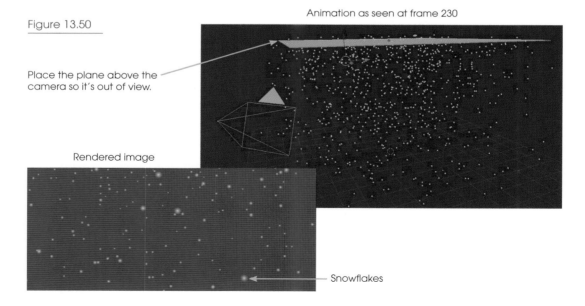

Animation as seen at frame 230

Place the plane above the camera so it's out of view.

Rendered image

Snowflakes

13.9.2 Fire

In a new scene, delete the cube and add a UV sphere. Add a material, make it a halo type, and use the color picker to change it to a yellow color. Set the halo size to 0.300. In the "Scene" button, untick the "Gravity" box. Add a particle system to the sphere and in the "Velocity" tab set "Normal: 0.000" and the "Emitter Object Z: 2.870." In the 3D window, move the sphere down the z-axis slightly to position it at the bottom of the camera view. Run the animation then cycle forward through the frames and render an image (Figure 13.51).

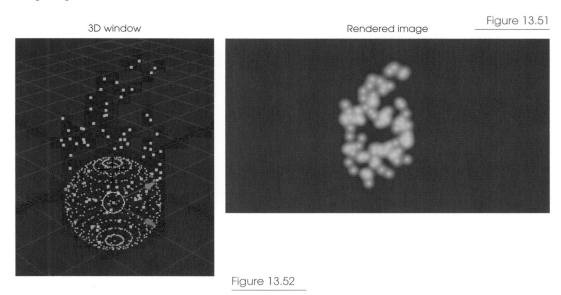

3D window   Rendered image   Figure 13.51

Figure 13.52

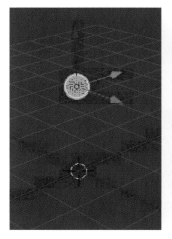

3D window   Figure 13.53

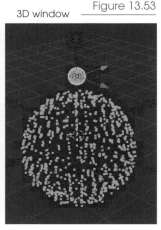

13.9.3 Simple Fireworks

Create a new scene, delete the default cube, and add a scaled down UV sphere. Position the sphere at the top of the camera view (Figure 13.52). In the "Material" button, add a material, make it a halo type, and change the color to yellow and the halo size to 1.000. In the "Particles" button, add a particle system. In the "Emission" tab, change "Lifetime: 100," "Start: 50," and "End: 51." In the "Velocity" tab, set "Normal: 2.000." Run the animation and then advance to

Figure 13.54

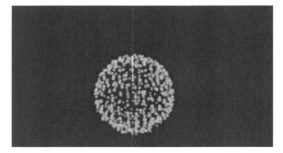

Camera view

Figure 13.55

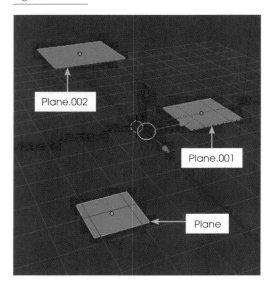

Plane.002

Plane.001

Plane

Figure 13.56

Rename the object here if necessary.

frame 67 (Figure 13.53). In the "Particles" button – "Render" tab, untick "Emitter" and render the scene (Figure 13.54).

13.10 Keyed Particle Systems

So far we have looked at particle systems of "Type: Emitter" with Newtonian physics. We will now consider "Type: Emitter" with keyed physics, which we call keyed particles. Keyed physics is a way of controlling the movement of particles by directing them from the original emitter object to a second object and onto a third and subsequent objects. The flow of particles may be used as an animation or used to create a static image. The following procedure for setting up a keyed system will demonstrate the principles involved.

Open a new scene in Blender and delete the default cube. Add three separate plane objects and position them as shown in Figure 13.55. A simple way to do this is to add one plane, then with the plane selected, press Shift + the D key to duplicate it. The new plane will be in grab mode (you'll see a white outline), so hit the Y key to confine movement to the *y*-axis and drag the new plane to one side. Click the mouse to exit grab mode, and then repeat the process to add a third plane (this time, hit the Z key to confine the third plane's movement to the *z*-axis). Note that the first plane was named "Plane" by Blender (you can see the names at the lower left of the screen when an object is selected). The second plane is named "Plane.001" and the third "Plane.002." Arrange the planes in the 3D window in order of name—it will help later on.

Note: You can go to the properties window – "Object Data" button and edit the name in the "Name" box at the top of the window (Figure 13.56). You could use any name you like; however, since the planes are all identical, it's probably best to stay with the "Plane" names.

Figure 13.57

Figure 13.58

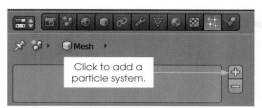

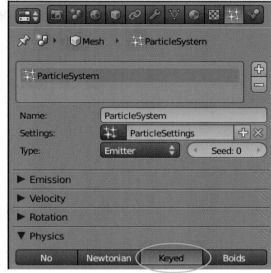

Select "Plane" and in the properties window – "Particles" button, click on the + sign to add a particle system (Figure 13.57). Go to the "Physics" tab and select "Keyed" (Figure 13.58). Click on the + sign next to the "Keys" panel to add a new particle target (Figure 13.59); Blender enters this in the panel and names it "Particle System." Note the small panel with the little cube in it just below the "Keys" panel. Leave this empty for the time being—the plane named "Plane" is going to be our emitter. Deselect "Plane" in the 3D window and select "Plane.001." Repeat the process to add a keyed particle system to "Plane.001" and "Plane.002."

Figure 13.59

Tip: When you select "Plane.001," all the buttons in the "Particles" tab disappear. Drag up the scroll bar at the right-hand side of the window to reveal the + sign to add a new system.

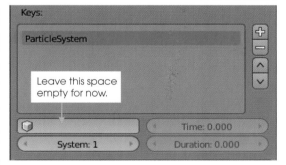

Select "Plane" and in the "Particles" button – "Physics" tab, click on the + sign next to the "Keys" panel to add a new particle target. Blender enters this as "Particle System" again. Click on the small panel with the little cube in it to display a drop down selection panel. Click on "Plane.001" and Blender changes the target to "Plane.001: Particle System" (Figure 13.60). You are telling the particle target for "Particle System" that its target object is "Plane.001." Still with "Plane" selected in the 3D window, click on the + sign next to the "Keys" panel again. Click on the cube and select "Plane.002." We now have particle targets named "Particle System," "Plane.001: Particle System," and "Plane.002: Particle System." This is simply telling the particles emitted from "Plane" to go to "Plane.001" and then to "Plane.002." Hit Alt + the A key to see the animation (Figure 13.61). Remember that all the rules for number of particles, lifetime, start, end, and normal velocity apply.

Figure 13.60

Figure 13.61

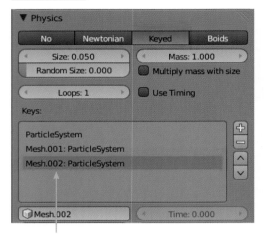

Particle targets

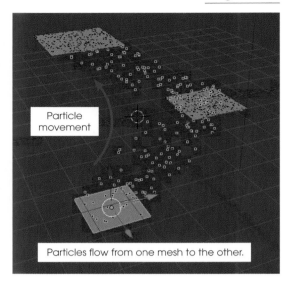

Particle movement

Particles flow from one mesh to the other.

13.11 Boids Particle Systems

Boids particle systems are used to simulate flocks, swarms, herds, and schools of various kinds of animals or anything that acts with similar behavior. Boids particle systems are of "Type: Emitter" but have boids physics applied. Boids particles in one particle system can react to particles in another system or they can react to particles within their own system. Boids are given rules of behavior, which are listed in a stack. The rules at the top of the stack take precedence over rules lower down in the stack, but the stack is able to be rearranged once it is written. Since only a certain amount of information is able to be evaluated if the memory capacity is exceeded, rules lower down the stack are ignored. The procedure for setting up boids particle systems will be demonstrated with the following examples.

13.11.1 Example: A Flock of Birds

Since we're still working with the basics, our particles will *act* like a flock of birds but won't actually look like birds. Open a new Blender scene and stick with the default cube: this will be our particle emitter. In the properties window – "Particles" button, add a new particle system. Leave all the button settings as their default values, except for the following:

- "Emission" tab
  - Amount: 30 (we'll have a small flock)
  - Lifetime: 250 (the default animation length in the timeline)
- "Physics" tab
  - Select "Boids."

Figure 13.62
Figure 13.63

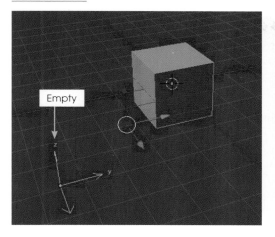

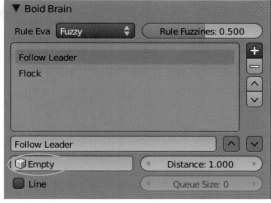

- "Boid Brain" tab
  - With "Separate" highlighted, hit the – sign to delete it. Click on the + sign at the RH side of the window to display a selection drop down menu for boids rules and select "Follow Leader." Click on the up arrow below the – sign to move "Follow Leader" to the top of the stack.

We have told the particles to follow the leader while flocking together. We will now give the particles a leader to follow. Deselect the cube in the 3D window (press the A key) and add an empty; an empty is a location point that can be animated to move in the scene but does not render. Grab the empty and move it to the side (Figure 13.62). Deselect the empty and select the cube. Go back to the "Boid Brain" tab and make sure "Follow Leader" is highlighted. Below the stack window you will see an empty box with a little cube in it. Click in this box and select "Empty" from the drop down menu that displays (Figure 13.63). We

Figure 13.64

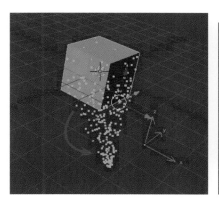

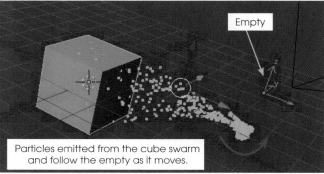

Particles emitted from the cube swarm and follow the empty as it moves.

have told the particles to follow the empty. Animate the empty to move across the screen (see Chapter 9 for a refresher on animation). When the animation is played, select the cube in the 3D window. Particles are emitted from the cube, head towards the empty, and attempt to follow it as it moves across the screen (Figure 13.64). Having the cube selected displays the particles as little orange squares; if it isn't selected, all you get are black dots, which are hard to see.

> Note: With a high particle amount, Blender may crash due to overload when calculating data. This of course depends on the capability of your computer.

13.11.2 Example: Directing Movement

In this example, I will demonstrate how to direct particles to move from one object to another. Start a new scene and add a second cube object by pressing Shift + the D key. Note that the default cube is named "Cube" (see the lower left side of the 3D window) and the new cube is named "Cube.001." Position the Cubes as shown in Figure 13.65, scaling the new cube down. Select the original cube and add a particle system with boids physics. In the "Emission" tab, reduce the "Amount" value to 10 and set the "Lifetime" value to 1500; we want to keep the number of particles low and have them visible for a fair amount of time in the animation. Go to the timeline window and set the animation "End" value to 1500 frames.

Now let's display the particles in a different way. In the "Particles" button – "Display" tab, select "Cross" and set the "Draw Size" value to 10; you will see a cross appear on the cube. In the "Boid Brain" tab, remove "Separate" and "Flock" and add "Goal." Click in the "Object" box below the rule window and select "Cube.001"—this tells the particles emitted from the original cube to go and find the target. Play the animation to see the result: crosses emitted from "Cube" migrate across to and accumulate on the target (Figure 13.66). Remember that the location of either or both of the cubes in the scene may be animated at the same time.

Figure 13.65

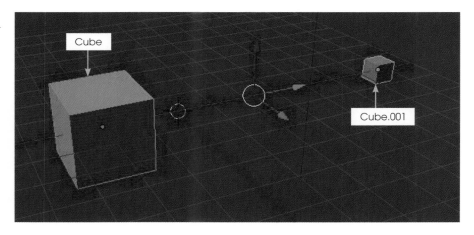

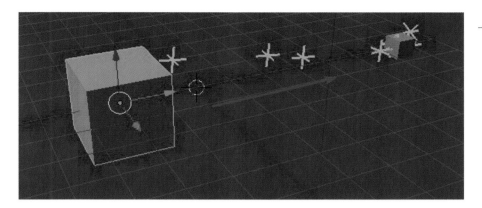

Figure 13.66

13.11.3 Example: Prey/Predator Relationship

Boids particles will not only act like swarms or flocks in their movement; they can also be made to react to one another. An example would be one flock of birds chasing off another flock. Let's set up an example in a new Blender scene with two cubes, as shown in Figure 13.67. Make the larger cube two times bigger than the smaller cube. The small cube will emit predator particles and the large cube will emit prey particles.

Predator particles. Select the small cube in the 3D window and add a particle system in the properties window – "Particles" tab. Change the following settings:

- "Emission" tab
    - Amount: 100 (the larger number becomes the aggressor)
    - Lifetime: 1500 (allows the particles to be visible for the duration of the animation)
- "Display" tab
    - Select "Point'" and set the "Draw Size" value to 3.

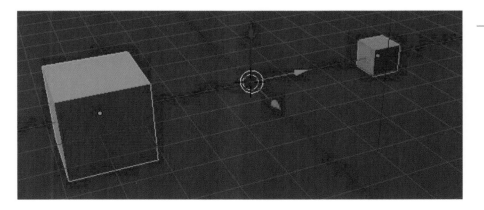

Figure 13.67

- "Physics" tab
  - Select "Boids."
  - Size: 0.030
  - Max Air Speed: 7.000 (gives an advantage over the slower prey particles)
  - Next to the "Relations" panel, click on the + sign and select "Enemy."
- "Boid Brain" tab
  - The default "Separate" and "Flock" rules are applied. Add a "Fight" rule and move it to the top of the stack.

Prey particles. Select the large cube in the 3D window, add a particle system, and change the following settings:

- "Emission" tab
  - Amount: 10
  - Lifetime: 1500
- "Display" tab
  - Select "Cross" and set the "Draw Size" value to 10.
- "Physics" tab
  - Select "Boids."
  - Size: 0.030
  - Max Air Speed: 1.000 (combined with its size, this makes the prey bigger and slower)
  - Relations: Click the + sign then click in the target selection box below the window and select "Cube"—now "Cube: Particle System" displays in the window. Select "Enemy."
- "Boid Brain" tab
  - The default "Separate" and "Flock" rules are applied. Add a "Fight" rule and move it to the top of the stack.

Figure 13.68

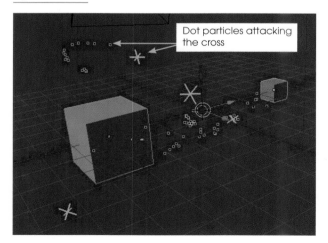

Dot particles attacking the cross

Go back to the predator and repeat the "Relations" setup, this time selecting "Cube.001" as the target (you cannot set up "Relations" until the other object has a particle system). Still in the "Physics" tab with the larger cube selected, change to Newtonian physics then tick in the "Die on hit" box. Change back to boids physics and change the "End" value to 1500 in the timeline. You may have to zoom out in the window. Changing to wireframe display mode gives a better view of the particle swarms. Shift select both cubes in the 3D window and play the animation to see the result; selecting both cubes draws orange lines around the particles and makes them more visible. The cross particles emitted from the large cube are attacked by the swarm of small particles from the small cube and the cross particles die when they are hit (Figure 13.68).

For simplicity, we are showing only dots and crosses as seen in the 3D window. A render could show anything you wish by choosing "Object" in the "Render" tab and assigning a preconstructed mesh object. A complex single frame can take a while to render and a complex animation can take an eternity.

13.11.4 Example: Follow Terrain

Boids particles can be made to emulate herds following a terrain. Set up a new Blender scene, as shown in Figure 13.69. The cube object is the default cube and will act as a target to which the particles will be directed. The other two objects in the scene are two planes with one being scaled up and shaped to act as our terrain. To create the terrain, delete the cube and add a plane. Scale the plane up four times, tab into edit mode, and subdivide it five times. Deselect all the vertices and press the C key for circle select mode. Click, hold, and drag the LMB, selecting a row of vertices from one side of the plane to the other. Press Esc to cancel the circle select. In the 3D window header, turn on proportional editing. Click on the blue arrow of the manipulation widget and drag down to form a ditch in the terrain. Repeat the procedure to form a rise along the side of the ditch.

With the scene assembled, select the objects as listed and perform the following setup in the properties window:

- Select "Plane.001" (the small plane rotated, which will act as our emitter).
- Add a particle system with boids physics; untick "Allow Flight" and tick "Allow Land."
- In the "Emission" tab, change the values to "Amount: 100" and "Lifetime: 1500" and change the animation length in the timeline to 1500 frames.
- In the "Boid Brain" tab, add a "Goal" rule, move it to the top of the stack, and select "Cube" as the goal.

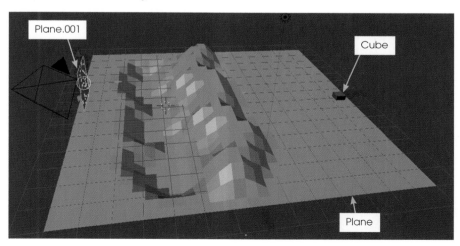

Figure 13.69

Figure 13.70

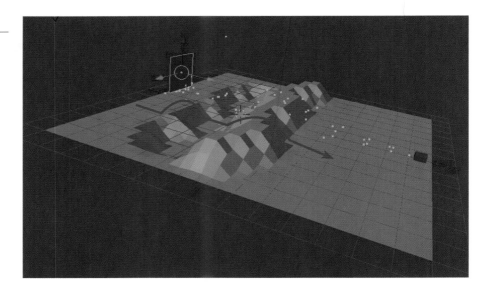

- Select "Plane" (the terrain).
- In the properties window – "Physics" button, click the "Collision" tab.
- The cube (target) requires no action other than to scale it down a bit.

Select "Plane.001" and play the animation; the particles emitted follow the contour of the terrain as they move to the target (Figure 13.70).

Figure 13.71

Click to add a
particle system.

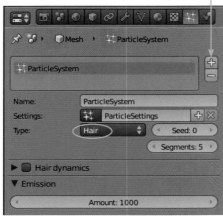

13.12 Hair Particle Systems

The previous pages describing particles have introduced particles of "Type: Emitter" with physics types "No," "Newtonian," "Keyed," and "Boids." We will now take a look at particles of "Type: Hair," where particles are rendered as strands and may be edited in the 3D window. Hair type particles may be used to represent such things as grass, fur, hair, or anything that has a surface with fibrous strands.

We will perform a quick demonstration to show what is meant by hair particles. In the 3D window, delete the default cube object, add a plane, and zoom in a bit. With the plane selected, go to the properties window – "Particles" button and click on the + sign to add a particle system (Figure 13.71). At the top of the "Particles" window, click on the drop down menu that says "Type: Emitter" and select "Hair." The plane in the 3D window will show long strands sticking up from the surface of the plane. Go to the "Hair Length" value in the "Emission" tab and decrease the default value of 1.000 to see the length of the strands shorten—we now have a hairy plane (Figure 13.72).

Let us proceed with something a little more exciting. Start a new Blender scene, delete the cube, and add a monkey. The monkey head always loads looking upwards, but we want him positioned with the top of his head pointing up (press the R key – the X key – 90 – "Enter" to rotate him about the x-axis 90 degrees). If we add a hair particle system, we will get a hairy-headed monkey with hair sticking out in every direction; however, let's try for a more clean-cut look

Figure 13.72

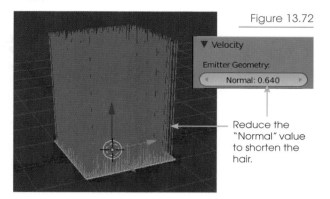

Reduce the "Normal" value to shorten the hair.

Limit selection to visible

Figure 13.73

with some hair on the head and a beard. Press the number pad 7 key to access a top view, looking down on the monkey's head. We will designate where we want the hair to grow by selecting a bunch of vertices; this bunch is called a vertex group. Tab into edit mode, zoom in so you can see what you are doing, and in the 3D window header click on the "Limit selection to visible" button (Figure 13.73).

Press the A key to deselect all the vertices, then select a group on the top of the monkey's head (Figure 13.74). You can do this by pressing Shift + the RMB on the individual vertices, by pressing the B key and the LMB to drag a box over the vertices, or by pressing the C key

Figure 13.75

Figure 13.74

Top view of the monkey head with the vertices selected

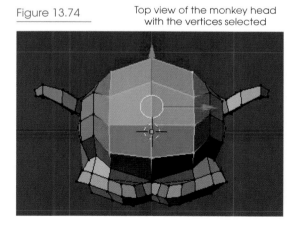

Click to add a vertex group.

Rename the group "Hair."

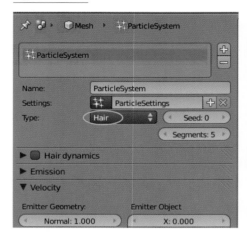

Figure 13.78

and the LMB to drag the circle to select (scroll the MMB to change the circle size and press Esc to cancel when your selection is finished). Leave the vertices selected and click on the "Object Data" button in the properties window. In the "Vertex Groups" tab, click on the + sign to add a vertex group. In the name box, click on "Group" and delete it (Blender names every new vertex group "Group"). Type in "Hair" and press Enter to rename the group (Figure 13.75). You will note that the group highlighted in blue in the window changes because we still have our vertices selected. Now in the "Vertex Groups" tab, just below "Name" click on the "Assign" button—this assigns the selected vertices to the vertex group named "Hair."

So far, there is a head and we have nominated an area on the head by selecting a group of vertices. We do not have hair. Go to the "Particles" button and click on the + sign to add a particle system. Change "Type: Emitter" to "Type: Hair" (Figure 13.76). Still, nothing hap-

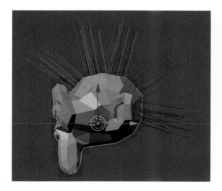

Figure 13.79

pens because we are in edit mode. Note that Blender has
named the particle system "Particle System." Tab to object
mode in the 3D window and you should see plenty of hair
(Figure 13.77). In fact, there is hair everywhere. To correct
this look, start in the "Hair Length" box in the "Emission"
tab and decrease the value until the hair strands look reasonable; say, about 0.820. Next, while still in the "Particles"
button, go down to the "Vertexgroups" tab and in the box
next to "Density" click and select "Hair" (Figure 13.78).
We now have hair only on the area we selected. Press number pad 3 to get a side view—what a scrawny bunch of
hair (Figure 13.79, left)! To fix the scrawny look, go to the
"Children" tab and click on "Simple"—now we have a bushy, mohawk hairdo
(Figure 13.79, right).

Figure 13.80

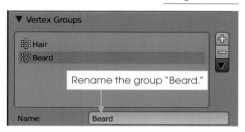

We will continue on and add a beard as promised. To make the process interesting but hopefully not difficult to understand, I will vary the procedure just a
little. We previously selected a bunch of vertices, created a vertex group, named
it, then assigned the selected vertices to the group. Let's create a new vertex group
first this time. With the monkey selected in object mode in the 3D window, go
to properties window – "Object Data" button and click on the + sign in the "Vertex Groups" tab to add a new vertex group. Blender again names the new group
"Group." Rename this to "Beard" as we did before for the hair (Figure 13.80). Now
we need to select the vertices to assign them to the new group. We could use the
procedures as outlined previously, but let's do it a different way.

Figure 13.81

First tab into edit mode and deselect all the vertices. In the 3D window
header, change to weight paint mode. Our monkey turns blue in the 3D window, which shows that no vertices are selected. Note that "Beard" is highlighted in blue in the "Object Data" button – "Vertex Groups" tab. Click on
"Hair." If you look closely amongst all that black hair (it may help to rotate
the view), you will see a red scalp; this is showing the area that was previously
selected by individual vertices. Tab to edit mode and click on "Select" in the
"Vertex Groups" tab and you'll see the vertices that were painted. Press the A
key in the 3D window to deselect, and click on "Beard" again in the "Object
Data" button – "Vertex Groups" tab. Tab to weight paint mode and look at
the tools panel at the left-hand side of the screen. In the "Brush" tab, click on
the + sign and drag the "Strength" slider all the way to the right so the value
is 1.000 (Figure 13.81). In the 3D window, drag the circle that appears as the
mouse cursor over the monkey's chin—you will see the color change as you
drag. Keep dragging until the chin is all red, which means that you have selected this area as the new vertex group for the beard (Figure 13.82). Tab to
edit mode, make sure all vertices are deselected, then in the "Vertex Groups"
tab click on "Assign" to assign the painted vertices to the beard vertex group.
Click "Select" to see them.

Go to the "Particles" button and add a new particle system. Note that
Blender names this system "Particle System 2." Select "Type: Hair," decrease

Figure 13.82

Figure 13.83

Figure 13.84

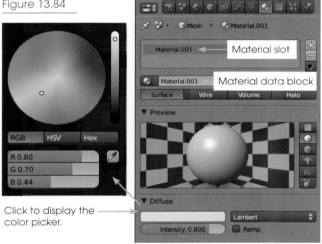

Click to display the
color picker.

Figure 13.85

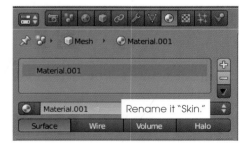

the "Hair Length" value in the "Emission" tab to 0.290, and go down to the "Vertexgroups" tab, click in the "Density" box, and select "Beard." We now have scrawny hair on the monkey's chin. Go to the "Children" tab and click "Simple" for a hairy monkey (Figure 13.83). It doesn't matter in which order you do it, the procedure is the same: select vertices to define the area, create a vertex group, assign vertices to the vertex group, create a hair particle system, and assign it to the vertex group.

A gray monkey with a black beard and hair in the 3D window is fine, but it isn't all that exciting in a render—let's jazz it up a bit. Select the monkey in object mode in the 3D window and go to the properties window – "Material" button. Click on "New" to add a material. Click in the diffuse color bar and select a color for the monkey with the color picker that displays (Figure 13.84). To start with, this color will be applied to everything on the monkey: his skin, hair, and beard. At the top of the "Material" window, note that "Material.001" is highlighted in blue and just below that "Material.001" is listed again. The blue highlighted "Material.001" is a material slot and the lower "Material.001" is a material data block. In the "Material" window's unique data

Figure 13.86

Click on the triangle to change the value.

Figure 13.87

block ID name, click on "Material.001," and delete and rename it "Skin" (Figure 13.85). Click on the + sign to add a new slot and name the next one "Hair." Repeat the process again and rename it "Beard." There are now three material slots, each with a separate data block. Click on slot "Hair" and "Beard" in turn and choose colors for them.

Go to the "Particles" button and at the top you will see "Particle System" and "Particle System 2." Remember that the first system is for the hair and the second is for the beard. Select "Particle System" (hair) and in the "Render" tab – "Material" button, click on the little triangle at the RHS until you get a value of 2. Now do the same for "Particle System 2," selecting a value of 3 for the beard (Figure 13.86). The beard and hair look strange, but at least the colors are pretty (Figure 13.87). As always there is much more to play with in Blender; try the hair tutorials at www.blendercookie.com.

13.12.1 Final Note

Adding hair to an object can add an awful lot of vertices, which when rendering can take an awful lot of time and may even cause your computer to stall out. If you are not doing anything serious and have a slow machine to start with, keep the number of strands low.

13.13 The Assignment Tab

When a particle system is first added to a scene by clicking on the + sign, Blender introduces a block of data to the scene that comprises a default particle system. Blender names this data block "Particle Settings," as seen in the "Settings" panel. The data block named "Particle Settings" is automatically linked to the default particle system that is named "Particle System." "Particle System" is placed in the assignment panel where it is assigned to an object in the 3D window. This explanation may be viewed in Figure 13.88. There is no "Assignment" tab or assignment panel as such, but for the purpose of this discussion we will consider the area marked in green as the "Assignment" tab and the panel displaying "Particle System" highlighted in blue as the assignment panel.

In the "Assignment" tab, there is a "Type" drop down menu that displays the options "Emitter" and "Hair." "Type: Emitter" is the default selection, which means that with the

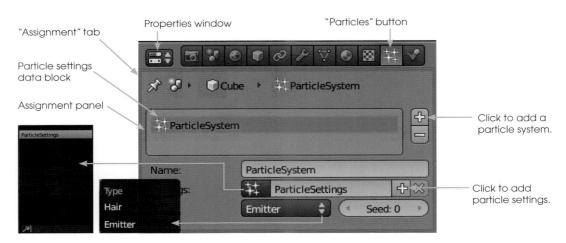

Figure 13.88

particle system assigned to an object in the scene, that object becomes the emitter of the particles. In either case, the object becomes an emitter with a particle system assigned. "Type: Hair" may be viewed as a specialized static emitter, which will be described later in the section.

Note that the names "Particle Settings" and "Particle Systems" may be renamed by clicking in the panels, deleting the name, and retyping a new name. This is useful when there are multiple objects, data blocks, and particle systems. Multiple objects in the 3D window can each have a different particle system assigned, and each object may have more than one particle system.

When a new particle system data block is added to the scene, Blender creates a new name for the data block. The default particle settings data block is named "Particle Settings" as previously stated. When a second data block is added, it is named "Particle Settings.001," a third would be named "Particle Settings.002," etc. Renaming data blocks to something more relevant to objects in the scene would be an advantage. When new data blocks are created, they are stored in a cache for reuse by other particle systems.

When a new particle system is added to the scene, Blender assigns that system to the object that is selected in the 3D window. If no objects are selected, the new particle system is assigned to the last object that was introduced to the scene. Particle systems added to a scene initially have the default "Particle Settings" data block linked and a new name applied as described previously. At this point, the data block settings may be altered to create a new unique data block or a previously created data block may be selected and linked to the new particle system. Clicking on the icon in front of the "Particle Settings" panel reveals a drop down menu showing the cache mentioned previously with data blocks for selection.

The foregoing statements may seem confusing and not easily related to what has been labeled the "Assignment" tab. The following exercise will attempt to clarify the statements and at the same time demonstrate the application of particle systems in practical terms.

13.13.1 Practical Exercise

Figure 13.89

Open a new scene in Blender and delete the cube from the 3D window. Add three separate plane objects and position them at the center of the scene so that they are all visible in camera view and an image containing all three may be rendered (Figure 13.89). Add a diffuse material color to each of the planes—let's make them red, green, and blue (the colors do not have to be accurate). Turn off the "Gravity" setting in the "Scene" tab and turn off the 3D manipulator widget in the 3D window

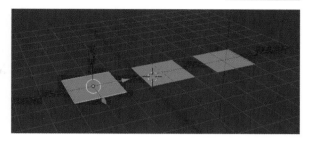

(Figure 13.90). At this time, the three plane objects have been named "Plane," "Plane.001," and "Plane.002" by Blender, as seen in the lower left-hand corner of the 3D window when each is selected (Figure 13.91). This naming is not all that relevant to what we have in the scene, so we will rename the objects.

Figure 13.90

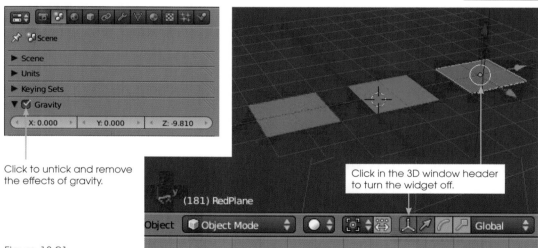

Click to untick and remove the effects of gravity.

Click in the 3D window header to turn the widget off.

Figure 13.91

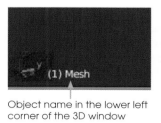

Object name in the lower left corner of the 3D window

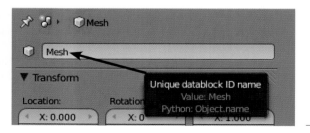

Unique datablock ID name
Value: Mesh
Python: Object.name

Figure 13.92

Figure 13.93

"Particles" button

Figure 13.94

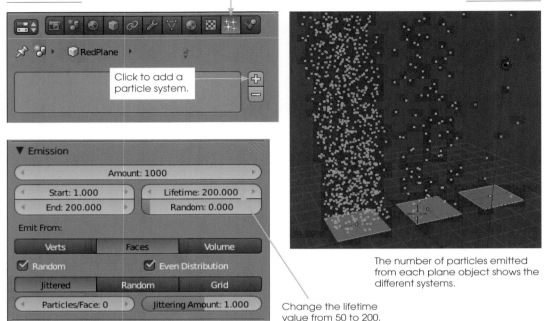

Click to add a particle system.

▼ Emission

Amount: 1000

Start: 1.000   Lifetime: 200.000
End: 200.000   Random: 0.000

Emit From:

Verts   Faces   Volume

☑ Random   ☑ Even Distribution

Jittered   Random   Grid

Particles/Face: 0   Jittering Amount: 1.000

The number of particles emitted from each plane object shows the different systems.

Change the lifetime value from 50 to 200.

In the 3D window, select the red plane and go to the properties window – "Object" button. At the top of the window you will see "Plane" in the unique data block ID name panel (Figure 13.92). Click on the name to highlight it, hit delete, type in "RedPlane," and press Enter. Select the green plane in the 3D window and rename it "GreenPlane," and then similarly for the blue plane.

We will now add particle systems to the planes. Select the red plane and click on the "Particles" button in the properties window. Click on the + sign to add a particle system. The particle system panel displays with all the tabs and buttons for controlling the settings and has been set up with default values. Leave all the values as is except for the "Lifetime" value in the "Emission" tab—change this value from the default 50 frames to 200 frames (Figure 13.93). This will give us a better view of particles being generated. Do the same for the other two planes and in addition change the "Amount" value in the "Emission" tab to 100 for the green plane and 10 for the blue plane. Shift select all three planes in the 3D window and hit Alt + the A key to play the animation of particles being generated. Cycle through the animation in the timeline window to frame 180 and observe the particles (Figure 13.94). We have three different planes with three different particle systems—red plane: 1000 particles, green plane: 100 particles, blue plane: 10 particles.

Now in the 3D window select each plane separately and note in the properties window – "Particles" button – "Assignment" tab the names that display in the "Name" and "Settings" panels (Figure 13.95).

- Red Plane
  - Name: Particle System
  - Settings: Particle Settings
- Green Plane
  - Name: Particle System
  - Settings: Particle Settings.001
- Blue Plane
  - Name: Particle System
  - Settings: Particle Settings.002

Figure 13.95

We previously stated that we have three separate particle systems; however, now we see that the three names are all "Particle System," but each one has a different settings name. It's probably a good idea to do some renaming. Change the names to the following:

- Red Plane
  - Name: RedPSystem
  - Settings: RedPSettings
- Green Plane
  - Name: GreenPSystem
  - Settings: GreenPSettings
- Blue Plane
  - Name: BluePSystem
  - Settings: BluePSettings

Click to reveal the drop down menu.

Figure 13.96

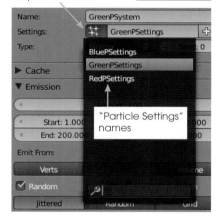

We should be able to see where we are now. To continue, in the 3D window select the green plane—we are going to reassign some settings. In the properties window – "Particles" button – "Assignment" tab, click on the button just in front of the name panel and next to "Settings." The drop down menu that displays has the names of the three particle settings data blocks (Figure 13.96). Whenever a new group of particle settings is created, Blender puts it into a cache for reuse. You can see these data blocks in the outliner window in data block mode. The green plane is selected, so in the data block drop down menu click on "BluePSettings." We now have the BluePSettings assigned to the GreenPSystem. If you replay the particle generation animation, the green and blue planes generate the same number of particles (Figure 13.97). Note that in the settings panel, a number 2 has appeared; this tells us that "BluePSettings" is being used by two systems. The color of the particles is controlled by the color of the plane object and the number of particles emitted is set by the particle system settings.

Figure 13.97

13.13. The Assignment Tab

Figure 13.98

Note: Shift select all three planes when replaying the animation to make the particles visible in the 3D window. If a plane is not selected, the particles appear as tiny black dots.

Figure 13.100

Figure 13.101

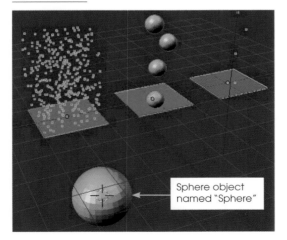

Sphere object named "Sphere"

I have demonstrated that you can select any data block of settings and assign it to any particle system. Continue by clicking on the number 2, which makes the data block a single user. Blender does this by leaving the original as it is and creating a new data block; however, the new data block is identical to the original. You can see that the settings name is now "BluePSettings.001" (Figure 13.98), but let's change some data in this new data block. Find the "Render" tab in the "Particles" window (scroll down a bit). In the bar containing the render type selection, click on "Object" (Figure 13.99). In the 3D window, add a UV sphere to the scene and give it a yellow color. Note that Blender has named the sphere "Sphere." Make sure it is off to one side in the scene away from the planes.

Reselect the green plane in the 3D window and then go back to the "Particles" button in the properties window. Check that you still have GreenP-System and BluePSettings.001. Now go back to the "Render" tab for BluePSettings.001 and where it says "Dupli Object" click on the little cube icon and then click on "Sphere" in the drop down menu—we are telling Blender to display and render the particles as spheres (Figure 13.100). Scroll up to the "Physics" tab and slightly increase the "Size" value; you will see a sphere appear on the green plane. Play the particle generation animation and you will see yellow spheres being generated (Figure 13.101).

With the green plane selected, click on the + sign to add a particle system in the properties window – "Particles" button – "Assignment" tab. You will see a new particle system highlighted in blue named "Particle System 2" with particle settings named "Particle Settings" (Figure 13.102)—this has created a new particle system. With the green plane selected in the 3D window, play the animation again. The green plane now emits yellow spheres and original particles together (Figure 13.103). The original particles only display for a short while since the "Lifetime" value is 50 frames. We have two separate particle systems with separate setting data blocks assigned to the same object. The best way to get the hang of all this is play, play, and more play.

Figure 13.102

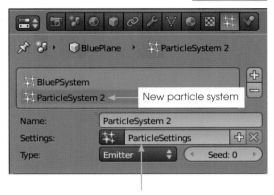

New particle system

Original default particle settings

Figure 13.103

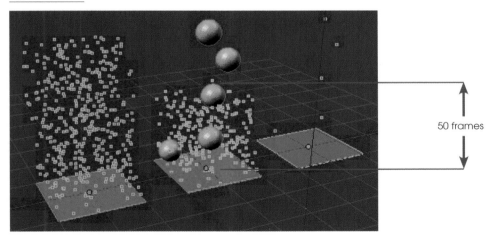

50 frames

14

Child/Parent Relationships and Constraints

14.1 Child/Parent Relationships

Child/parent relationships are used when there are several parts connected together that are required to move independently. Examples include a robot arm or a humanoid limb: the components of the arm move, but are connected to the body. The hand is a child of the forearm, the forearm is a child of the bicep, and the bicep is a child of the body—they are all linked together but move separately in their own way.

Learning Unit 4 Parenting Objects

We will demonstrate the application of this in Blender by connecting several scaled cubes together. Start with the default Blender scene, scale the cube as shown in Figure 14.1, then tab to edit mode and shift the vertices, positioning the center towards one end. Duplicate the scaled cube twice (press Shift + the D key twice) (Figure 14.2).

Figure 14.1

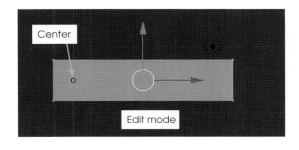
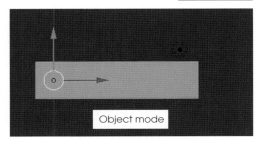

Figure 14.2

Figure 14.3

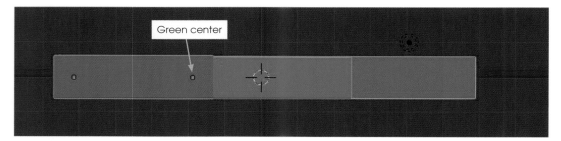

Green center

Note: In Figure 14.2, a separate cube has been added to the scene instead of duplicating the original. This has allowed different material colors to be applied. If you duplicate an object, you also duplicate its material and then the objects are all the same color.

Shift each cube and overlap the ends (Figure 14.3). Create the child/parent relationship by first selecting the red cube, then shift selecting the green cube, then pressing Ctrl + the P key and selecting "Object" in the "Set Parent To" panel that displays (Figure 14.4). Deselect then repeat the process for the green and blue cubes. The first object selected is always the child of the second object selected. Therefore, in Figure 14.4 red is the child of green, which in turn is the child of blue.

To see the relationship in action, select the red cube and rotate it. Select the green cube and rotate it, and you'll see that the red cube will follow. Select the blue cube and rotate it, and both the red and green cubes will follow. You can add a child/parent relationship to any object in Blender. For instance, a camera can be parented to another object so that when the object moves, the camera moves with it.

Figure 14.4

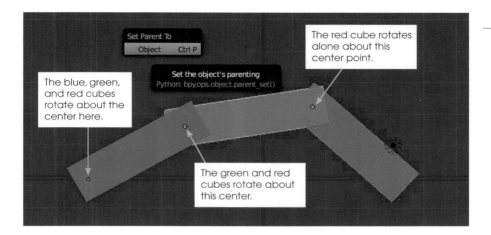

14.2 Introduction to Constraints

Constraints are object features that define spatial relationships between objects. They are the standard method for controlling characters among all 3D animation packages that still implement a more traditional approach to digital character animation. In Blender, constraints can be associated with objects; note, however, that not all constraints work with all objects. Constraints are associated with an object by selecting the object in the 3D window then clicking on "Add Constraint" in the properties window – "Object Constraints" tab

Figure 14.5

and selecting the constraint from the drop down menu that displays (Figure 14.5). In many cases a control object will be required to make the constraint function. There are control values to be inserted to regulate the function.

The following pages in this chapter contain a brief description of constraint functions. Most constraints are self explanatory, therefore a detailed explanation will only be given for a few common constraints or where it is not self evident.

14.2.1 Constraint Stacks

It should be noted that in some cases it is appropriate to apply

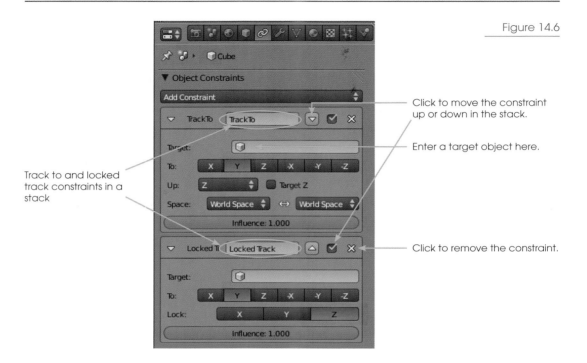

Figure 14.6

Click to move the constraint up or down in the stack.

Enter a target object here.

Track to and locked track constraints in a stack

Click to remove the constraint.

more than one constraint to an object. When this is done, the constraints are placed in a stack in order of priority and the priority can be changed by moving a constraint up or down in the stack (Figure 14.6).

14.3 Transform Constraints

Here are a list of the transform constraints available in Blender and their functions:

- Copy Location. Forces the object with the constraint added to take up the location of the target object.
- Copy Rotation. Forces the object with the constraint added to copy the rotation of the target object. When the target rotates, the object rotates.
- Copy Scale. Forces the object with the constraint added to copy the scale of the target object
- Copy Transforms. Similar to the copy location constraint.
- Limit Distance. Constrains the object to remain within a set distance from the target object. The distance is a spherical field surrounding the target and the object is constrained within or outside the spherical field.
- Limit Location. Constrains the object's location between a minimum and maximum distance on a specific axis. The distance is relative to either the world center or a parented object.

- Limit Rotation. Constrains an object's rotation about a specific axis between limits.
- Limit Scale. Constrains the scale of an object between limits on a specified axis.
- Maintain Volume. Constrains the dimensions of a side on a specified axis.
- Transformation. See Section 14.3.1.

Figure 14.7

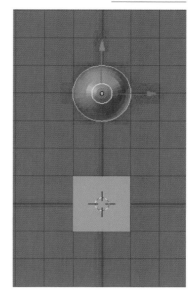

14.3.1 The Transformation Constraint

The transformation constraint allows you to control the location, rotation, and scale of an object or part of an object by adjusting the location, rotation, or scale of another object. The object to be controlled is termed the "source" and has the constraint applied to it while the other object (the controlling object) is termed the "target object." The transformation constraint is more complex and versatile than the other transform constraints. The location, rotation, or scale of the target object can be set to affect the location, rotation, or scale of the source object with the constraint applied. The location, rotation, or scale values in either case can be set to operate within a specific range.

To demonstrate this constraint, add a UV sphere to the default scene and move it four Blender units along the *y*-axis (Figure 14.7). Place the 3D window in top orthographic view (number pad 7 – number pad 5). Select the cube and go to the properties window – "Object Constraints" button, click "Add Constraint," and select "Transformation" from the drop down menu (Figure 14.8). In the con-

Figure 14.8

straint panel, set the values as shown in Figure 14.9. The location of the source (in this case, the UV sphere) is set to operate on the *x*-axis between 0.000 and 2.000 Blender units. Note that the *x*-axis of the source is set to affect the *z*-axis of the destination. The destination (the cube) will rotate about the *z*-axis from 0.000 to 60.000 degrees.

By translating the sphere along the *x*-axis between 0.000 and 2.000 Blender units, the cube rotates about the *z*-axis between 0.000 and 60.000 degrees (Figure 14.10). The control transformation of the sphere and the rotation of the cube only takes effect within the set limits. By adding additional transformation constraints and setting different parameters such as the scale of the sphere to affect the

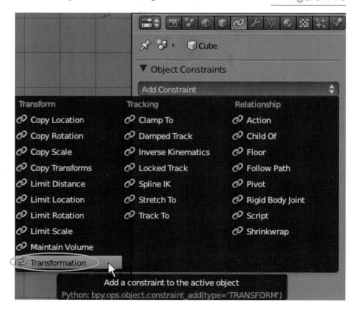

Figure 14.9   Figure 14.10

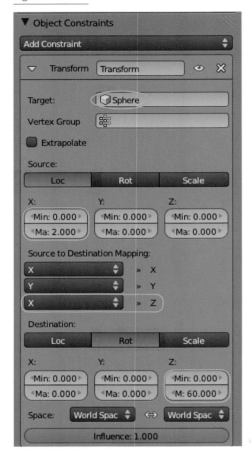

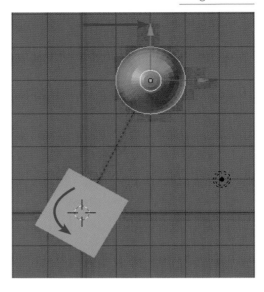

translation of the cube, multiple transformation controls can be established. Adding constraints places them in a stack and the position in the stack may be adjusted.

14.4 Tracking Constraints

Here are a list of the tracking constraints available in Blender and their functions:

- Clamp To. Clamps or locks the position of the object to a target curve.
- Damped Track. Constrains one local axis of the object to always point towards the target object (Figure 14.11).
- Inverse Kinematics. Can only be applied to bones (see Chapter 15 on armatures).
- Locked Track. Similar to a damped track constraint with more axis control.
- Spline IK. Can only be applied to bones (see Chapter 15 on armatures).
- Stretch To. Stretches the object towards the target object or compresses the object away from the target object.
- Track To. Causes the object to always point towards the target object no matter where either the object or the target is positioned. For example, you can track a camera to follow an object that is animated to move. Start with the default blender scene in top view (number pad 7 – number pad 5). Select the camera

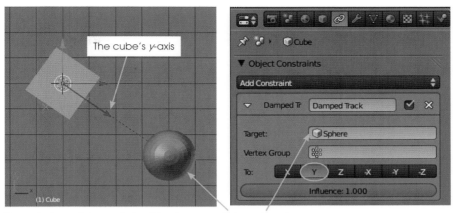

Figure 14.11

The cube's y-axis is constrained to always point towards the sphere.

Sphere target

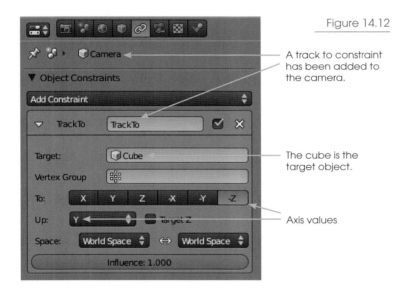

Figure 14.12

A track to constraint has been added to the camera.

The cube is the target object.

Axis values

and press Alt + the R key to clear the rotation and align the camera axis with the world axis. With the camera still selected, go to the properties window – "Object Constraints" button, click "Add Constraint," and select "Track To" (Figure 14.12). Enter the cube as the target object, and set "Axis To = –Z" and "Axis Up = Y" to orientate the camera in the world. The camera will now point at the cube when the camera or the cube is moved, and during an animation playback (Figure 14.13).

Learning Unit 4

Empty Object

Figure 14.13

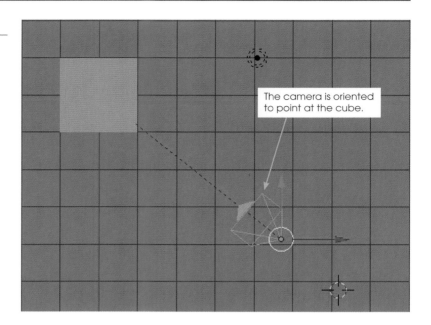

The camera is oriented to point at the cube.

14.5 Relationship Constraints

Learning Unit 4

Parenting Objects

Here are a list of the relationship constraints available in Blender and their functions:

- Action. See Section 14.5.1.
- Child Of. See Section 14.1.
- Floor. Allows the target object to obstruct the movement of the object. For example, a sphere animated to descend in a scene will not pass through a plane that has been set as a target object.
- Follow Path. Causes the object to be animated to follow a curve path nominated as the target. This constraint also has the feature to follow the curve, which means that the object will rotate and bank as it follows the curve. This constraint can also be employed to duplicate objects along a curve path. (See Sections 14.6–14.8.)
- Pivot. Causes the object to leapfrog to the opposite side of the target object along an axis between the object and the target centers. The location can be offset on either side of the axis by inserting offset values.
- Rigid Body Joint. See Section 14.5.3.
- Shrinkwrap. See Section 14.5.2.

14.5.1 The Action Constraint

An action constraint allows you to control the action of one object by manipulating the action of another. For the purpose of this explanation, consider an action to mean a translation,

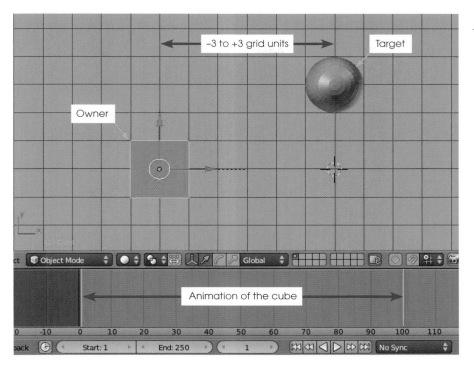

Figure 14.14

Figure 14.15

rotation, or scale of an object in an animation. We will use the translation of a sphere to control the translation of a cube.

Set up a scene as shown in Figure 14.14. The object to which the constraint is applied is called the owner. This is the object that will be controlled; in this case, it's the cube. The controlling object (the sphere) is the target. Set up an animation of the cube to translate along the *x*-axis from −3 grid units at frame 1.00 to +3 grid units at frame 100.00 (see Chapter 9 for a refresher on animation basics).

With the animation of the cube created, select the cube in the 3D window and add an action constraint by going to the properties window – "Object Constraints" button, clicking on "Add Constraint," and selecting "Action" from the drop down menu. Set the values in the action constraint panel as shown in Figure 14.15.

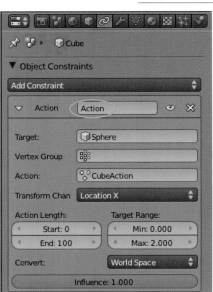

- Target. The controlling object (sphere).
- Action. The animation of the cube ("CubeAction").
- Translation. "Location X," movement along the *x*-axis.

14.5. Relationship Constraints

Figure 14.16

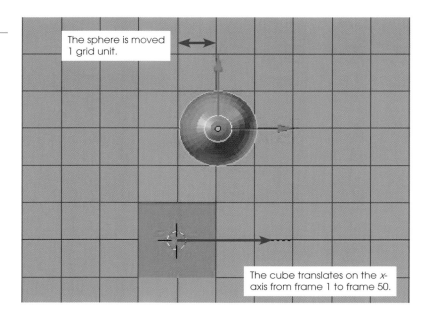

The sphere is moved 1 grid unit.

The cube translates on the *x*-axis from frame 1 to frame 50.

- Action Length. The animation length, frame 1 to 100.
- Target Range. The translation range in Blender grid units of the target (sphere) that will control the movement of the cube. In other words, moving the sphere along the *x*-axis from its original location two Blender units will move the cube from its location at frame 1 to its location at frame 100 (Figure 14.16). Note that the "Target Range" values (movement of the sphere) must be in the positive direction (0.00 to 2.00).

Figure 14.17

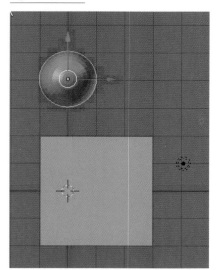

This is a basic introduction to the action constraint. For a more detailed explanation, refer to the Blender Wiki manual at wiki. blender.org/index/php/Doc:Manual.

14.5.2 The Shrinkwrap Constraint

The shrinkwrap constraint could be more aptly named the mesh surface lock since the constraint locks an object to the surface of another mesh object that's set as the target. Do not confuse this constraint with the shrinkwrap modifier. To demonstrate how the constraint operates, follow these procedures. In the default Blender scene in top orthographic view, add a UV sphere, scale the cube up, and arrange the objects as shown in Figure 14.17. Select the sphere and in the properties window – "Object Constraints" button, add a shrinkwrap constraint (Figure 14.18). In the "Object Constraints"

Figure 14.18

Figure 14.19

Figure 14.20

tab, click in the "Target" selection bar and select "Cube" as the target (Figure 14.19). The sphere relocates, positioning its center on the surface of the cube (Figure 14.20).

Note: In the "Object Constraints" tab, the "Shrinkwrap Type" is "Nearest Surface Point." The sphere has therefore located at the nearest point on the surface of the cube (the target).

In the "Object Constraints" tab, change the "Shrinkwrap Type" to "Nearest Vertex" (Figure 14.21). With this option, the sphere relocates to the nearest vertex on the target object. If the "Shrinkwrap Type: Project" option is selected, the sphere will revert to its original location ("Project'" means to project an axis to the surface). In our setup, the sphere's axes are represented by the red, green, and blue arrows of the transformation widget. By default, the axes are the global axes of the imaginary 3D world and with the sphere located in its original position you see that neither of these axes are directed towards a surface on the cube.

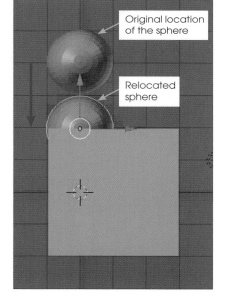

Original location of the sphere

Relocated sphere

Note that the direction of the widget arrows represent the positive direction. With "Shrinkwrap Type: Project" selected, "Axis X," "Axis Y," and "Axis Z" buttons are present in the properties window – "Object Constraints" tab. Check the "Axis X" button. In order to project an axis towards a surface of the cube, we must rotate the

Figure 14.21

Figure 14.22

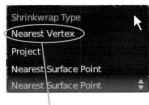

Change to "Local."

Figure 14.23

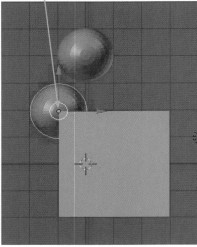

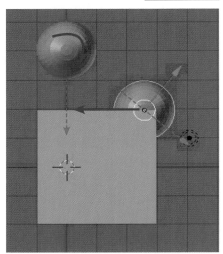

sphere's local axes. To do this, with the sphere selected, press the N key with the mouse cursor in the 3D window to display the numeric panel. In the "Transformation Orientation" tab, click on the "Transform" selection drop down menu and select "Local" (Figure 14.22). Rotate the sphere until the *x*-axis points at the cube (Figure 14.23). As soon as the axis projects to a surface on the cube, the sphere is located on the surface. By slowly rotating the sphere you will see it move along the surface as the direction of the axis changes. In the "Object Constraints" panel, the "Distance" and "Influence" sliders affect how far the sphere is located between its original position and the surface of the cube. By checking "Axis X" and "Axis Y," the projection line is at 45 degrees between the axes.

14.5.3 The Rigid Body Joint Constraint

The rigid body joint is used to constrain the movement of objects in the Blender game engine (see Chapter 19 for more on the game engine). It is not intended to be used for the manipulation of objects in the 3D window or in an animation. To provide an insight into the use of this constraint, we will demonstrate a simple hinge constraint. In the game engine, a hinged object such as a door would require a force to open and close it. To make our demonstration as simple as possible, we will hinge a trapdoor and use the default gravity force in Blender.

14. Child/Parent Relationships and Constraints

In the properties window – "Scene" button, ensure that "Gravity" is checked in the "Gravity" tab. Set up a scene as shown in Figure 14.24 by scaling the default cube object and then duplicating and transposing the duplication (see Chapter 3 for a refresher). By duplicating the cube you will have one cube named "Cube" and another named "Cube.001."

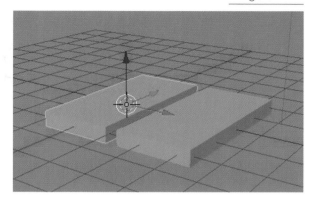

Figure 14.24

Select "Cube" in the 3D window, then in the properties window – "Object Constraints" button click on "Add Constraint" and select "Rigid Body Joint." Note that the constraint type is highlighted in red, indicating that although a constraint has been added, it is not active (Figure 14.25). To activate the constraint, click in the "Target" selection bar and select "Cube.001"—this links the owner of the constraint to a fixed object in the scene (i.e., "Cube.001"). The constraint panel that displays will have "Pivot Type: Ball" selected, so change this to "Hinge." Check "Display Pivot" to display the hinge pivot axes in the 3D window. To see the axes more clearly, rotate the screen, turn off the manipulation widget, change to wireframe viewport shading, and zoom in on the window (Figure 14.26). You should now see *px*, *py*, and *pz* hinge pivot axes displayed as broken orange lines; the length of the lines are proportional to the sides of the cube sides.

The object will only pivot about the *px*-axis when using the "Hinge" type constraint. We want "Cube" to pivot

Figure 14.25

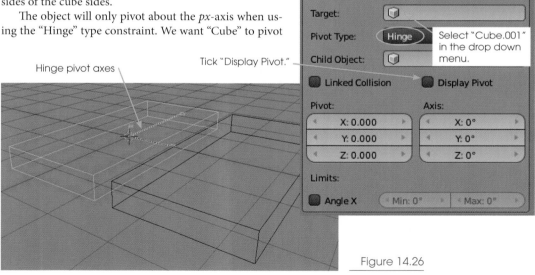

Hinge pivot axes

Tick "Display Pivot."

Figure 14.26

Figure 14.27

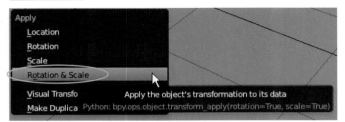

on a hinge located between the two cubes at the lower edges. It is important to note that before you adjust the location and orientation of the pivot, it is essential to press Ctrl + the A key and select "Rotation & Scale" to apply the pivot scale and rotation (Figure 14.27). Failing to do this results in the pivot working off some ghost location.

Figure 14.28

Note: Upon selecting "Rotation & Scale," the axes lines are scaled in proportion to the original default Blender cube (Figure 14.28).

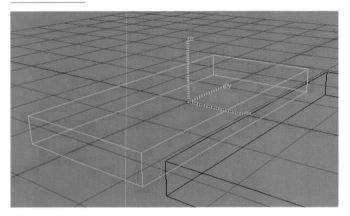

Adjust the location and orientation of the pivot by first rotating the pivot axes. In the constraint panel, enter "Z: 90" in the "Axis" bar. Next adjust the "X" and "Z" values in the "Pivot" bar, which locates the *px*-axis as shown in Figure 14.29. The foregoing has set the scene to allow "Cube" to pivot down on the *px*-axis (Figure 14.30). We now have to enter the Blender game engine. Change the Blender screen from the default to the game logic arrangement and change "Blender Render" to "Blender Game"

Figure 14.29

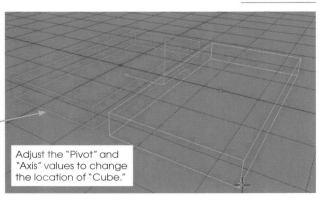

Adjust the "Pivot" and "Axis" values to change the location of "Cube."

14. Child/Parent Relationships and Constraints

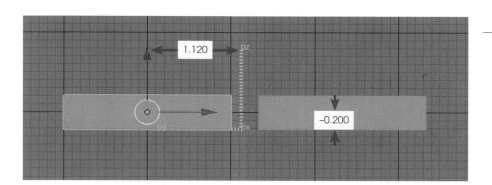

Figure 14.30

1.120

−0.200

Figure 14.31

"Physics" tab

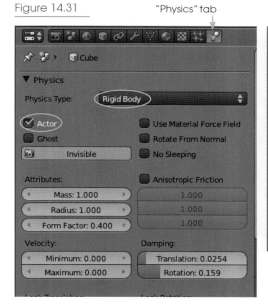

Figure 14.32

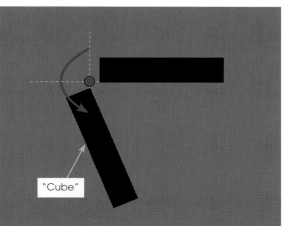

"Cube"

in the info window header. Zoom in and change the 3D window from top orthographic to front orthographic view. In the properties window – "Physics" button, select "Physics Type: Rigid Body" and check that "Actor" is ticked (Figure 14.31). Place the cursor in the 3D window and press the P key to see "Cube" swing down on the pivot (Figure 14.32).

14.6 Duplicating along Curves

The follow path constraint can be used to duplicate an object along a curve. For example, start with the default scene with the cube object selected, add a Bezier curve to the scene, and shape it in edit mode as shown in Figure 14.33. Select the cube and scale it down very small. In the properties window – "Object Constraints" button, press "Add Constraint" and

Learning Unit 4

Spin Duplicate

Figure 14.33

Figure 14.34

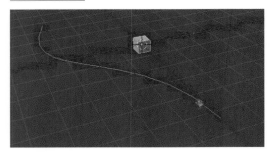

Default scene with a cube and Bezier curve

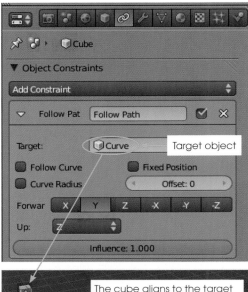

Target object

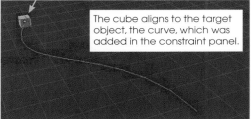

The cube aligns to the target object, the curve, which was added in the constraint panel.

Figure 14.35

"Object" tab

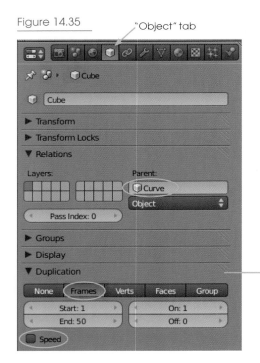

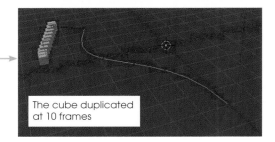

The cube duplicated at 10 frames

select "Follow Path." In the "Object Constraints" panel, set the target object as "Curve" (Figure 14.34). In the properties window – "Object" button – "Relations" tab, select "Parent: Curve" and in the "Duplication" tab, select "Frames" and untick "Speed" (Figure 14.35). You may want to scale and reposition the cube at this point. Changing the "End" value will produce a different array of cubes (Figure 14.36).

14. Child/Parent Relationships and Constraints

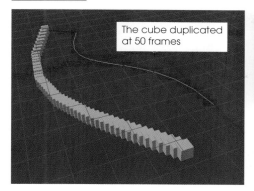

The cube duplicated at 50 frames

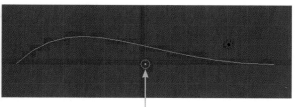

Scale the circle down.

Figure 14.38

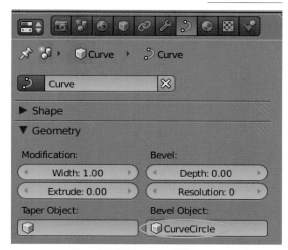

14.7 Extruding along Curves

A shape can be extruded along a curve to produce a different shape. For example, start with the default Blender scene and delete the cube object. Add a Bezier curve and scale it up along the *x*-axis. For simplicity, put the window into top view (number pad 7 – number pad 5). The curve may be scaled and shaped in edit mode to produce a shape for your extrusion to follow.

Deselect the curve and add a Bezier or NURBS circle; the circle may be shaped in edit mode to produce a cross section shape for your extrusion. Scale the circle way down (Figure 14.37). Deselect the circle and select the curve. In the properties window – "Object Data" button – "Geometry" tab, enter "Curve Circle" in the "Bevel Object" data panel and adjust the scale as required (Figure 14.38).

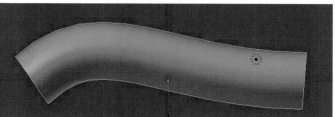

14.8 The Follow Path Constraint

The follow path constraint causes an object in an animation to follow a path that has been set as the target. This constraint is combined with the follow curve constraint that, when set, causes the object to rotate and bank as it follows the path. The follow path constraint can also be used to duplicate objects along a path and to extrude an object along a path. In an animation, the motion of the object is set by inserting key frames (see Chapter 9 for a refresher). When using the follow path constraint, the key frames are set in the properties

Figure 14.39

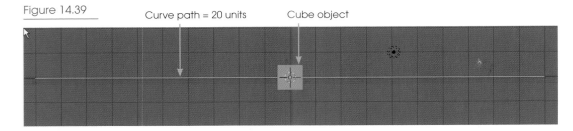

Curve path = 20 units   Cube object

window – "Object Data" button – "Path Animation" tab. As always, an example is the best way to demonstrate the process.

14.8.1 Scene Setup

Start with the default Blender scene with the default cube object selected and perform the following actions. Press number pad 7 followed by number pad 5 to place the 3D window in top orthographic view. With the cube selected, press the S key, type 0.5, and press Enter to scale the cube down to half its original size. Deselect the cube with the A key and press Shift + the A key – "Add" – "Curve" – "Path." A curve path is added to the scene, which is four Blender grid units long. With the curve path selected press the S key + 5 and then Enter to scale the path up to 20 units long (Figure 14.39). How you scale your object and set the path length and shape will depend on what you are attempting to achieve in your animation. Here we are merely creating a path that will have some relevance to the values that will be added in our demonstration.

14.8.2 Add a Constraint

Figure 14.40

Deselect the curve path and select the cube object. Go to the properties window – "Object Constraints" button – "Add Constraint" and select "Follow Path" to assign the follow path

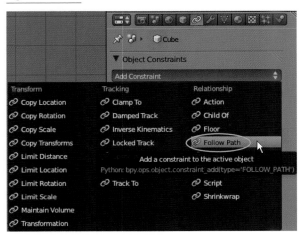

constraint and display the constraint panel (Figure 14.40). In the panel, click on the little cube icon in the "Target" bar and then click on "NurbsPath" in the drop down selection menu that displays—this assigns the target object (Figure 14.41). At this point, the cube moves to the left-hand end of the path. Deselect the cube.

In earlier versions of Blender, pressing Alt + the A key would play an animation showing the cube moving along the path; however, in the latest version key frames have to be manually inserted. Key frames are inserted by manipulating values in the path's "Path Animation" tab, and then they are displayed in the timeline window at the bottom

Figure 14.41

Set "NurbsPath" as the target object.

Figure 14.42

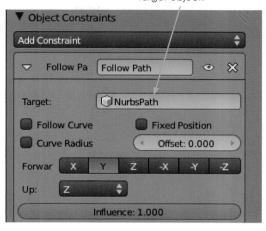

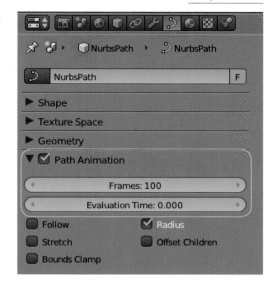

of the screen. Therefore, select the curve path in the 3D window then go to the properties window – "Object Data" button – "Path Animation" tab. Make sure "Path Animation" is checked in the tab and note the values "Frames: 100" and "Evaluation Time: 0.000" (Figure 14.42). Consider the "Frames: 100" value to mean that the curve path length in the 3D window is divided into 100 intervals. Consider the "Evaluation Time" value to mean the interval at which the linked object is residing along the curve path at a given time. The default range is 0.00 to 100.00. If the number of intervals (frames) is increased, adjust the evaluation time range accordingly. With the cube at the start of the path, the "Evaluation Time" value is 0.000. By default, the timeline window shows a 250-frame animation timeline with values "Start: 1" and "End: 250" and the vertical green cursor at frame 1 (Figure 14.43).

Figure 14.43

Timeline window

Green cursor at frame 1

The curve path and the animation timeline are two separate identities. The object's movement along the path may coincide with the timeline, but not necessarily. To demonstrate this we will set the object to move along the path midway in the animation. In the timeline window, move the cursor to frame 25. In the properties window – "Object Constraints" button – "Path Animation" tab, click the RMB on the "Evaluation Time" bar and

Figure 14.44

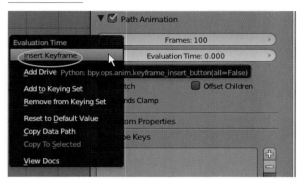

then select "Insert Keyframe" (Figure 14.44). The bar will turn yellow and a vertical yellow line is added in the timeline window under the green cursor to show that a key frame has been set at frame 25. In the timeline window, move the green cursor to frame 125. In the properties window – "Path Animation" tab, change the "Evaluation Time" value to 100. The cube moves along the path as you drag the mouse. At "Evaluation Time: 100," the cube is at the end of the path. Repeat the process for adding a key frame.

14.8.3 Timeline Animation Play Control Buttons

In the timeline window, return to frame 1 and play the animation (press Esc to stop the animation). Consult Figure 14.45 for an explanation of the timeline animation control buttons. The animation plays but the cube remains stationary until frame 25, then it moves along the path and reaches the end at frame 125. The animation continues to play in the timeline until frame 250. In the 3D window, carefully observe the motion of the cube as it moves along the path. At the start, there is a definite acceleration followed by a constant velocity then a deceleration as the cube approaches the end of the path. We can see a graphical representation of this movement in the graph editor window. Divide the 3D window in two and change one half to the graph editor window; you will probably have to zoom in on the window (press the number pad - key several times or scroll the MMB) and also drag the window to centralize the graph (hold and drag the MMB). Scale the graph horizontally and vertically by holding Ctrl + the MMB and dragging the mouse (Figure 14.46).

Figure 14.45

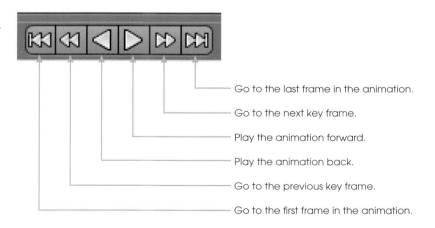

Go to the last frame in the animation.

Go to the next key frame.

Play the animation forward.

Play the animation back.

Go to the previous key frame.

Go to the first frame in the animation.

Figure 14.46

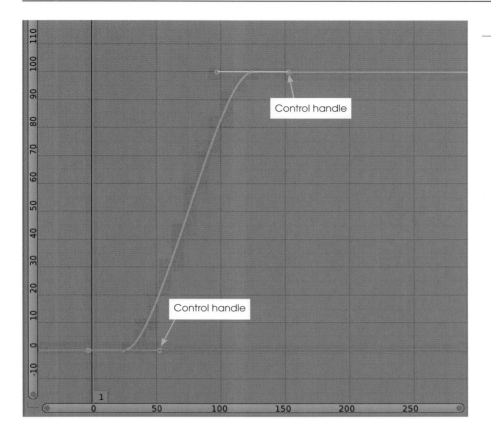

The graph editor window shows the frames of the timeline window across the bottom and the curve path length (intervals) vertically up the LHS. The green horizontal and vertical lines are cursors: the vertical green cursor represents the position of the cube. Click, hold, and drag the vertical line until it's at frame 125; you can see the cube is now at interval 100 of the curve path length (which is the end of the animation). The graph shows a Bezier curve with control handles at frame 25 and frame 125. With the cursor located at frame 70, change the "Evaluation Time" value to 30, and note that the cube relocates to interval 30 along the path. Add a key frame and you'll see that a third control handle is added to the graph in the graph editor window (Figure 14.47). If the animation is played at this point, the cube appears to move in the animation as it moved previously. There is no perceivable change to the movement, but since the shape of the graph is slightly different, there is in fact a change of velocity.

In the graph editor window, the graph is in edit mode with all the control handles selected. Press the A key to deselect the handles, click the RMB on the new middle handle, then click the RMB again on the upper end of the handle. Press the G key and drag the handle until it is horizontal (Figure 14.48). Play the animation from frame 1 and you will observe

Figure 14.47

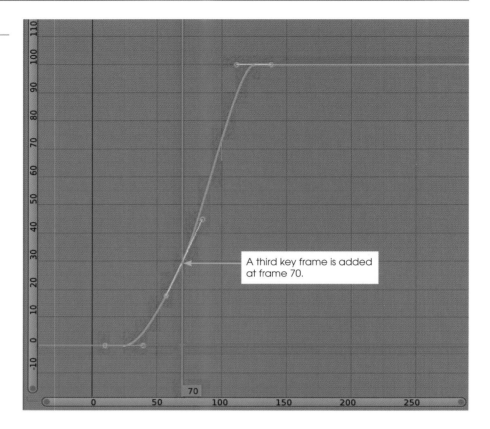

A third key frame is added at frame 70.

that the cube will stop momentarily at frame 70 with the cube 30 intervals along the path, then continue on to the end. By dragging and rotating the middle control handle, you can control how the cube moves along the path. Note that as you reposition the control handle, the key frame in the timeline window repositions.

This demonstration has employed a straight line path in the 3D window, but the path can be shaped into a curve and extruded. You may add key frames as required and in doing so add control handles to the graph in the graph editor window. Manipulating the control handles allows control over how your object moves at intervals along the path. You can therefore set the movement of an object to decelerate into a curve and accelerate out of a curve, giving it an extremely realistic motion. With the cube selected in the 3D window, check "Follow Curve" in the "Object Constraints" panel. With the curve path reshaped (reposition the curve path's control handles in the 3D window), the object following the curve path will be aligned to the path (Figure 14.49).

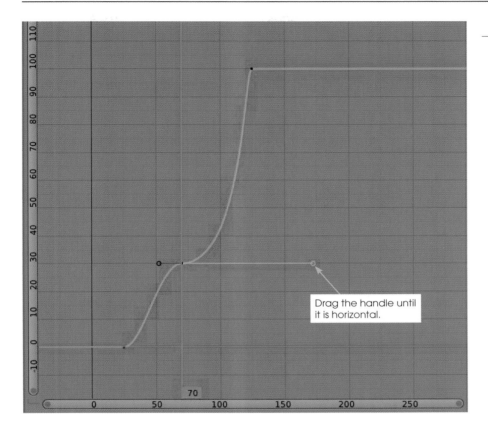

Figure 14.48

Drag the handle until it is horizontal.

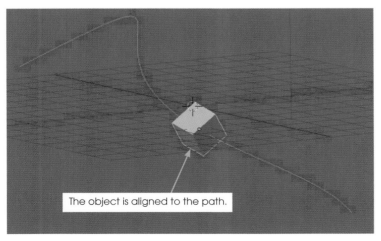

Figure 14.49

The object is aligned to the path.

15

Armatures

15.1 Adding an Armature

In Blender, "armature" refers to an object type that is used to deform a mesh. Think of your finger and the skin covering it and the bones inside. The skin would be the mesh and the bones are the armature; when the bone moves, the skin moves with it.

To begin the instruction on armatures, start with the default Blender scene, delete the cube object, and add an armature object (press Shift + the A Key – "Armature" – "Single Bone"). Zoom in (with the number pad + key) and press number pad 1 then number pad 5 to get the front elevation orthographic view.

15.2 Single Bone Armatures

What you see is a single bone armature (Figure 15.1). Armatures can, and usually do, comprise multiple bones, but before we complicate anything we should start with an understanding of bone manipulation. The default single bone armature is displayed in type octahedral due to the object having eight surfaces: it appears as two four-sided pyramids conjoined at the base with spheres at the apexes. For the purpose of the demonstration, we will name the parts of the armature tip, body, and base.

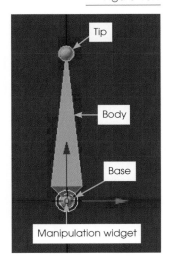

Figure 15.1

Note: Although the armature is an object in Blender, it is not a mesh object. Its shape cannot be edited other than scaling it larger or smaller. It can be rotated and translated. It has a center like any other object, which may be repositioned, but for use in a multibone armature it is best to maintain the center at the apex of the lower (smaller) pyramid in the center of the sphere. With the manipulation widget turned on, the widget is also positioned at the center.

15.3 Armature Display Types

The default armature display type is octahedral but there are four alternative display types: stick, b-bone, envelope, and wire (Figure 15.2). The wire display option appears much the same as stick. With the armature bone selected, see the properties window – "Object Data" button – "Display" tab to choose these options (Figure 15.3). Which display type is used depends on what you are doing with the armature. I won't go into the different uses at this time but since the basic function of an armature is to deform a mesh object, we need to understand how this happens.

15.3.1 Basic Procedure

The basic procedure for deforming a mesh object with an armature is to apply an armature modifier to the object and then, in the modifier, name the armature that will do the defor-

Figure 15.2

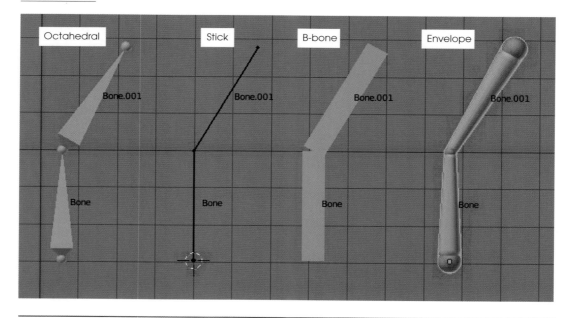

Figure 15.3 Figure 15.4

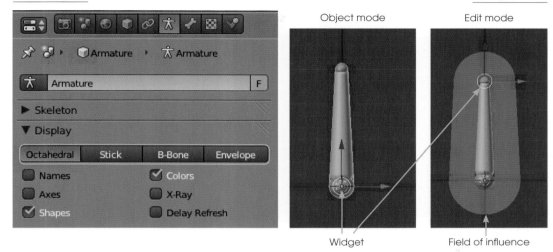

Object mode Edit mode

Widget Field of influence

mation. It doesn't matter which armature display type is used; each armature has a field of influence in which mesh vertices must reside in order to be influenced.

Change the armature display type to "Envelope" and you will see a shape like a cylinder with a sphere at each end (Figure 15.4). Tab into edit mode, and you will see the field of influence surrounding the armature (you can only see this in envelope display type in edit mode). In edit mode, you can select the whole armature or the spheres at either end separately, then scale them. This has the effect of reshaping the field of influence to encompass vertices in a mesh.

Just file this information in your memory bank for the time being and go back to the default single bone armature in octahedral display type in object mode. Tab into edit mode and select the tip—now the widget is located at the tip, which shows that the tip of the armature is selected (Figure 15.5). Turn the widget off and you'll see that the sphere at the tip is orange; having the widget on just makes it easier to see for demonstration purposes. With the widget on you can translate the tip in the 3D window, which also changes the length of the armature. The rotate and scale functions of the widget have no effect.

15.4 Multibone Armatures

Turn the widget off but leave the tip selected. Now press the E key (extrude) and drag the mouse; you will see a new bone being extruded from the tip (Figure 15.6). Select the tip of the new bone, press the E key, and drag the mouse and a new bone is extruded. Select the base of the original bone and repeat the process, creating a multibone armature (Figure 15.7).

Figure 15.5

With the widget off, the tip is orange.

Edit mode

Figure 15.6 New bones extruded from the tip Figure 15.7

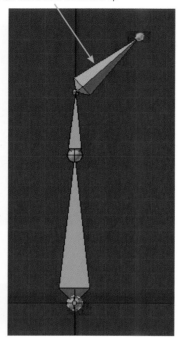

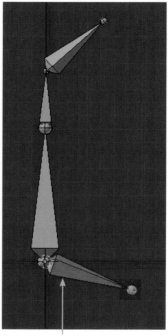

New bone extruded from the base

15.5 Deforming a Mesh Object

So far, I have demonstrated the very basics of what an armature is and how to expand a single bone into a multibone armature. It's time to see how to deform a mesh. To demonstrate the armature principle in Blender, we will make something akin to a finger on your hand and make it deform with an armature.

Start with the default Blender scene, delete the cube, and add a mesh circle. In the tool shelf (the panel at the lower LHS of the 3D window), reduce the number of vertices from 32 to 8. When creating a mesh for use with armatures, use as few vertices as possible. A high number of vertices will give you a better surface look and a better render, but too many vertices will slow down the computer considerably in an animation.

Note: When you add a primitive to a scene, it is in object mode and the tool panel at the lower left of the screen provides the facility to edit the size and vertex count. Once you tab to edit mode, the tool panel no longer has this feature.

Edit mode in front view   Object mode in front view   Figure 15.8

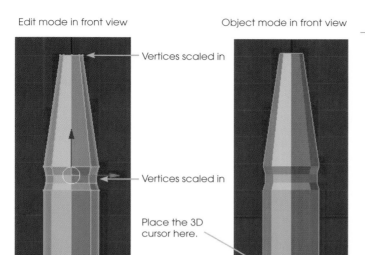

Vertices scaled in

Vertices scaled in

Place the 3D
cursor here.

Tab into edit mode and extrude the circle on the *z*-axis to produce a cylinder. With the top ring of vertices selected, extrude the shape again. With the third ring selected, press the S key and move the cursor in towards the center of the cylinder. Continue on extruding and scaling until you get a shape like the one in Figure 15.8 (left). The finger will only have two parts, with a joint in the middle. The vertices close together in the middle of the mesh are where the joint will be; they act like a concertina hose on a vacuum cleaner, allowing the mesh to bend. With the mesh selected, tab into object mode and place the 3D cursor as shown in Figure 15.8 (right).

Figure 15.9

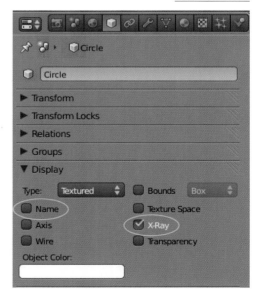

Note: For the purpose of the demonstration, leave the default circle object with the default radius of 1.000 Blender grid units. If the circle is scaled, the finger mesh vertices may fall outside the armature's field of influence, producing some unexpected results.

Deselect the mesh finger with the A key and add a single bone armature as previously described. Since the cursor was placed at the base of the finger on the centerline,

Figure 15.10

Figure 15.11

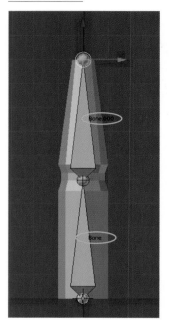

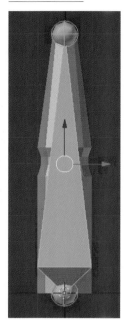

Figure 15.12

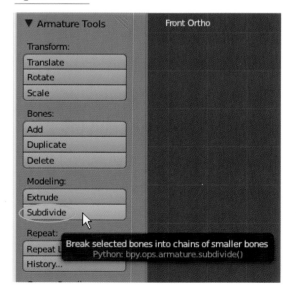

you probably won't see the armature. Go to the properties window – "Object Data" button – "Display" tab and tick "X-Ray" (Figure 15.9). This makes the armature visible in object mode in solid display. It actually makes the armature display on top of the mesh. With the armature selected, tab to edit mode, select the tip of the bone, and drag it up to the middle of the bend point of the finger. Press the E key and extrude the bone, which creates a second bone, up to the top of the mesh finger (Figure 15.10). In the properties window – "Object Data" button – "Display" tab, tick "Name" to show the names of the bones in the 3D window (Figure 15.9). The names will be "Bone" and "Bone.001." Press the A key to deselect the armature bones and remain in object mode.

15.5.1 Alternative Method for Creating a Multibone Armature

There is an alternative method for creating a multibone armature. With a single bone armature added, tab to edit mode and drag the tip up to the top of the finger (Figure 15.11). Make sure you have the body of the bone selected (right click on the body), go to the tool shelf at the left of the screen, and click "Subdivide" (Figure 15.12). Successive clicks will subdivide the bone and create a multibone armature.

15.6 Armature Modifiers

We will now add an armature modifier to the finger mesh object. Deselect the armature and select the finger in object mode. In the properties window – "Object Modifiers" button, click "Add Modifier" and select "Armature" (Figure 15.13). Click in the "Object" panel and select "Armature" (Blender named your armature "Armature") (Figure 15.14). It is time to test the deformation process. In the 3D window, deselect the finger and select the armature. (Depending on how you positioned the armature in the finger, you may have difficulty selecting. If this is the case, go to the outliner window at the upper right of the screen and right click on "Arma-

Figure 15.13   Figure 15.14

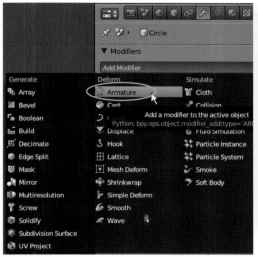

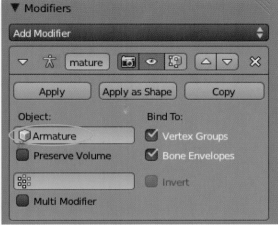

ture" in the display.) With the armature selected, change from object mode to pose mode in the 3D window header—select "Bone.001," which should be highlighted in blue. Press the R key and rotate the bone and you'll see the top of the finger rotate with the bone (Figure 15.15). Next, select a bone and press the S key to scale (Figure 15.16). Then, change the armature to envelope display (Figure 15.17).

Figure 15.15

Rotated bone

Figure 15.16

Scaled bone

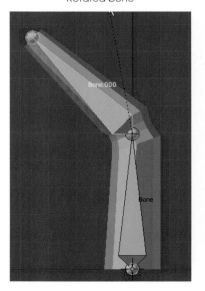

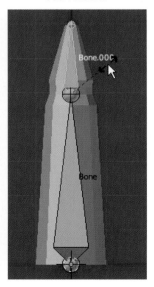

The foregoing has demonstrated how to deform a mesh object using armatures and the armature modifier. The ultimate use of armatures is in character animation, which involves rigging a mesh (the character) with a multiboned armature and then animating the movement of the armature to simulate the character's movement. Rigging a character can be a tedious and sometimes complicated process. Blender has a ready-made humanoid armature rig stowed away in the user preferences window.

Figure 15.17

Rotated bone in envelope display

Scaled bone in envelope display

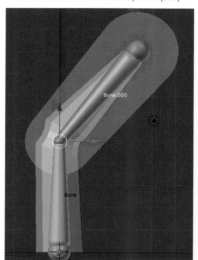

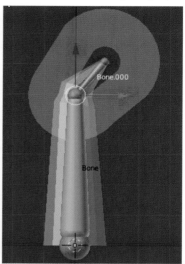

15.7 Humanoid Armatures

In the user preferences window of a new scene, click on "Addons" at the top of the window. In the panel at the LHS, click "Rigging" and you will have a single-line entry named

Figure 15.18

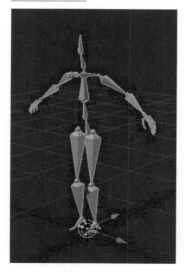

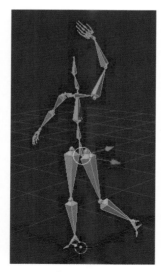

"Rigging Rigify." Tick the little box at the end of the line. Go back to the 3D window and press Shift + the A key. Select "Armature" and you will see that "Human (Meta-Rig)" has been added to the selection options. Click on the new entry and a multiboned humanoid armature is introduced to the scene. On my computer it is entered rather small. If this is the same for you, zoom in or scale the rig up. Pan the window around and have a good look at the rig. If you go into pose mode and select individual bones, you will be able to move them about to create different poses (Figure 15.18).

It may be a little ambitious at this stage to construct a model of a human figure and rig it for animation. Of course you could use the Make

Object mode

Pose mode

Human program (www.makehuman.org/) to create a figure then import it into Blender and rig for animation, but unless you have a reasonable computer you may be disappointed. Make Human models have a pretty high vertex count so there is a lot of stuff to move about in an animation. You would also have to go find a rigging tutorial on the internet and study this topic in detail. What we have covered so far is the very basics; while on the subject of armatures, let's demonstrate a few more basics.

Figure 15.19

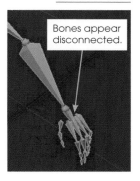

Bones appear disconnected.

15.8 Disconnected Bones

You may have noticed that in the humanoid armature, some of the bones appear to be disconnected because they are separated from adjoining bones (Figure 15.19). To demonstrate how this occurs, follow this procedure. In a new scene, add a single bone armature, tab into edit mode, select the tip, and extrude another bone. Select the body of the new bone and, in the properties window – "Bone" button – "Relations" tab, untick "Connected" (Figure 15.20). The new bone may now be translated (use the G key to grab) and repositioned away from the original bone, although it remains part of the armature (Figure 15.21). If "Connected" is reticked, the new bone will be repositioned with its base connected to the original bone.

Figure 15.20

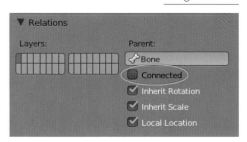

In the previous examples of deforming a mesh with an armature, the mesh vertices had to be located within the field of influence of the armature. An alternative to this is to manually nominate which vertices will be affected by the armature. There are basically two methods:

1. Select and assign vertices to a vertex group and nominate the control armature bone.

2. Perform this same operation using Blender's weight paint tool.

Figure 15.21

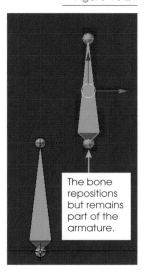

The bone repositions but remains part of the armature.

15.8.1 Method 1: Manually Assign Vertices

In a new scene, construct a finger as previously described. Add a two bone armature as before, but position it as shown in Figure 15.22. Select the armature and in the properties window – "Object Data" button – "Display" tab, tick "Names" to show the bones named "Bone" and "Bone.001." Deselect the armature. Select the finger, tab into edit mode, and press the A key to deselect the vertices. In the properties window – "Object Data" button – "Vertex Groups" tab, click the + sign to add a new vertex group; a vertex group is added and named "Group" (Figure 15.23). The aim here is to select vertices and add them to the vertex group. The movement of the group is to be controlled by a bone in the armature. By renaming "Group" to "Bone.001," the vertex group will automatically be controlled by the bone named "Bone.001." Groups and bones may be renamed to whatever you want, but for a group to be controlled by a bone, the names must be identical.

Figure 15.22

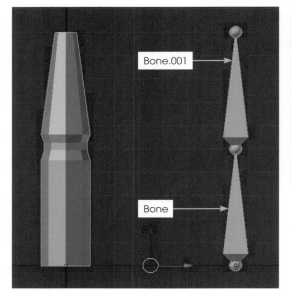

Bone.001

Bone

Figure 15.23

Click the + sign to add a group.

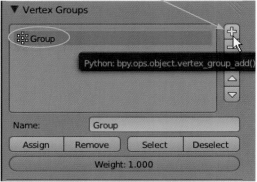

▼ Vertex Groups

Group

Python: bpy.ops.object.vertex_group_add()

Name: | Group

Assign | Remove | Select | Deselect

Weight: 1.000

Figure 15.24

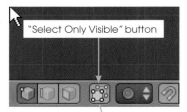

"Select Only Visible" button

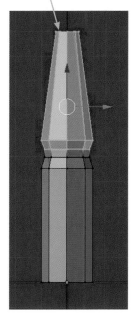

In the 3D window, select the vertices in the upper part of the finger (press the B key – drag a rectangle). Make sure you have the "Select Only Visible" button turned off in the 3D window header or you will only be selecting the front vertices of the finger (Figure 15.24). In the "Vertex Groups" tab, click "Assign" to assign the selected vertices to the group. Check out the assignment by alternately clicking on "Deselect" and "Select" in the tab (Figure 15.25).

Figure 15.25

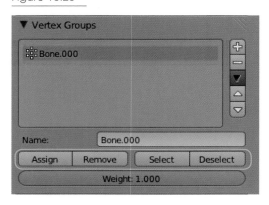

▼ Vertex Groups

Bone.000

Name: | Bone.000

Assign | Remove | Select | Deselect

Weight: 1.000

Tab into object mode and deselect the finger with the A key. Select the armature and change to pose mode. Select "Bone.001" and press the R key to rotate (Figure 15.26). Nothing happens because we haven't applied an armature modifier to the finger. Go back and select the finger and in the properties window – "Object Modifiers" button,

Figure 15.26

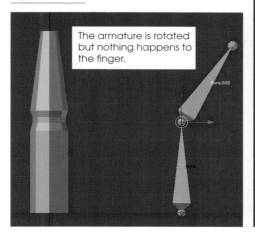

The armature is rotated but nothing happens to the finger.

Figure 15.27

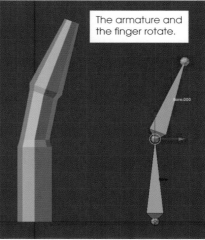

The armature and the finger rotate.

click "Add Modifier" and select "Armature." In the armature "Object" panel, click and select "Armature." Deselect the finger and select the armature in pose mode. Select "Bone.001" and rotate it—the upper part of the finger will now deform as the bone is rotated (Figure 15.27). Since the armature is located well away from the finger, the field of influence of the armature is not enforced (Figure 15.28).

Figure 15.28

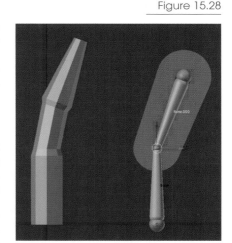

15.8.2 Method 2: Weight Paint

Instead of selecting vertices, Blender has a painting method that selects and assigns vertices to a group, automatically linking them to an armature bone. The paint method allows a graduated weight to be given to vertices that dictates how much influence the armature bone will have over the deformation of the mesh.

To begin, set up a new scene the same way you did for Method 1. Select the finger in object mode and add an armature modifier in the properties window. Don't forget to enter "Armature" in the "Object" panel. Select the armature and enter pose mode. In the properties window – "Object Data" button – "Display" tab, tick "Names" to display the bone names in the 3D window; the names should be "Bone" and "Bone.001" as before. Select "Bone.001" and right click the finger to select it. With the finger selected, go to the 3D window header and change from object mode to weight paint mode (Figure 15.29). The finger displays in blue, which indicates that no vertices are selected (Figure 15.30).

Figure 15.29

Figure 15.30

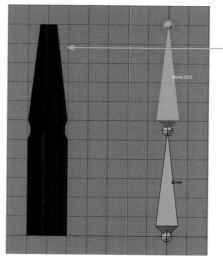

The finger is blue because no vertices are selected.

Figure 15.31

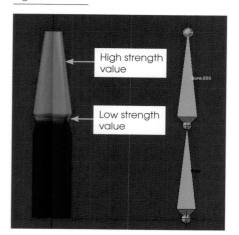

Paint circle size

Strength slider

Figure 15.32

Figure 15.33

High strength value

Low strength value

In the panel at the left-hand side of the window, drag the "Strength" slider up to 0.9000 (Figure 15.31). We are about to paint over the finger mesh to select vertices, and by setting the strength to a high value we are telling Blender that the selected vertices are to be rigorously controlled by "Bone.001." In weight paint mode, the cursor in the 3D window has a circle attached to it (Figure 15.32). The size of the circle is the size of the paint tool, which can be altered in the panel at the left. We want the upper part of the finger to be transformed by "Bone.001" so click, hold, and drag the cursor circle over the top part of the finger. The part of the finger painted turns red, which indicates a rigorous control (Figure 15.33). Altering the "Strength" value changes the control strength and will display as some other color.

Painting only selects vertices on the visible surface of the mesh. You have to turn the mesh around and paint the back side to select the whole top part of the finger (pan the 3D view around). Having painted the finger, note that in the properties window – "Object Data" button – "Vertex Groups" tab a vertex group has been created and named "Bone.001." Selecting "Bone.001" in pose mode and translating it will move the top part of the finger.

15.9 Vertex Groups or Field of Influence

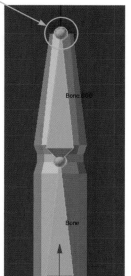

Having described the deformation of a mesh by employing vertex groups and field of influence, the question arises as to which is being employed when the armature is located inside the mesh. If we follow the preceding examples by either selecting vertices or weight painting, we assign vertices to a vertex group. It is unclear whether the vertex group or the field of influence is controlling the deformation of the mesh. If the armature is moved away from the mesh posing, the bone will still cause a deformation; therefore, the vertex group is in control. But when the armature is inside the mesh, is it the field of influence or the vertex group?

Follow this example to clarify this dilemma. Create the same scene as in Methods 1 and 2, select only the vertices at the tip of the finger, and assign them to a vertex group (Figure 15.34). Make sure you have added an armature modifier to the finger and have assigned "Armature" in the "Object" panel. Rotate "Bone.001" in pose mode and the whole top of the finger deforms. Place the armature in object mode and move it away from the finger. Rotate the bone again and only the tip of the finger deforms—this only proves that both the vertex group and the field of influence are active.

Place the armature back inside the finger. Select the finger and take a look at the armature modifier. Under the heading "Bind To" there are the two boxes labelled "Vertex Group" and "Bone Envelope." Untick "Bone Envelope"; rotating the bone now only deforms the tip of the finger (Figure 15.35). Obviously you have turned the field of influence off, so herein lies the control for selecting either the field of influence or the vertex group.

Another way of negating the field of influence is to set the "Distance" and "Weight" values to 0.000 in the properties window – "Bone" button – "Deform" tab (Figure 15.36). In the properties window – "Object Data" button – "Skeleton" tab, under "Deform" there are also boxes ticked and labelled "Vertex Group" and "Bone Envelope." Ticking or unticking these seems to have no effect.

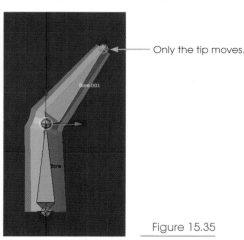

Only the tip moves.

Figure 15.35

Figure 15.36

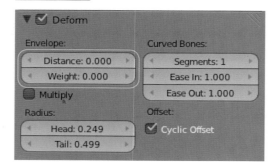

Figure 15.37

15.10 Inverse Kinematics

The inverse kinematics (IK) solver constraint is a wonderful tool for animators. IK is the opposite of FK, or forward kinematics, and both IK and FK are ways of controlling the posing and animation of a chain of bones. With FK, you have to rotate the chain of bones one by one to pose it for animation; this is a tedious process but gives you full control. With IK, dragging the end of the chain will result in the chain following the selected bone.

An example would be to create a chain of bones as shown in Figure 15.37. With the chain (armature) selected, go into pose mode, select the last bone in the chain, and in the properties window – "Bone Constraints" button, click on "Add Constraint" and select "Inverse Kinematics" (Figure 15.38). In the 3D window in pose mode, with the end bone still selected, press the G key and move the bone (Figure 15.39). Even in this single constraint, there are plenty of settings to play with.

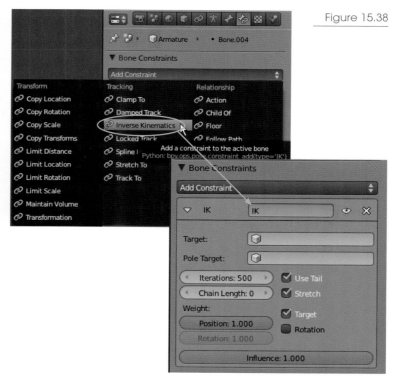

Figure 15.38

Figure 15.39

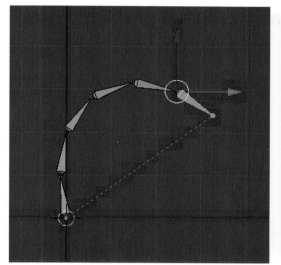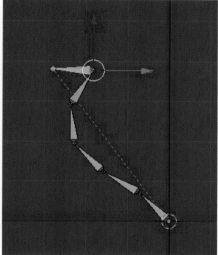

16

Shape Key and Action Editors

16.1 Introduction

The shape key and action editors provide an easy method of animating shapes and objects, and both editors are located in the dope sheet window. The shape key editor allows you to control the animation of vertices or groups of vertices, while the action editor allows you to set up an animation of an object's movement and scale.

To demonstrate both methods, start with the default Blender scene, delete the cube, and add a simple plane object with four vertices. Go into top view (number pad 7 – number pad 5) and zoom in on the view with the number pad + key. Split the 3D window into two windows and change the bottom one to the dope sheet window.

16.2 Shape Key Editor

In the dope sheet window, click on the drop down mode selection and select "ShapeKey Editor" (Figure 16.1). With the editor selected, the window has become an animation timeline.

Figure 16.1

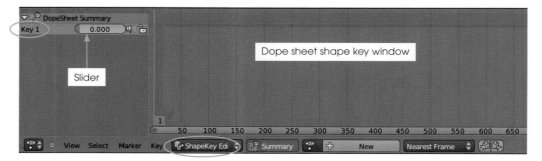

Figure 16.2

Figure 16.3

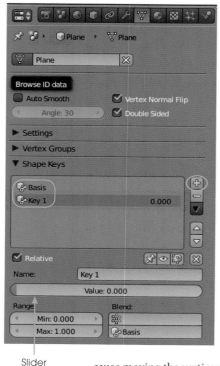

Slider

Vertex moved in edit mode

Original shape in object mode

Select the plane in the 3D widow and click on the + sign in the properties window – "Object Data" button – "Shape Keys" tab. The tab expands, showing that a "Basis Key" has been inserted. Additionally, a summary line is added in the dope sheet window. Click on the + sign again and "Key 1" will be added (Figure 16.2). Note that in the dope sheet shape key window, "Key 1" is also displayed (at the upper LH side of the window). With the cursor in the 3D window, tab to edit mode and deselect all the vertices with the A key. Select one of the vertices and drag it (press the G key and drag the mouse) and tab to object mode—the plane reverts to its original shape (Figure 16.3) because moving the vertices in edit mode has set the limits for their motion.

In the properties window – "Object Data" button – "Shape Keys" tab, changing "Value" by moving the slider changes the shape of the plane in the 3D window (Figure 16.2). You can also change the shape by moving the slider next to "Key 1" in the dope sheet shape

Figure 16.4

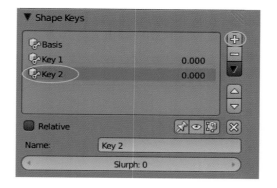

A new vertex moved in edit mode

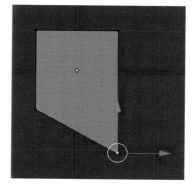

Figure 16.5

Figure 16.6

"Key 2" has been added to the shape key editor.

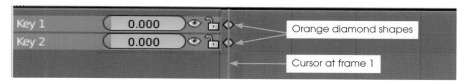

Figure 16.7

Orange diamond shapes

Cursor at frame 1

Figure 16.8

Cursor at new frame

Value of shape key at the current frame
Python: ShapeKey.value

key editor; by doing so, a key frame is automatically inserted at the frame where the cursor is located. In the properties window – "Shape Key" tab, click on the + sign again to add "Key 2" (Figure 16.4). In the 3D window, tab to edit mode, select a different vertex, and move it somewhere to set the limit of movement (Figure 16.5). Tab back to object mode and you'll notice that "Key 2" has been added to the shape key editor (Figure 16.6).

In the shape key editor, move each slider to see the plane change shape in the 3D window, then return each slider to the 0.000 position. Moving the sliders has inserted key locations in the timeline of the shape key editor at frame 1, as indicated by the orange diamond shapes (Figure 16.7). Drag the green line to a new frame, move the key sliders (to 0.787 and 0.600, respectively). New key frames are inserted, marked again by orange diamond shapes (Figure 16.8). Scrub the timeline (drag the green line) to see the animation. You can also press Alt + the A key with the cursor in the 3D window to play the animation, and Esc to stop.

16.3 Action Editor

To demonstrate the action editor, begin with the same setup as you used for the shape key editor, except this time select "Action Editor" mode in the dope sheet window. Select the plane in the 3D window in object mode and insert a key frame (with the I key) and select "LocRotScale."

In the dope sheet action editor, you will see the key frame displayed in the upper LHS of the window. Clicking on the little triangle in front of "LocRotScale" expands the key frame to show the individual components (Figure 16.9). In the action editor window header, click on "View" and tick "Show Sliders"; there are now value sliders in each component of the key frame (Figure 16.10). By repositioning the cursor in the action editor to a new frame and moving the sliders, you can manipulate the plane in the 3D window (Figure 16.11). When the slider value changes, key frames are inserted, which produces an animation. As I mentioned previously, you can scrub the animation or press Alt + the A key to play it.

Figure 16.9

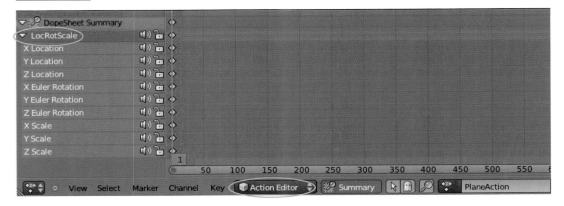

Figure 16.10

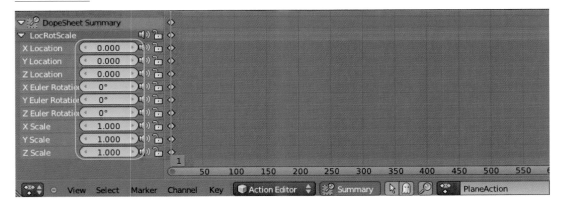

Figure 16.11

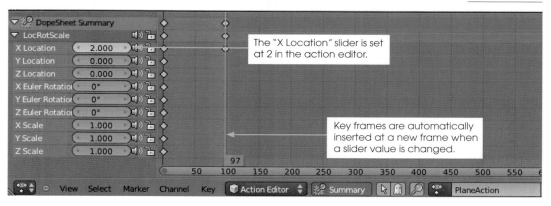

The "X Location" slider is set at 2 in the action editor.

Key frames are automatically inserted at a new frame when a slider value is changed.

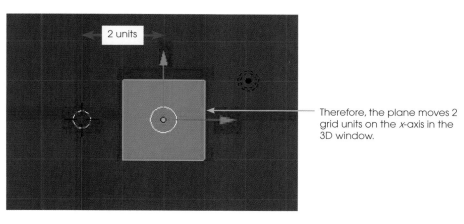

2 units

Therefore, the plane moves 2 grid units on the x-axis in the 3D window.

17

Fluid Simulation

17.1 Introduction to Fluid Simulation

Fluid simulation physics provides a means of simulating fluid flow. In this discussion, we will consider two scenarios. The first scenario is animating a volume of fluid such as a droplet of water or larger single volume, which is initially suspended in space and allowed to drop into a container or onto a surface. The second scenario is animating a stream of fluid such as fluid running from a tap or out of a container in a controlled flow. The latter scenario will provide a recap on the former one.

For detailed procedures, see the Blender Wiki PDF, which is obtainable at wiki.blender. org/index.php/Doc:2.6/Manual/Physics/Fluid.

17.2 Basic Setup (Scenario 1)

The setup in Figure 17.1 represents a basic 3D window scene in wireframe mode, constructed for a fluid simulation. As with all Blender scenes, there must be a light to provide illumination and a camera before anything can be rendered. The scene has been constructed with a fluid object (a default sphere with 32 segments and rings), a domain cube (a default cube scaled up three times), and an obstacle object (a cup extruded from a circle).

In the scene, a volume of liquid (the fluid object) is suspended in space and it will be released and then dropped into a cup (the obstacle object). The falling fluid (fluid simulation) takes place within the confines of the domain—the domain is a segment of space defined

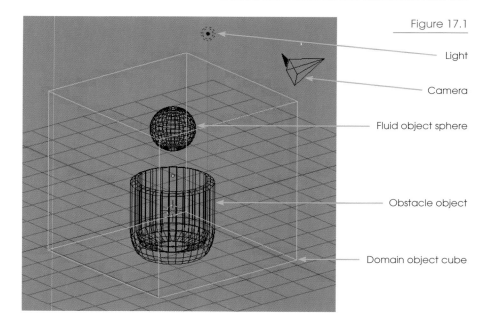

Figure 17.1

Light

Camera

Fluid object sphere

Obstacle object

Domain object cube

by a cubic volume (in this case, the cube). There must be a domain for a simulation to take place and all objects participating in the simulation must be within the domain. Any object partially outside of the domain will not function.

In this simulation, the fluid is represented by a sphere positioned somewhere towards the top of the domain and immediately above the cup. The size of the sphere relative to the domain and to the other objects within the domain determines the volume of the fluid; for instance, a large sphere relative to the domain and the cup produces a large fluid volume.

Figure 17.2

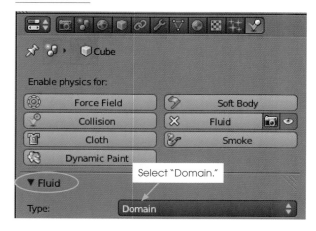

Select "Domain."

The cup is an obstacle that obstructs the movement of the fluid. In this example, the fluid is simply falling in space until it is obstructed by the cup. If the cup did not exist, the fluid would fall until it reached the bottom of the domain and then it would come to rest as if enclosed in a transparent rectangular container, which is defined by the shape of the domain. With the objects placed in the scene, nothing will happen until all the objects have values assigned. This sets up the simulation.

17.2.1 Domain Object Setup

In this scenario, the domain is a cube that has been scaled to enclose the sphere and the cup.

Figure 17.3

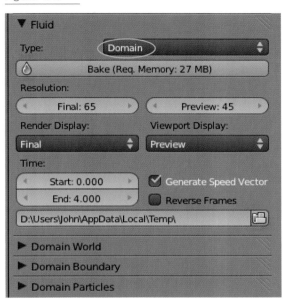

To assign fluid simulation values to the domain, first select the cube in the 3D window. Go to the properties window – "Physics" button – "Fluid" tab and select "Domain" from the "Type" drop down selection menu (Figure 17.2). The "Fluid: Domain" settings panel displays (Figure 17.3). Selecting the cube in the 3D window applies the domain characteristics to the cube and displays "Domain" options. Three further tabs can now be opened (Figure 17.4). While discussing this first scenario of fluid simulation, default values will be used, with one exception: in the "Time" settings, change the "End" value to 0.30, which reduces the bake time to something more reasonable for a demonstration.

Baking is similar to rendering images for an animated movie; it's the process of simulating a fluid flow and can take a considerable time depending on the complexity of the simulation setup. When baking, Blender looks at the "Start" and "End" values set in the "Fluid" tab, calculates the time period, then computes how the volume of fluid would react to the environment during that time. In our example, the time period is 0.30 seconds. The "Start" and "End" values have nothing to do with how many frames will be produced in the animation of the fluid flow, but instead are concerned with the physical force and the fluid viscosity—in other words, how the fluid will react to its environment in the given time period.

Figure 17.4

In the properties window – "Render" button – "Dimensions" tab, the default animation length is set at 250 frames and the animation will display at 24 frames per second. The animation frame range is also displayed in the timeline window. These values produce an animation of approximately 10 seconds. Thus, the behavior of the volume of water in this scenario over 0.30 seconds will be spread over the animation time of 10 seconds. Imagine dumping a cup of water and observing its action over 0.30 seconds then stretching that behavior over 10 seconds—a slow motion effect will result. Therefore, a 0.30-second bake will suffice to demonstrate simulating a fluid flow, even though it does not produce a real-time animation.

What is real-time animation? Real-time animation with respect to fluid flow is an animation that shows precisely how the fluid reacts in real time as opposed to our slow motion effect. If you are interested in real time, set the "Start" and "End" values in the "Fluid" tab to match the length of the animation. For example, with the default animation of 250 frames at 24 frames per second equaling approximately 10 seconds, you would set the time values to provide a 10-second period. Be warned: there will be a long wait while your Blender bakes. Varying the "Start" and "End" values of the fluid action therefore affects how the behavior of the fluid is seen in the final animation. For now, leave all the values in the standard domain tab set per the defaults, except for the "End" time setting.

One last point in the domain settings: note the directory name at the bottom of the "Fluid" tab. This gives the location of where the bake files will be saved, but you may change this to whatever you wish. I have already noted that baking takes a long time and with that comes a lot of files. If a simulation is rebaked, the files are overwritten, but after messing about with some trial and error in the learning process, you will still accumulate a whole slew of files.

17.2.2 Fluid Object Setup

See Blender Wiki PDF Manual, p. 1060, step 2

In this scenario, the fluid is represented by a sphere that has been placed in the domain immediately above the cup. As I said before, the size of the sphere relative to the domain and the cup determines the volume of the fluid in the simulation. For this demonstration, make sure the sphere is much smaller than the cup, otherwise you'll have some mopping up to do. Select the sphere in the 3D window, go to the properties window – "Physics" button – "Fluid" tab, and select type "Fluid" in the drop down menu (Figure 17.5). You can leave the settings as they are, but it is worth noting that the "Initial Velocity" values will give your fluid a kick start in whatever direction you set.

Figure 17.5

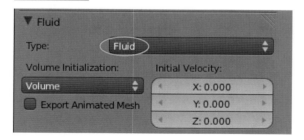

17.2.3 Obstacle Object Setup

See Blender Wiki PDF Manual, p. 1060, step 2

In this scenario, the obstacle to the fluid flow will be the cup. The cup is produced by extruding a circle in edit mode. Add a mesh circle object and tab into edit mode wireframe display. Leave the circle with the default 32 vertices and a radius of 1.000. Change the 3D view to front view (number pad 1 – number pad 5). With all vertices in the circle selected, press the

E key then the Z key and drag the mouse to extrude the circle up the *z*-axis. Press the S key and scale the new circle of vertices out. Repeat this process to shape the outside of the cup. When you reach the rim of the cup, extrude and scale circles of vertices in and down the *z* axis to form the inner surface of the cup. At the bottom of the interior with the final circle of vertices selected, scale the circle in and zoom in on the view (number pad - key) as far as you can go. When you are scaled all the way in, press "Remove Doubles" in the tool panel to leave a single vertex at the center. Tab back to object mode solid display and add a subdivision surface modifier to make the surface of the cup nice and smooth.

Figure 17.6

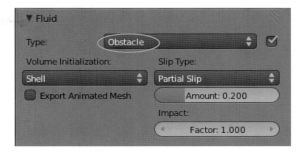

With the cup selected in the 3D window, go to the properties window – "Physics" button – "Fluid" tab and select type "Obstacle" (Figure 17.6). Change the "Volume Initialization" from "Volume" to "Shell"—with "Volume," Blender considers the shape to be solid with no interior. Now that all the objects required for the simulation have settings assigned, the fluid simulation setup is now complete and ready to be baked.

17.2.4 Baking

In the 3D window in wireframe mode, select the domain cube. The "Domain" properties tab will be displayed with the values that were previously set. Make note that baking a simulation can take a long time depending on the complexity of the simulation, the resolution, the length of the animation, and the speed of the computer. For the purpose of this scenario in which the default values have been used, set the length of the animation to 50 frames in the animation timeline window. At a display rate of 24 frames per second, this will produce an animation lasting approximately 2 seconds.

See Blender Wiki PDF Manual, p. 1062

Go back to the properties window – "Physics" button – "Fluid" tab. With the domain object (the cube) selected in the 3D window, click on the "Bake" button. The bake progress can be observed at the top of the 3D window in the fluid simulation progress bar; the bar only appears when you bake and will be located in the information window header adjacent to "Blender Render." If you want to cancel a bake, click on the × next to the bar. The bake takes a considerable time; it is akin to creating an image for each frame of an animation, so be prepared to sit back and wait a while. In this scenario, the bake should take about 30 seconds.

Figure 17.7

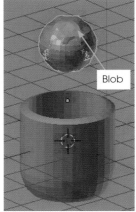

Note what happens in the 3D window. The domain has changed into a blob that attaches itself to the sphere fluid object (Figure 17.7). When the bake is completed, change to solid mode and press Alt + the A key to view the animation of the simulation. The blob descends, deforming as it goes, and splashes into the cup. If the bake is not performing as expected, it can be terminated by pressing the Esc key or the cancel button in the header and settings can be adjusted to correct the action. To rebake the simulation, select the domain (which is now the blob attached to the sphere) and press "Bake" again in the "Domain" properties

Figure 17.8

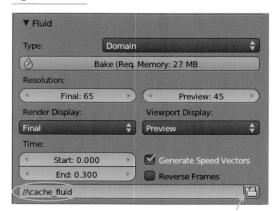

Click to open the file browser window to change
where the bake is saved.

tab. When a simulation is baked, it is similar to rendering files for an animation sequence. Files are created and saved to a folder on the computer's hard drive (refer to wiki.blender.org/index.php/Doc:2.6/Manual/Physics/Fluid/Domain#Baking). The path to the folder where the baked files are saved can be seen in the "Fluid: Domain" tab (Figure 17.8).

The folder for the storage of bake files can be changed to any folder you wish by clicking on the file browser icon and navigating to a folder in the file browser window (see the navigation section in Chapter 2 for a refresher). If the bake is executed without altering the path, the bake file will be saved in the default folder. When a simulation is baked without altering the destination folder, any existing bake file is overwritten. To delete a bake file, select the storage folder and delete the files or shred the folder.

17.3 Basic Setup (Scenario 2)

The setup in Figure 17.9 is a basic scene configuration to demonstrate a fluid simulation in accordance with Scenario 2. The camera and light are not shown in the screenshot, but they must exist in the scene. In this scenario, the fluid will flow in a stream from the inflow object sphere, down the obstacle object trough, and into the obstacle object cup. All objects participating in the simulation must be within the confines of the domain (Figure 17.10).

Figure 17.9

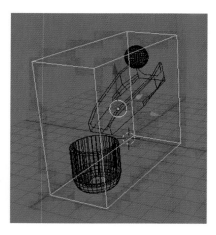
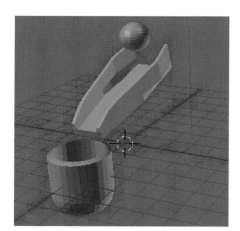

17.3.1 Domain Object Setup

You'll notice that the domain cube has been scaled to confine the participating objects in a restricted volume of space. The procedure for assigning the cube as the domain and setting

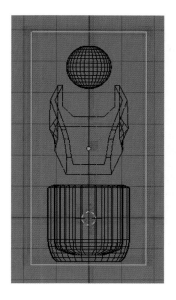

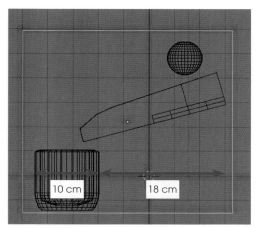

Figure 17.10

10 cm   18 cm

Figure 17.11

its values is identical to that of Scenario 1, with the exception that the "End" time value has been changed to 8.00 and the "Real World Size" has been set at 0.280 meters in the "Domain World" tab (Figure 17.11).

When setting up this fluid simulation, the length of the final animation in real time and the physical size of the scene in real terms must be considered. The Blender scene viewed on the computer screen is seen in Blender units and an animation is measured in the number of frames viewed at a set frame rate. In this simulation, the animation will be 200 frames long viewed at 24 frames per second, as seen in the properties window – "Render" button – "Dimensions" tab (Figure 17.12). Two hundred frames at 24 frames per second produces an animation of approximately 8 seconds duration. Setting "Start" at 0.00 and "End" at 8.00 in the "Fluid" tab computes the action of the fluid over a 8-second time period, i.e., over the length of the animation—this produces a real-time animation. If, for example, the "End" value was set at 4.00 seconds, then how the fluid behaved in 4.00 seconds would be spread over the 8.00 seconds of animation (in other words, it would be slowed down).

In regards to the size of the scene, consider that the diameter of the cup is something like 10 centimeters and the horizontal length of the trough extending past the edge of the cup is 18 cm. We then require a domain length of 28 cm. Thus, the "Real World Size" value is set at 0.280 (0.280 m = 28 cm), which is the longest side of the domain (Figure 17.10).

Figure 17.12

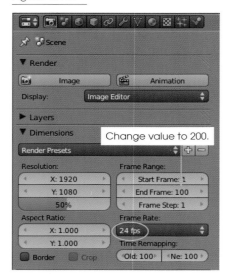

17.3.2 Fluid Object Setup

In this scenario, there is no fluid object; instead, we use an inflow object (the sphere) to provide a continuous flow of fluid.

17.3.3 Inflow Object Setup

Make particular note of the scale of the inflow object relative to the obstacle objects; the scale of the inflow object determines the physical volume of the fluid in the scene (Figure 17.13). If the inflow object is too large, the volume of fluid will spill over the sides of the trough and cup.

With the inflow object selected in the 3D window, go to the properties window – "Physics" button – "Fluid" tab. Since the domain object has been previously set, the "Fluid" options in the "Type" tab should already be available. Select "Inflow" to display the inflow options (Figure 17.14). To give the fluid a small amount of momentum, set the "Z" initial velocity at 0.20. In doing this, the fluid will move before the acceleration due to the effects of gravity. Leaving the "Z" velocity at 0 produces a rather sluggish fluid flow.

17.3.4 Obstacle Object Setup (Trough)

Make particular note of the construction of the trough; it has been modeled by extruding and scaling a cube into a rectangular U shape, rotated to provide an incline, and positioned

Figure 17.13

Figure 17.14

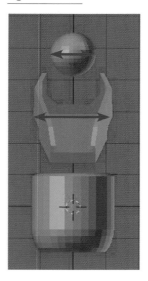

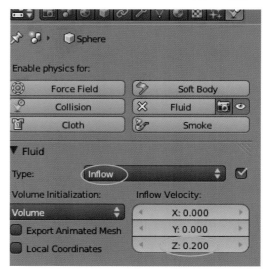

below the inflow object and above the cup. In this demonstration, the trough construction does not have to be exactly as shown in the diagrams. Start with a cube object and scale it along the *x*-axis. Tab into edit mode and turn off "Limit selection to visible" in the 3D window header. In end view, progressively select vertices to form a cube face and extrude, as shown in Figure 17.9(right). You can modify the profile as you wish (scale the ends of the trough to fit the cup and inflow), then when completed tab back to object mode and add a subdivision surface modifier. Without the modifier, the fluid tends to break through the trough surface.

With the trough constructed, select it in the 3D window, go to the "Fluid" tab, and select "Obstacle" (Figure 17.15). Set the "Volume Initialization" option to "Shell" and the "Slip Type" to "Free." The "Volume Initialization" and "Shell" options initialize a thin layer for all the faces of the mesh, which prevents fluid breakthrough. The "Free" option allows fluid movement along the obstacle. For other options, see the Blender Wiki manual.

17.3.5 Obstacle Object Setup (Cup)

The model of the cup is identical to that used in the first scenario. Set the value options the same as for the trough obstacle object, except set the "Volume Initialization" option to "Shell" and the "Slip Type" to "Partial Slip" (Figure 17.16). All objects included in the simulation

Figure 17.15

Figure 17.16

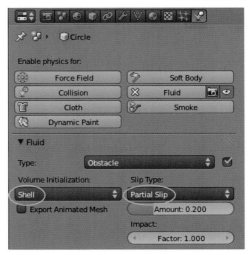

Frame 30

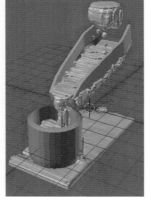

Frame 80

Note: In these examples, fluid is seen breaking through the trough and cup. Applying a subdivision surface modifier to the trough and cup mesh and increasing the "Resolution" – "Final" value in the "Physics" – "Fluid" tab will resolve this.

Figure 17.17

have been assigned and the process can be baked, so you can now follow the procedure as outlined in the first scenario.

The bake process takes a fair while and no action is observed in the 3D window other than the small bake progress bar at the top of the screen. When the bake has completed, the progress bar disappears. Play the animation or step through the animation in the timeline to see the result (Figure 17.17).

Figure 17.18

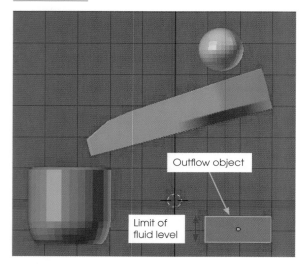

17.3.6 Outflow Object

An outflow object is used to limit the buildup of fluid to a certain level within the confines of the domain (Figure 17.18). The outflow would be used if you wanted the fluid to overflow from the cup and you only wanted the fluid level in the domain to reach a certain level.

17.4 Fluid Simulation with Particle Objects

So far, domain, obstacle, inflow, and outflow objects have been considered. Now let's consider the application of particle objects. Start with the fluid system that you used in the second scenario. Add a sphere to the scene and position it within the confines of the domain,

Figure 17.19

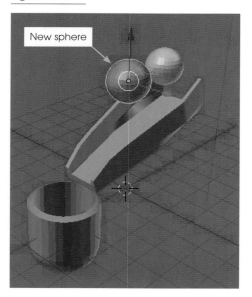

Figure 17.20

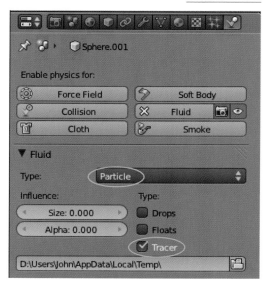

as shown in Figure 17.19. With the new sphere selected in the 3D window, go to the properties window – "Physics" button – "Fluid" tab, select "Type: Particle," and tick "Tracer" (Figure 17.20).

In the 3D window, select the domain, which is now the blob attached to the side of the inflow sphere object. Go to the "Fluid" tab – "Domain Particles" tab and set the "Tracer Particles" value to 3000 and the "Generate Particles" value to 1.000 (Figure 17.21). Setting these values instructs the system to generate 3000 particles over the length of the animation and turns the generation on to normal (0 = off, 1 = normal, greater than 1 = more).

In the "Fluid" tab under "Type: Domain," click on "Bake." The system will now rebake the simulation, taking as long as it did the first time. Notice that there are dots distributed randomly amongst the fluid as the fluid is being generated; these dots are the particles and will show as halos when rendered (Figure 17.22). In Figure 17.23, a material color and a spotlight have been added.

Note: The domain has been moved to level 2, therefore only the particle halos render.

Figure 17.21

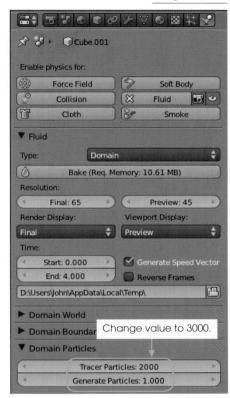

Figure 17.22

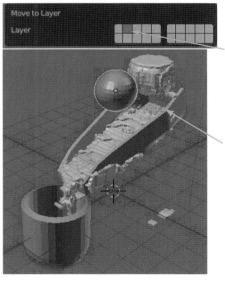

Particles can be better seen with the domain moved to level 2.

Particles shown as dots.

Change value to 3000.

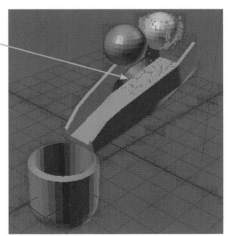

Figure 17.23

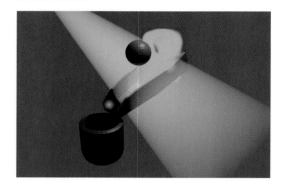

17.5 Fluid Simulation with Control Objects

Besides domain, fluid, obstacle, inflow, and particle objects, there is also the control object. Control objects are placed in the scene within the domain to influence the flow of fluid. In Figure 17.24, a domain has been set up containing an inflow cube object and an outflow cylinder object. The inflow provides a continuous flow of fluid, which simply accumulates on the floor of the domain until it reaches the level of the outflow object.

In Figure 17.25, a cone object has been added to the domain as a control object. With the control cone added, the fluid flows towards the cone before seeking the outflow object. By placing control objects within the domain, the flow of fluid can be directed.

Figure 17.24

Figure 17.25

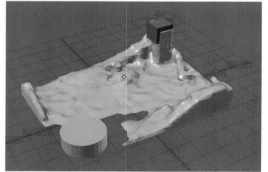

Scene at frame 80 without the control object

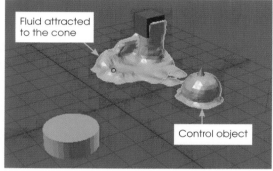

Scene at frame 80 with the control object

17. Fluid Simulation

18

Nodes

18.1 Introduction to Nodes

The Blender node system allows for the creation of materials and textures for application to objects and allows for the output of data affecting the rendered image or movie. In Blender, every button, value slider, pop-up menu, and tick box provides the user a means of entering data that affects the program's output display. Nodes do exactly the same thing—they are graphical displays where data can be entered. The displays can be arranged and linked together in combinations providing an array of options, and the nodes are accessed using the node editor window.

Start a new Blender scene and leave the default cube object selected. Change the 3D window to the node editor window; the window will display as blank. Blender nodes are arranged in three categories: material nodes, texture nodes, and compositing nodes (Figure 18.1). Each category can be selected in the window's header. Material nodes allow the

Figure 18.1

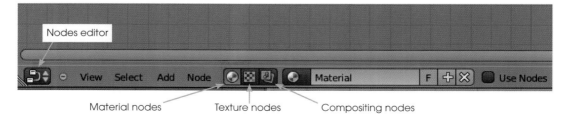

Nodes editor

Material nodes   Texture nodes   Compositing nodes

Figure 18.2

Properties window   "Material" button

The material in the slot is applied to the cube object.

The material named "Material" is selected.

Default material color

creation of materials, texture nodes allow the creation of textures, while compositing nodes provide a means of assembling and enhancing images or movies.

Before attempting to use nodes for any specific task, it is essential to know how to add, arrange, and link nodes. The first step is to open the node editor window. By default, the material node category is selected, so to demonstrate the process of using nodes we will start with this category. Make sure an object is selected in the 3D window and that a material has been assigned. If you use the default Blender scene, the default cube object is selected and in the properties window – "Material" button, the preview panel shows a gray sphere; this sphere is showing the default color of the default material named "Material," which is applied to the cube (Figure 18.2).

Figure 18.3

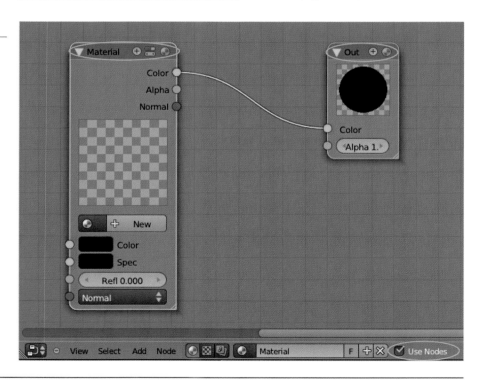

The node editor cannot be activated unless a material has been applied to the selected object in the 3D window. In the node editor window header, tick the "Use Nodes" box and two nodes will display in the window: material and output (Figure 18.3). Note that the sphere in the "Material" button – preview panel is now a black circle, which is what is displayed in the output node panel.

18.1.1 Resizing Nodes

Click and hold on the little cross hatched triangle in the lower RH corner of the node and drag your mouse to resize the node panel. You should now see the word "Output" in the header of the output node.

18.1.2 Expanding and Collapsing Nodes

Besides changing the size of a node panel, you can also expand and collapse it to save space on the screen. Look at the material node header: there is a + sign in a circle, an icon like the properties window icon, and a sphere like the "Material" button icon. Clicking on any of these icons will toggle between expanding and collapsing the node panel in different ways, so click and experiment to determine the difference (Figure 18.4). Node systems can become very complex so it is very handy to be able to minimize the size of the nodes. To toggle between expanding and collapsing the node entirely, click on the gray triangle at the LHS of the header.

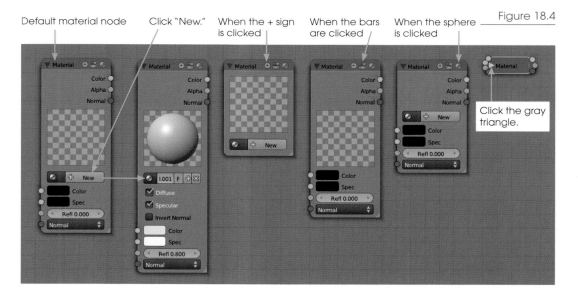

Figure 18.4

Default material node   Click "New."   When the + sign is clicked   When the bars are clicked   When the sphere is clicked   Click the gray triangle.

18.1.3 Moving and Arranging Nodes

Click and hold anywhere in the node panel and drag the mouse to move the node.

18.1. Introduction to Nodes

343

Figure 18.5

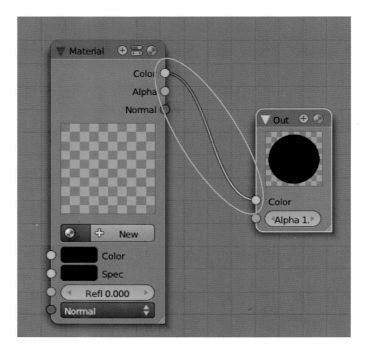

18.1.4 Zoom Window

Scrolling the mouse wheel or pressing the number pad + and - keys will zoom in and out in the node editor window. Click and hold the MMB to pan the window.

18.1.5 Connecting and Disconnecting Nodes

You will see that the material node is connected to the output node by a curved line between the two yellow "Color" sockets (Figure 18.5). Click and hold on the output node's yellow socket and drag your mouse away from the socket; release the hold, and you will have disconnected the nodes (the connecting line disappears). Click and hold on the material node's yellow socket, drag the mouse to the output node's yellow socket, and release the hold to reconnect the nodes. In general, sockets should be connected yellow to yellow, gray to gray, and blue to blue.

Figure 18.6

18.2 Node Groups

Several nodes may be grouped together; this is a way of saving space on the screen since the group is able to be expanded and collapsed. To group nodes, press the B key, drag a rectangle around the nodes you wish to group, then press Ctrl + the G key (Figure 18.6). Selecting the group and pressing Alt + the G key ungroups the selection, and pressing Tab toggles between expanding and collapsing the group.

Figure 18.7

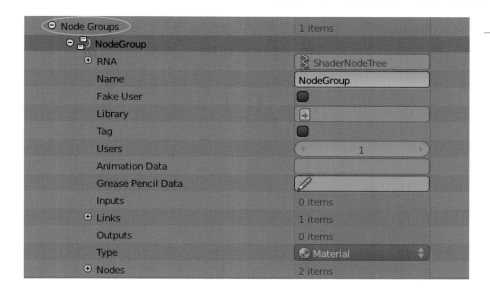

Grouping nodes provides a means of saving a particular node combination and thus the means of creating an effect and then appending this for use in other Blender files. In this way, you can build a library of node combinations for reuse. Once a node group is created, you can select it and then add, remove, link and unlink, and move nodes around within the group—in other words, you can edit the group. When you have finished editing a group, press Tab to collapse it and the A key to deselect it. You can now add more nodes to the screen.

18.2.1 Naming Node Groups

You may wish to change the names of the node groups to something more meaningful, which you can do in the outliner window. Blender's default scene opens with an outliner window in the upper RH side of the screen, but this is an abridged version of the full window. Divide one of your larger windows in two and change one part to the outliner window—it should display in data blocks mode showing entries for everything in your scene. Scroll down and find "Node Groups"; if you have just created a node group, you will find it as a subentry (Figure 18.7). Expand the subentry and change the name of the group in the "Name" panel. A name change here will be reflected in the node editor window.

18.3 Material Nodes

Material nodes allow the creation of materials and once a material node is created in Blender, it is saved for future use in the Blender file. You can use an object that is selected in the 3D window in conjunction with the node editor when dealing with material nodes.

We will work through a simple exercise and create a material using nodes. Start with the default Blender scene with the default cube object selected. The cube will have the default

Figure 18.8

material applied to it, as seen in the properties window – "Material" button; the material displays as the default gray color. At this point, it is worth taking a look at what we have in terms of the material. Look at the properties window – "Material" button. The preview tab shows a sphere with the gray color and a material named "Material" is selected and assigned to the material slot (Figure 18.8). The material slot is linked to the selected cube object in the 3D window, which renders as the gray color. Clicking on the "Browse ID data" button shows the material cache with only the material named "Material" stored in it.

18.3.1 What Is a Material?

A material in Blender is a bunch of data that tells the program to display the surface of an object in a certain way (i.e., gray in color, reflecting a certain color under a light source, having bumps or spots, etc.). The data is grouped together in a block called a data block.

18.3.2 Data Blocks

If you change the 3D window to the outliner window in data blocks mode, you will see the "Materials" data block as one of the entries (Figure 18.9). Click on the + sign next to "Materials" to see the data block for the material named "Material." Note that Blender's default screen arrangement has an outliner window in the upper RH side of the screen—as I mentioned before, this window is an abridged version of the full outliner window. It's worth mentioning here that you can change the name of the material in the name slot in the data block. Just click in the slot, delete, and retype a new name and the name change will be reflected in the properties window – "Material" button. This is very useful when creating multiple materials.

Figure 18.9

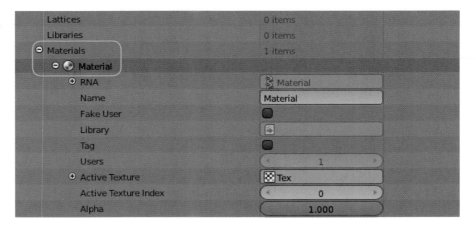

Change the outliner window to the 3D window to get us back to square one. Make sure the cube is selected and make note that Blender has assigned the material named "Material" to the cube (material nodes will not work unless a material has been assigned to the selected object). Change the 3D window to the node editor window and you will get a blank window. At the start of this chapter, I said that nodes were accessed through the node editor window. By default, material nodes mode is selected but to activate the nodes you must tick the "Use Nodes" box in the window header. The material node shows a blank chequerboard preview panel, the output node shows a black circle, and in the properties window – "Material" button – preview tab, you should see the same black circle.

If you click on the "Browse ID data" button you will see that the default material named "Material" is still the only thing in the cache; note that "Material" is still shown selected and in the material slot. If you render an image (by pressing F12), however, all you get is a black profile of the cube. Activating "Use Nodes" has taken over the render process and at this stage we have not created any new material. In the material node, click on "New"; the material node expands and the "Color" and "Spec" color selection bars show white. If you click on the "Color" bar, you will see RGB values of 0.800 (gray) and the "Spec" bar shows RGB values of 1.000 (white)—this is why you see gray spheres in all the preview windows. Render an image (F12) and you should see a gray cube.

Note that in the "Material" button, "Material" is still showing as selected and in the material slot. Click on the "Browse ID data" button and you will now see two materials: "Material" and "Material.001." Clicking on "New" in the material node has created a new material; since "Material" and "Material.001" are identical, you can only render a gray cube.

Click on the the color selection bar in the material node and pick a new color. All the previews display the new color, but in the 3D window the cube is still gray. Note that in the material node the name of the material is showing "Material.001," which shows that the node is editing "Material.001." Untick "Use Nodes" in the header, go to the "Material" button in the properties window, and in the "Browse ID data" button drop down menu, select "Material.001." This places "Material.001" in the material slot and assigns it to the cube in the 3D window. The cube will now display the color you chose.

These are the very basics of using material nodes, but of course there is much more. Clicking on "Add" in the node editor window header reveals a pop-up selection menu with seven categories of node types. Each category has individual node type options. It is not possible to demonstrate all of the possible node combinations, but the following examples should give you the idea. Remember, when you create a node arrangement that produces a desired result, create a node group and save the .blend file for future use. The node group can be appended to any new Blender scene and applied to any object in the scene. Therefore, it's possible to create a single .blend file containing many node groups for future appending.

18.3.3 Example 1

Figure 18.10 shows a material color mixed with a magic texture, which has "Mapping" settings applied. The new material has been applied to a sphere, which has been scaled down along the z-axis to create a disk (Figure 18.11).

Figure 18.10

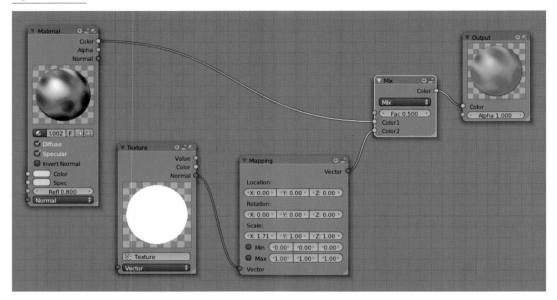

Figure 18.11

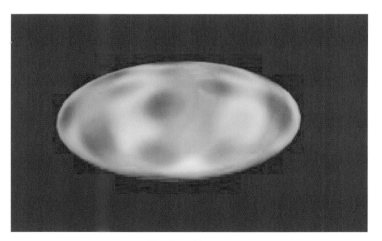

Rendered image

18.3.4 Example 2

Figure 18.12 shows another variation on Example 1, this time with a marble texture. Figure 18.13 shows the rendered image.

Figure 18.12

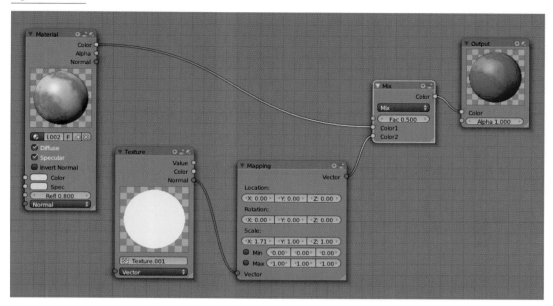

Figure 18.13

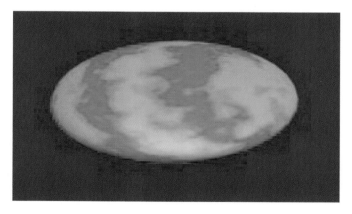

Rendered image

18.3.5 Example 3

Figure 18.14 shows two RGB inputs connected to a "Mix" panel with a "ColorRamp" panel applied and Figure 18.15 shows the rendered image. Note that the three examples shown so far simply create a material and apply it to a selected object in the 3D window. The default settings for the lamp and camera are used with no other influence.

Figure 18.14

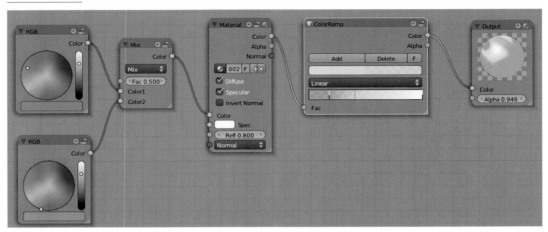

Figure 18.15   Rendered image

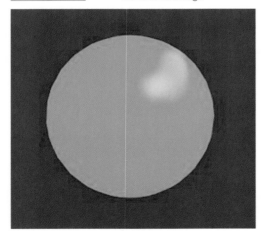

18.3.6 Example 4

This example demonstrates the use of material nodes in combination with other objects in the scene. The objective here is to create a simple graduated material. First, we have to set up the scene as shown in Figure 18.16; the default cube has been elongated into a vertical column, and a simple plane object has been added to the scene, scaled up, and positioned behind the elongated cube, forming a backdrop in the camera view (Figure 18.17). Make sure the lamp is positioned on the camera side of the plane. Select the plane in the 3D window and assign the default material and a marble texture to it in the properties window – "Material" button. Deselect the plane then select the elongated cube. In the properties window – "Material" button – "Diffuse" tab, pick a diffuse color, and in the "Specular" tab, pick a specular color. In the "Transparency" tab, tick "Transparency" and change the "Alpha" value to 0.000. While still in the "Transparency" tab, click "Raytrace" and set the "IOR" value to 1.2. In the properties window – "Render" button – "Shading" tab, untick "Shadows." The diffuse and specular colors can be anything you want. Obviously, "Transparency" makes the cube transparent; with the "Alpha" value at 0.000, it is fully transparent. The "IOR" value is an angular index of refraction for ray traced refraction; the value of 1.200 makes the cube appear to look something like glass. Only by experimenting with different values will you understand how to achieve the outcome you want.

Figure 18.16

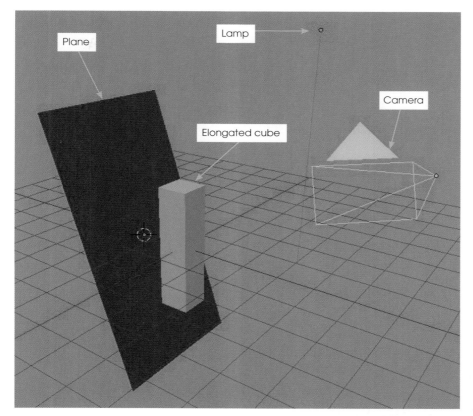

Figure 18.17

Make sure the cube is selected in the 3D window and then in the node editor window – material nodes mode, tick "Use Nodes" and set up the arrangement seen in Figure 18.18. Note that the "Separate R" node in the figure is actually "Separate RGB" and the "Extend" node is "Extended Material." Note also all the unconnected sockets on the extended material node. The rule here is that an unconnected input socket will relay the value in its adjacent panel to the output. If an input node is connected then that node overrides the value. For example, "Refl 0.800" is the value used since there is no input connected to the socket.

It's worth remembering that in any scene, the lamp or number of lamps, the type of lamp, and the energy settings and color of the lamp light can have a dramatic effect on the rendered image. Something else to note in

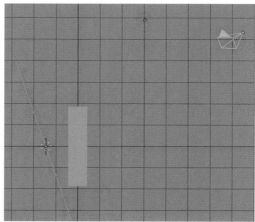

Side view of the scene

Figure 18.18

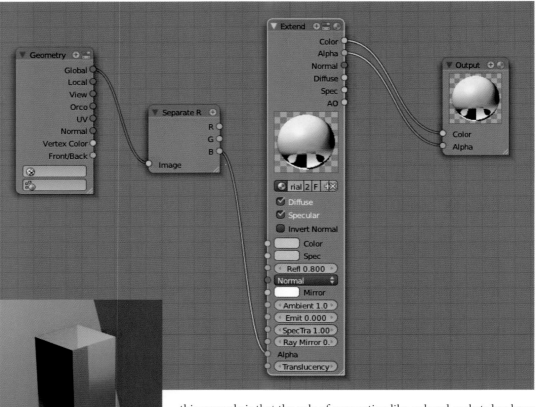

Figure 18.19

this example is that the rule of connecting like-colored sockets has been broken: the blue "Global" socket on the geometry node is connected to the yellow "Image" socket on the separate RGB node.

"Separate RGB" tells Blender to separate the red, green, and blue values; it is being used to separate the coordinates that are vector values. RGB in this case represents *x,y,z* coordinate values that are fed to the "Alpha" value in the extended material node. "B" corresponds to the *z* value, or the vertical coordinate. Therefore, we are applying the material to a vertical cube column. The value is fed into the "Alpha" socket on the extended material node, which is the value that controls transparency. "Geometry" – "Global" is telling Blender to use global coordinates. The combination is telling Blender to apply the diffuse color and the transparency to the elongated cube on the *z*-axis.

We have ray tracing applied and we have given the elongated cube the characteristics of glass. The cube is therefore refracting the light reflected from the backdrop in the scene (the plane); Figure 18.19 shows the application. This example shows how you can mix and match nodes, lamp settings, and objects in the scene to produce stunning effects. Bear in mind that in this type of setup, the proximity of objects in the scene, the position of the lamp and its settings, the number of lamps, and the color and type of texture, all have an effect on the rendered output. When following this example, you probably won't produce the same image as shown.

18.4 Texture Nodes

Texture nodes allow you to create textures and apply them to a selected object in the 3D window. As far as adding nodes to the node editor, manipulating them, and connecting them, the process is the same as for material nodes. However, activating the node editor in texture mode is slightly different.

Start a new Blender scene and delete the default cube object. Add a simple plane object and scale it up a bit; a plane will provide a nice flat surface on which to place the texture. In the properties window – "Material" button, click "New" to add the default material. As with material nodes, texture nodes cannot be activated unless a material has been applied to the selected object. Change the 3D window to node editor and note that the material node option in the header is selected by default. Change this to texture node mode and click on "New"—this is the same as clicking on "New" in the properties window – "Textures" button. Now tick "Use Nodes."

Two nodes appear in the editor window: checker and output (Figure 18.20). In all texture node arrangements, there must be an output node. If you render an image (F12), you will see the checker texture applied to the plane object, which is selected in the 3D window (Figure 18.21). In the properties window – "Textures" button, you will see that a texture named "Texture" is selected and placed in the texture slot. Click on the "Browse ID data" button and see that there are two textures in the cache: "Tex" and "Texture." "Texture" is the new

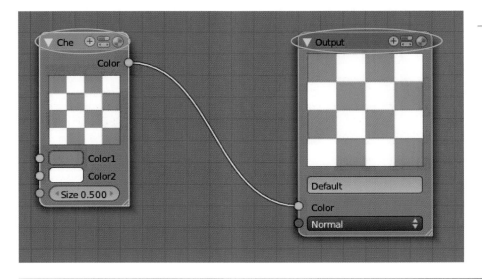

Figure 18.20

Figure 18.21

Rendered image

texture you have just created using nodes and "Tex" is Blender's hidden default texture data block. As with everything else in Blender, entering data for a new material or texture is in fact modifying something that already exists.

At this stage, you have "Use Nodes" active so the node editor is applying the new texture to the object. If you untick "Use Nodes," a render will only show the plane object as having the default gray material color. In the properties window – "Textures" button, click on the "F" next to "Texture" to save the texture data block. A "2" appears, indicating that there are two users of the data, so click on the "2" to make a single user. The "2" disappears and if you look in the cache (click the "Browse ID data" button), you will see "Tex," "Tex.001," and "Texture.001." "Tex" and "Tex.001" just render a gray plane while "Texture" displays the nodes in the node editor. You still have to tick "Use Nodes" to render the checker texture to the object.

This has demonstrated the basic application of texture nodes. There are many combinations of node arrangements that will produce many textures. The following examples will show simple arrangements. Note that complicated node arrangements consume computer power and unless you are working on a powerful machine, rendering an image will take forever or will just never happen.

Figure 18.22

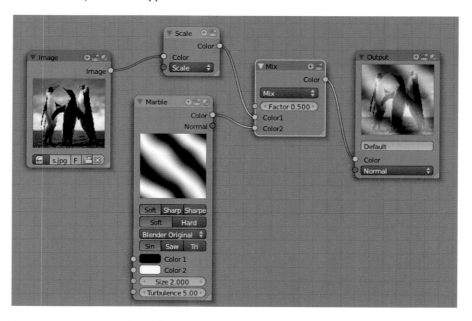

18.4.1 Example 1

In Figure 18.22, an image has been loaded into the image node and mixed with a wood texture node. The scale node resizes the image, and the texture created is mapped onto a sphere object selected in the 3D window (Figure 18.23 shows the rendered image).

18.4.2 Example 2

In Figure 18.24, the compose RGB node creates a color and the mix node combines the color with an image from the image node to produce a texture, as seen in the output node. The texture is applied to a plane object selected in the 3D window (Figure 18.25 shows the rendered image).

Rendered image

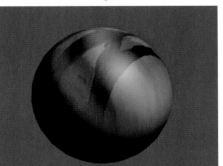

Figure 18.23

Figure 18.24

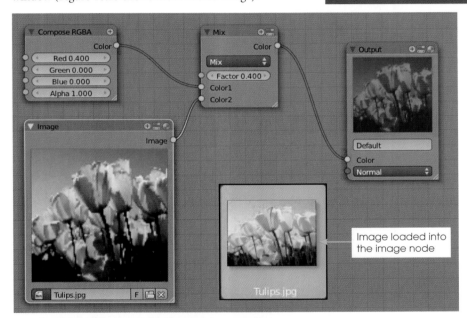

Image loaded into the image node

Figure 18.25

18.5 Compositing Nodes

Compositing nodes (or composite, for short) allow you to create and enhance an image. The contents of the Blender scene can be the basis for the image or an image already saved on the hard drive can be used. A presaved image can be combined with other images or the Blender scene to create a new image. Unlike material and texture nodes, it is not necessary to have an object selected in the 3D window or to have a material applied to an object. Of course by default, any object added to a scene has the default material added to it even though this does not display in the properties window until the "New" button is pressed.

To demonstrate the activation of the compositing node editor, start with a new Blender scene and delete the default cube. Add a monkey object and deselect the object in the 3D window. Change the 3D window to node editor and select the compositing mode in the window header. Tick "Use Nodes" and two nodes will display in the window: render layers and composite (Figure 18.26). Render an image (F12) to create a picture of the camera view with the monkey (Figure 18.27). Remember that the monkey is not selected in the 3D window and no material has been applied. Through the render layer and composite nodes, Blender is rendering an image of the camera view in the scene. Rendering places the image of the camera view into the nodes (Figure 18.28). Note that for Blender to render an image, there must be a compositing node in the node editor. The following are two examples of simple compositing node arrangements.

Figure 18.26

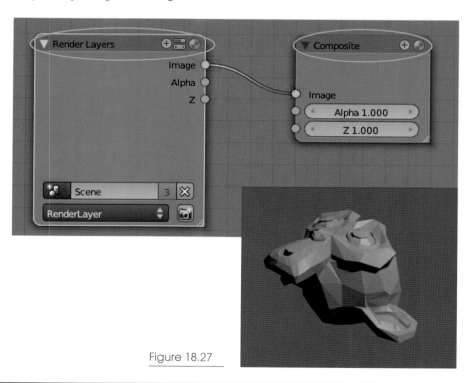

Figure 18.27

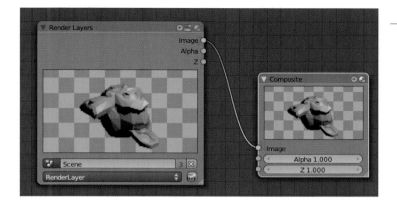

Figure 18.28

18.5.1 Example 1

When activating composite nodes as previously described, the 3D camera view is introduced to the render layers node and the composite node. Click on "Add" in the node editor window header and select "Input" – "Image" node and then a color–mix node. Connect the nodes as shown in Figure 18.29. In the image node, click on "Open Image" to open the file browser then navigate to an image stored on your hard drive. Select the image then click on "Open Image."

With the nodes linked, the 3D camera view and the new image are combined. Adjust the values in the mix and composite nodes as shown in Figure 18.29. Press F12 to render the combined image (Figure 18.30).

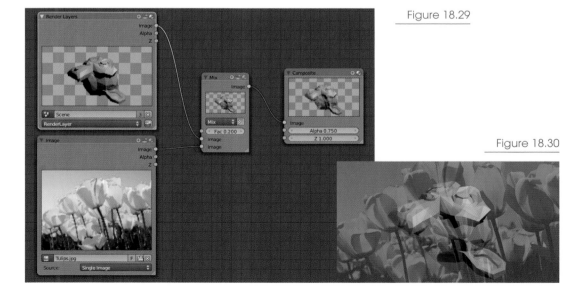

Figure 18.29

Figure 18.30

Figure 18.31

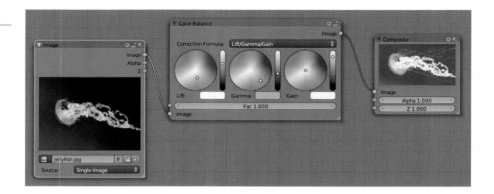

Figure 18.32

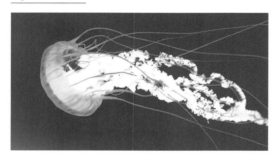

18.5.2 Example 2

By entering an image node, a color balance node, and a composite node, the color of a rendered image can be adjusted to produce a variety of effects. Figure 18.31 shows an example. The effects are limitless (Figure 18.32), as you will discover by experimenting with combinations of values in the color balance and composite nodes.

19

The Blender Game Engine

19.1 Introduction to the Game Engine

Blender has the functionality to create interactive video games. The program integrates real-time motion with physics and logic blocks, allowing you to turn objects into actors and move them around. This process also incorporates character animation and allows interactive walkthroughs to be created where doors open and close. The game engine is extensive in its application and it is not possible to cover all of its intricacies in this manual. You will have to research and experiment beyond the scope of this very brief introduction to become proficient.

Figure 19.1

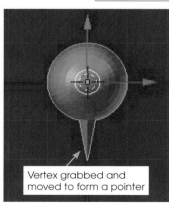

Vertex grabbed and moved to form a pointer

To get you started and to whet your appetite for gaming, follow this very basic example. Begin with the default Blender scene, delete the cube, and add a UV sphere. Gaming is a form of animation, therefore—as with all animation—it is best to keep animated objects with a low vertex count. To keep things simple, the default UV sphere will suffice. In the 3D window, tab into edit mode with the sphere selected and grab one single vertex on the side and make a pointer, as shown in Figure 19.1. This will provide an indicator showing which direction you are pointing when moving around. The sphere with the pointer will be our actor.

Go to the information window header and change the screen arrangement from the "Default" screen to the "Game Logic" screen (Figure 19.2). This arrangement has the logic editor window, 3D window, properties window, and the outliner window displayed. The information window header

Figure 19.2

Figure 19.3

is across the top of the screen. The screen is configured for setting up the game engine, but Blender is not ready yet. In the information window header, change "Blender Render" to "Blender Game" (Figure 19.3). With the sphere selected in the 3D window, go to the properties window – "Physics" button – "Physics" tab and set the "Physics Type" to "Dynamic." Note that in doing this, the "Actor" box is ticked, which indicates that the sphere is an actor. If it is not ticked, tick it.

To check if the sphere is behaving itself and is going to cooperate as an actor in this drama, set the 3D window to front view (number pad 1) and with the cursor in the 3D window press the P key. This puts the 3D window into play mode. The sphere should descend in the window and disappear out of sight. Press Esc to return the sphere to center stage in the window. You have just proved that the sphere actor is behaving itself; gravity has taken hold of the sphere and caused it to fall. Since there is nothing below the sphere to obstruct its motion, it falls to infinity. We had better do something to correct this.

Figure 19.4

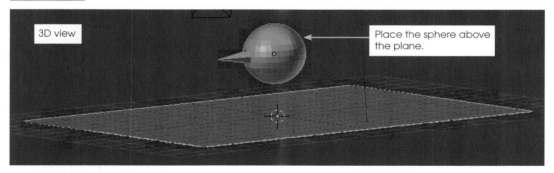

3D view

Place the sphere above the plane.

Figure 19.5

Game play view

The sphere is now sitting on the plane.

Figure 19.6

Put the 3D window into top view and add a plane to the scene. Scale the plane up six times, go back to front view, and move the sphere up above the plane (Figure 19.4). Move to user perspective view (number pad 0 then number pad 5 twice). Press the P key to see the sphere descend and sit on the plane, and press Esc to go back to object mode (Figure 19.5). It is time to tell Blender when and how we want our actor to move. In the logic editor window at the bottom of the screen, you should see three logic blocks: "Sensors," "Controllers," and "Actuators" (Figure 19.6). The sensor is what will trigger an action, so click on the "Add Sensor" drop down menu to see the options (Figure 19.7). The controller is what will control the action; click on "Add Controller" to see these options (Figure 19.8). Finally, the actuator tells the actor what to do, so click on "Add Actuator" to see these options (Figure 19.9). We will choose some settings and make something happen to give you an idea how this all works. In the "Sensors" logic block, click "Add Sensor" and select "Mouse." Therefore, our mouse will be the device we use to trigger the action. If you want to change your mind about this, click on the drop down menu and select something else. For now, let's stick with the mouse.

Figure 19.7

Figure 19.8

Figure 19.9

Where it says "Mouse Event" in the "Sensor" panel, you should select what part of the mouse will be responsible for the trigger. Click "Left Button" to see your options, but stick with "Left Button" as the final selection. In the "Controller" logic block, click "Add Controller" and select "And." In the "Actuator" logic block, click "Add Actuator" and select "Motion" since we want our actor to do some moving about. Leave the "Motion" type as "Simple Motion" and you should see two slots: "Loc" (location) and "Rot" (rotation) with "X," "Y," and "Z" values (Figure 19.10). "X," "Y," and "Z" indicate the axis and the value will give the speed of the action. Enter "Loc Y" as 0.20, which tells the actor to move along the y-axis at a speed of 0.20—note that this is in the positive y direction. To move in the opposite direction, enter –0.20. The last step for now is to connect the logic blocks. Click on the little black dot at the RHS of "Sensor" and drag over to the little circle next to "Controller," then do the same between "Controller" and "Actuator."

Time for a test run. Put your mouse in the 3D window and press the P key. Give your LMB a click and you will see the sphere move. It may not be in the direction of the pointy bit

Figure 19.10

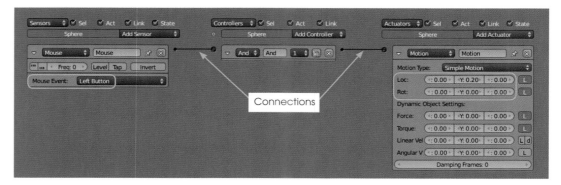

on the sphere, but that can be adjusted. If you hold the LMB down, the sphere will continue moving, fall off the side of the plane, and disappear into infinity. Press Esc to end the game.

Let's now add a few more controls. Adding controls (or logic blocks) soon fills up the logic editor window, so to save space you can click on the little triangles at the upper LHS of the panels and collapse them. Click again to expand. Add more sensors, controllers, and actuators, as shown in Figure 19.11, paying particular attention to the values in the motion actuators. Do not forget to connect them together.

Figure 19.11

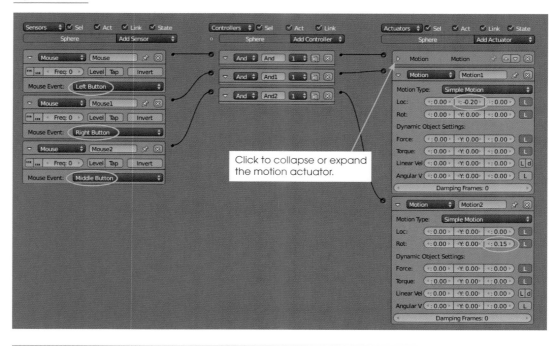

With the controls set as shown in Figure 19.11, you can drive the actor around the plane. Play with the mouse buttons and you will soon get the hang of it. Note that the sphere only rotates in one direction, but you can add another set of controls to rotate it in the opposite direction. Maybe change the mouse sensor to keyboard and use the A and S keys for rotation. You could also change all the sensor controls to keyboard and use a pattern of keys. The foregoing is about as simple as it gets, so it's now your responsibility to research and experiment further.

Figure 19.12

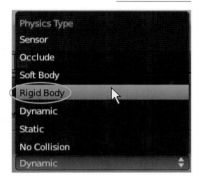

19.2 Game Animation

The game engine physics may be used to record an animation. In Chapter 9, we discussed animating the complex movement of an object by following a curve path; this procedure saved time by negating the application of key frames and allowed the movement to be easily modified by changing the shape of the curve path. Sometimes you won't be in a position to set a predetermined path, so you may wish to experiment to find the best movement to depict what you wish to show. This is where game physics is useful; you can drive your object around the scene and have the movement recorded.

Figure 19.13

Continue with the previous game engine setup and in the properties window – "Physics" button – "Physics" tab, click on the "Physics Type" drop down menu and change "Dynamic" to "Rigid Body" (Figure 19.12). In the information window header at the top of the screen, click on "Game" and tick "Record Animation" (Figure 19.13)—when your object is driven using the game engine, the movement will now be recorded. When you exit the game (by pressing Esc) and return to the 3D window, pressing Alt + the A key will replay the movement in the 3D window.

Before doing any driving, bear in mind that as soon as you press the P key to start the game, the animation recording is up and running. Look at the properties window – "World" button – "Physics" tab and note that the "Physics Steps: FPS" value is 60 (Figure 19.14). In the "Render" button – "Stand Alone Player" tab, note that the "Quality: FPS" value is also 60, so the animation is recording at 60 frames per

Figure 19.14

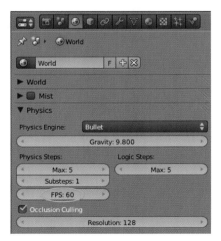

Figure 19.15

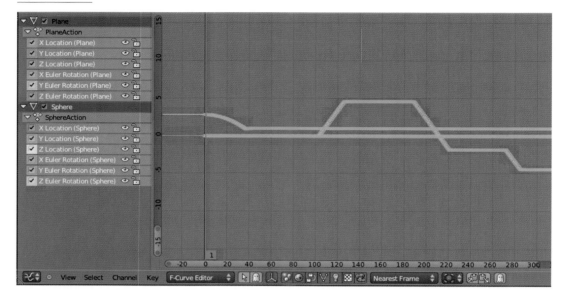

second. In no time at all, you will record many frames, so I suggest that you limit your driving in the game to a few seconds of simple short moves.

Now run your game with the P key, but remember to keep it simple and short, and press Esc to quit. After this short burst of tentative experimentation, with your actor returned to the center of the scene in the 3D window, press Alt + the A key to see the animation of your game movement. You probably see your object move, but it doesn't complete all the movement you made in the game. Change the text editor window at the RHS of the screen to the graph editor window and you will see your animation displayed as a graph with many lines and numerous channels entered in the dope sheet panel on the LHS of the window (Figure 19.15). Change the logic editor window at the bottom to the timeline window, which is now full of vertical yellow stripes (key frames) (Figure 19.16). Blender has recorded key frames at each frame of the animation. If you played the game for 8 seconds at 60 FPS, you have recorded 480 frames, each having a key frame.

In the timeline window, your animation is set with the values "Start: 1" and "End: 250," therefore when you play the animation in the 3D window, you only play the first 250 frames. Change the "End" value to equal the number of key frames shown in the timeline to see the full animation of the game movement.

Figure 19.16

Video Sequence Editing

20.1 Making a Movie
20.2 The Video Editing Screen

20.1 Making a Movie

Movies are made by piecing together video clips, which are the short segments of video you produce when you render an animation. It follows that you can only make a movie when you have video clips saved on your computer. How to render animation to video has been covered in Chapter 9 and I will assume that you have some clips saved. Make a note of where you have saved your clips and make sure you are conversant with the file browser window.

The first step in the moviemaking process is to set the video output format and to set the file path to the folder where you want to save your movie file. Start Blender, and in the default screen arrangement go to the properties window – "Render" button (Figure 20.1). In the "Output" tab, set your file path by clicking on the "Browse Folder" button. In the file browser, navigate to your folder. Next, set your movie video file type (the default output setting is PNG). Change "PNG" to

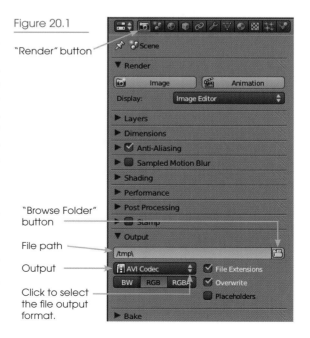

Figure 20.1

"Render" button

"Browse Folder" button

File path

Output

Click to select the file output format.

"AVI Codec," which will give you a file you can burn to DVD and play in a video player. Once you have set these options, click next to "Default" in the information window header and change the display screen to "Video Editing" (Figure 20.2).

Figure 20.2

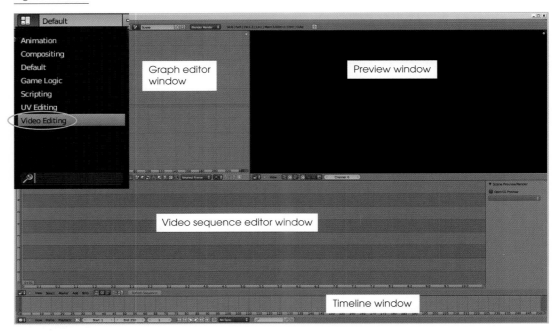

Figure 20.3

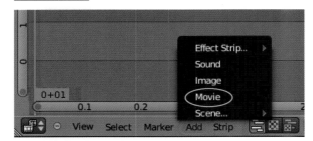

20.2 The Video Editing Screen

In the video sequence editor, click on "Add" in the header and select "Movie" (Figure 20.3). The file browser window displays. Navigate to the folder containing your video clips. On my computer, my clips are in "C:\SubAnim\"— you can see that I have five clips that form a movie when spliced together (Figure 20.4). Click on your first clip to highlight it (it's shown in orange) then click on "Add Movie Strip" in the upper RH corner of the file browser. The video clip is entered into the video sequence editor as a blue strip with a white border; the white border indicates that it is selected (Figure 20.5). If you press the E key, you can drag the clip right or left along the screen. The vertical green line is a cursor and is located at position 0+01 in the figure, which is the beginning of the timeline. Drag the clip until the start of the clip is at position 0.00 (Figure 20.6).

Figure 20.4

File selected   Other video clips

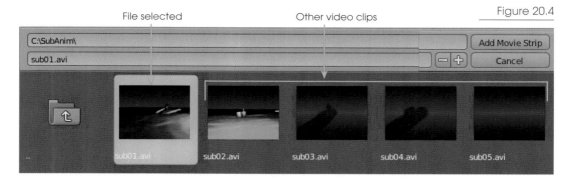

Figure 20.5

Video clip

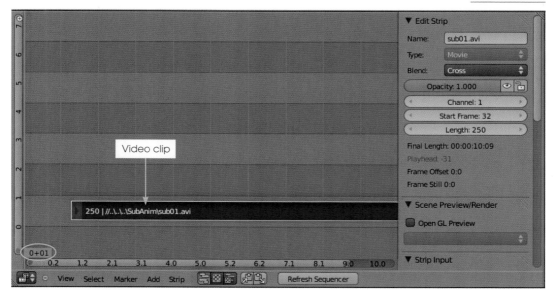

Figure 20.6

Drag the clip to 0.00.

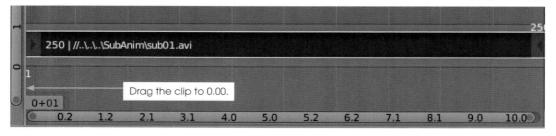

Figure 20.7

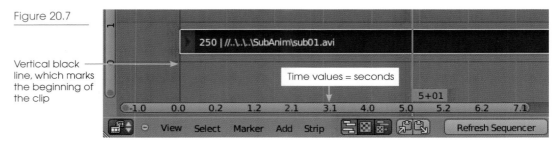

Vertical black line, which marks the beginning of the clip

Figure 20.8

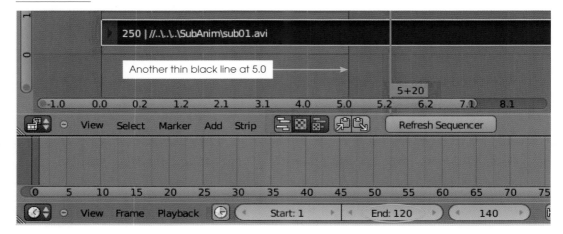

After positioning the clip at the start of the timeline, move the green cursor to the right. At position 0.00, you will see a thin vertical black line, which is the marker for position 0.00 (Figure 20.7). Dragging the green cursor allows you to scrub through your video clip, which you will observe in the preview window. With your normal cursor in the preview window, pressing Alt + the A key plays the clip. The graduations across the bottom of the video sequence editor are seconds.

In the timeline window at the bottom of the screen, change the "End" value to 120, and you will see another thin black line move in from the RHS of the window and locate at position 5.00 seconds (Figure 20.8). This line will represent the end of the render in the final movie output. Remember that in the render setup in the properties window, the frame rate for the animation was 24 frames per second; 120 frames played at 24 frames per second equals 5 seconds.

Place the cursor in the video sequence editor window and zoom in with the number pad + sign. Click on the time graduation bar and drag it to the right to move the editor window to the left. Click "Add" again and select your second video clip; the second clip is placed on the same line as the first clip (these lines are called channels). At the RHS of the window, there's an "Edit Strip" tab; change the channel number from 1 to 2 and you should see your

Figure 20.9

Second clip

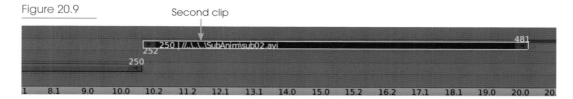

second clip move up a channel (Figure 20.9). Another way to do this is to right click on the clip and drag it up, but be sure to line up the end of clip 1 with the start of clip 2. Then, right click on strip 2 and drag it. Numeric values showing the end and start frames of the clips display, which allow you to align the ends accurately. You can align the clips on the same frame number, a slight gap is tolerated, or you can overlap the clips slightly.

After aligning all your clips (I'm only using two clips for this demonstration), go to the timeline window at the bottom of the screen and change the "End" frame so that the thin vertical black line in the video sequence editor window lines up with the end of your last clip—this sets the end frame for the movie file render (Figure 20.10). Before you render the movie, you can add a sound file (MP3 or wave) (Figure 20.11). You can also play a preview by putting the cursor in the preview window and pressing Alt + the A key (Figure 20.12).

Figure 20.10

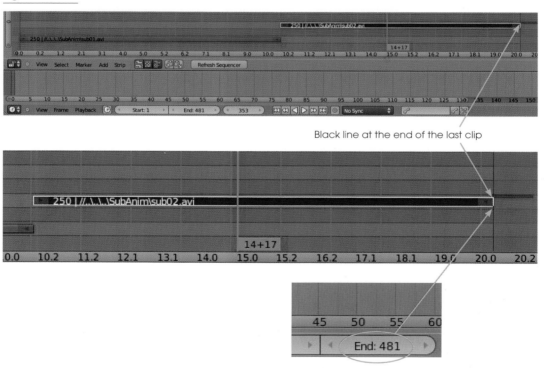

Black line at the end of the last clip

Figure 20.11

Sound file

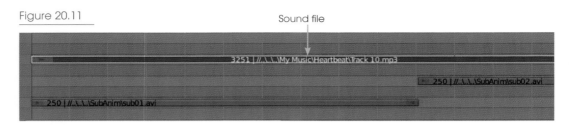

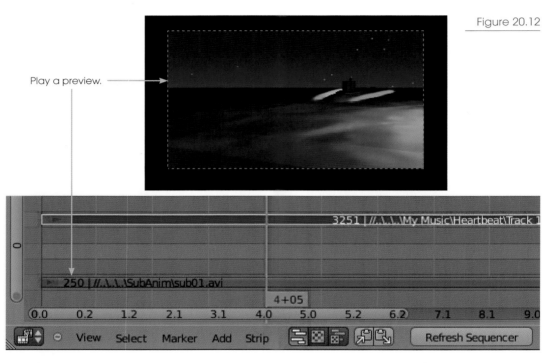

Play a preview.

Figure 20.12

Figure 20.13

Output folder

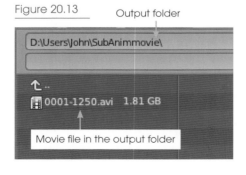

D:\Users\John\SubAnimmovie\

0001-1250.avi   1.81 GB

Movie file in the output folder

It's time to render. In the information window header, click on "Render" and select "Render Animation." Wait for the render to complete (it plays as it proceeds in the editor window). After completion, find the movie file in the output folder you set and give it a test run in a media player (Figure 20.13).

Basic Blender Commands

This is just a partial list of Blender commands. Please visit www.blender.org for more details.

- A key. Selects all; press again to deselect the selected.
- B key. Gives you a box (window drag) to select multiple objects in edit mode.
- C key. Gives you a circle to select multiple objects. The circle can be sized by scrolling the mouse wheel.
- E key. While in edit mode, selected vertices, edges, and faces can be extruded.
- G key. Press the G key and drag the mouse to move an object or selected vertices.
- I key. Inserts an animation key.
- M key. In object mode, it opens the "Move to Layer" option.
- N key. Toggles between showing and hiding the numeric data display for the selected object.
- O key. While in edit mode, it puts you into proportional vertex editing.
- P key. In edit mode, it opens the "Separate" menu in order to separate the selected vertices. In object mode, the game engine enters play mode.

- R key. Press the R key and drag the mouse to rotate an object or selected vertices.

- S key. Press the S key and drag the mouse to scale an object or selected vertices.

- U key. In edit mode, it opens the "UV Mapping" menu. In object mode, it opens the "Make Single User" menu.

- W key. Opens the "Specials" menu.

- X key/Delete key. Deletes a selection.

- Z key. Toggles the view between wireframe and solid.

- Alt + the A key. Plays an animation in the selected window (your cursor must be in that window for it to play).

- Alt + the C key. Opens the "Convert to" menu to convert between a mesh and a curve.

- Alt + the Z key. Toggles between a texture view and a shaded view.

- Arrow keys. Used to advance frames in an animation: left and right arrows = 1-frame increments, up and down arrows = 10-frame increments.

- Ctrl + the A key. After an object has been resized and/or rotated, it opens the "Apply" menu; this can reset the object's data.

- Ctrl + the J key. Joins two selected objects.

- Ctrl + the S key. Opens the file browser to save a file.

- Ctrl + the T key. Displays the "Make Track" menu.

- Ctrl + the Z key. The global undo command; with each press, one step will be undone (up to 32 steps are possible by default). If you are in edit mode, it will only undo editing steps on the selected object.

- Esc. Cancels an action and ends an animation.

- F1. Opens the file browser window.

- F2. Saves a file.

- F3. Saves a rendered image.

- F12. Renders an image.

- Left mouse button (LMB). Click to manipulate the 3D manipulator widget, to locate the 3D cursor, to activate functions, to enter values, etc.

- Right mouse button (RMB). Click to select.

- Middle mouse button (MMB). Click to manipulate specified options.

- Mouse scroll wheel. Zooms in and out and scrolls to expand/contract selection options.

- Number pad. Controls the view.
  - 7: Top.
  - 1: Front.
  - 3: Side.
  - 0: Camera.
  - 5: Perspective.
  - + and – : Zoom in and out and control the affected vertex size in proportional vertex editing.
- Shift key. Hold down while clicking the RMB to make multiple selections.
- Shift + the A key. Displays the "Add" menu to add objects to the scene such as meshes, cameras, lights, etc.
- Shift + the D key. Duplicates or copies selected objects or vertices.
- Shift + the S key. Displays the "Snap" menu.
- Shift + the space bar. Toggles between a view with multiple windows and a full screen view.
- Shift + the RMB. Selects multiple objects or vertices.
- Space bar. Displays the tool search window.
- Tab. Toggles between edit mode (vertex editing) and object select mode.

Supplements

B.1 Installing Add-Ons

Add-ons are additional Blender functions, hidden away in the user preferences window to prevent cluttering the interface. Add-ons are Python scripts (pieces of code in the Python programming language) that, when activated, provide additional functionality to the Blender program. Blender comes preloaded with a selection of add-ons, but there are literally hundreds of scripts available for download on the internet—the Blender website contains a link to the scripts repository where a great number can be found.

When you download an add-on (Python script), you have to install it into Blender; the best way to show this process is to provide an example. A very interesting add-on in Blender is called BlenRig 4, which is a script for manipulating a model of the human body. You will have to study the sections in this book on modeling, animation, rigging, and applying modifiers before you can possibly understand how this amazing piece of code works, but I am sure installing it will demonstrate how powerful Blender is. This exercise will show you how to download a compressed (.zip) file and extract it to a folder, find a Python script contained in the decompressed file, then install the script into Blender. This is an exercise in manipulating files to add functionality to Blender. For a beginner, the exercise may appear daunting but is well worth pursuing.

To begin, we will go to the internet and download a folder containing the Python script and a demonstration Blender (.blend) file. The download will be a compressed (.zip) file, so you must have a program installed on your computer to unzip it: either WinZip, WinRar, or Zzip will do the trick.

Before you download, keep in mind where on your hard drive you want to save your download and into which folder you want to unzip it. Windows usually has a default folder such as "Downloads" or "My Documents" where it saves downloaded files. If you want to download somewhere else or create a new folder, head to the section on navigation and Windows Explorer in Chapter 2. Whatever you do, remember where your files are located; if you have a memory like mine, it's best to create a log file somewhere and remember where you keep it.

Go online, open a browser window, and search "BlenRig 4." Select the "jpbovza.com. ar" site and find the downloads/tutorials page. The full site address is: jpbovza.com.ar/wp/ downloads/blenrig/current-release/blenrig-4-0/. In the tutorials section on this site, you have the option to download three demonstrations (Figure B.1):

- Zepam model
- Human male athletic model
- Gilgamesh model

Figure B.1

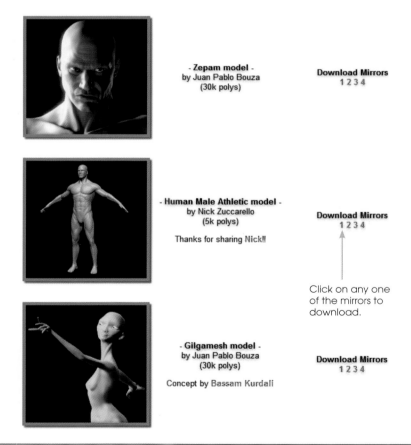

\- **Zepam model** -
by Juan Pablo Bouza
(30k polys)

Download Mirrors
1 2 3 4

\- **Human Male Athletic model** -
by Nick Zuccarello
(5k polys)

Thanks for sharing Nick!!

Download Mirrors
1 2 3 4

Click on any one
of the mirrors to
download.

\- **Gilgamesh model** -
by Juan Pablo Bouza
(30k polys)

Concept by Bassam Kurdali

Download Mirrors
1 2 3 4

Each of these demonstrations may be obtained from one of four "Download Mirrors"—it doesn't matter which mirror is used, the file will be the same. Once unzipped (or decompressed), you will have a folder containing two subfolders. For example, the Gilgamesh demonstration unzips into a folder called BlenRig4_01_Gilgamesh, and two subfolders called BlenRig_Addon and BlenRig4_01_Gilgamesh. The subfolder called BlenRig_Addon contains the file BlenRig_scripts_122.py, which is the Python script we are going to install into Blender. The subfolder called BlenRig4_01_Gilgamesh contains a file named BlenRig4_01_Gilgamesh.blend, which is a Blender file.

Once the Python script BlenRig_scripts_122.py is installed into Blender, it will provide controls in the form of sliders for manipulating the pose of a model of the human figure. These controls will only be of use to you once you have a model created in your scene and the model has been rigged for animation. The basics of modeling and rigging are covered in separate sections of this manual, but they are not adequately presented to describe the complex procedure for creating a human figure and rigging; that will require further study. This is merely a demonstration on installing a script and showing an example of the power of Blender.

Download BlenRig4_01_Gilgamesh and once the zip file is downloaded, unzip it to a folder. To unzip, simply double click on the file name and your default zip program will activate. There should be an option to extract the contents of the zip file to a folder of your choice.

B.1.1 How to Install the Script

Open Blender and change the 3D window to the user preferences window. Click on the "Add-Ons" tab at the top of the window; by default, the tab will display all the add-ons that have been included with the program. We are going to install the BlenRig_scripts_122.py script, which is associated with rigging. Before we install the script, we had better note what scripts are already installed under this category. At the LHS of the window there is a selection list with "All" highlighted in blue. Click on "Rigging," and the list will now only display one entry: "Rigging: Rigify" (Figure B.2). Look at the lower LHS of the window and click on the "Install Add-On" button, which opens a file browser window.

Now you have to navigate to the script saved on your hard drive. With the script located, click on it to highlight and then press the "Install Add-On" button in the upper RH corner of the window. The new script will be installed in the user preferences – "Add-Ons" window as "Rigging: BlenRig" script, but will not immediately display.

Note: In Blender 2.58, you have to close then restart the program before the new add-on will display in the user preferences window. Remember, you have to save user settings before closing Blender otherwise any changes to the default settings will be lost. After installing the script, even though it is not displayed, change back to the 3D window. In the information window header, click "File" – "Save User Settings," then close and restart the program. The script now displays.

Figure B.2

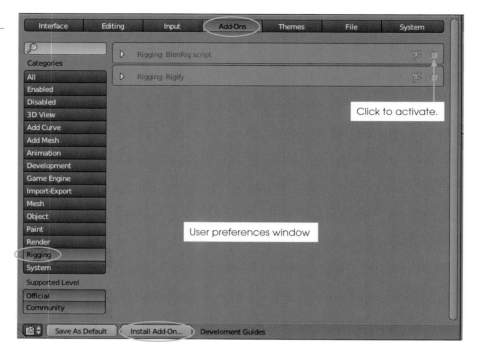

At this point, the script is not active. To activate the script you have to tick the little box at the RHS of the script entry in the user preferences window – "Add-Ons" tab. Before ticking the box, check the 3D window – properties panel (press the N key to display it) to see what's there before activation so you can compare what you get after. Change back to the 3D window and add an armature (a single bone will do for now); we require the armature since our add-on deals with controlling armature movement. The add-on won't do anything for us just now, but we just want to prove that it is installed and functioning. In the 3D window, press the N key to display the transform properties panel and note the seven tabs in the panel. Now tick the box in the user preferences window to activate the script. Click on any of the tabs in the transform properties panel and a new "BlenRig Controls" tab displays— we have just proved that the script is installed and active.

In the information window header, press "File" – "Open" and navigate to the Blen-Rig4_01_Gilgamesh.blend file. Click on the file to highlight it and press "Open Blender file" in the upper RH corner of the window. We now see Gilgamesh, a 3D model of a humanoid figure (Figure B.3). The transform properties panel is displayed and the "BlenRig Controls" tab is opened with a new bunch of tabs included. Clicking on a tab and ticking the "All" box displays several sliders; these sliders control the posing of the model. You can also click on control elements on the model and manipulate the pose for animation.

When you locate your script and click on the "Install Add-On" button, Blender copies the script into the "addons" folder located as follows (this is for a Windows system): C:\Users\%Name%\AppData\Roaming\BlenderFoundation\Blender\2.58\scripts\addons.

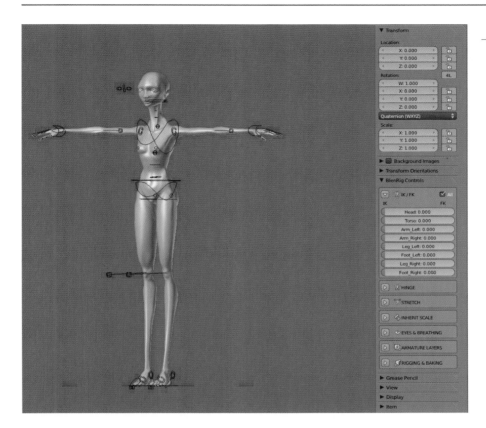

Note that the "AppData" folder in Windows is a hidden folder by default and you will have to reconfigure Windows to show it. To do this, click "Start" from the desktop then "Control Panel." In the search bar at the upper right of the control panel window, type in "Folders." In the window that displays, under "Folder Options" click "Show hidden files and folders." Click "Apply" then click "OK." In Windows Explorer, you will now be able to navigate to the "...scripts\addons" folder and see the installed script.

I hope the foregoing has demonstrated the versatility and shown the potential power of Blender by installing add-ons. The manipulation of files and folders is a part of Blender life, so being conversant with your computer file system will add new dimensions to your Blender experience.

B.2 The Outliner Window

In Chapter 1, the outliner window was briefly mentioned. It was stated that the outliner window gives you a display of everything in your scene. It does, but it also does much more. Follow this procedure to discover a little about how the window is arranged and how you can use it.

The outliner window

B.2.1 Step 1

Start with the default Blender screen showing the five default windows. The outliner window is displayed in the upper right hand corner of the screen (Figure B.4).

B.2.2 Step 2

To make life a little easier, divide the 3D window in two and change the left hand section into a copy of the outliner window (Figure B.5). The outliner window contains information about the current scene, which in this case is what is shown in the default 3D window. You can see that the default scene comprises a render layer, a world, a camera, a cube, and a lamp. Each line of information represents a data block, which is a group of data pertaining to something in the scene. The default outliner window shows five groupings, but note that before each line there is a small circle with a + sign in it; this is showing that some information is hidden. After the data block name, you can see a vertical bar followed by an icon; the icon represents a subdata block, so click on the + sign to reveal the subdata.

Figure B.5

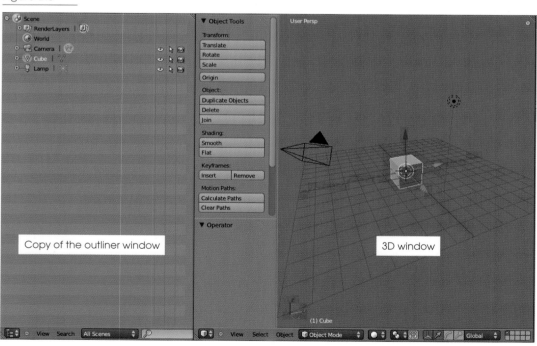

Copy of the outliner window

3D window

In the case of our default scene, instead of clicking on each + sign place the cursor in the outliner window and press the number pad + key three times—you will see all the data blocks and subdata blocks revealed (Figure B.6).

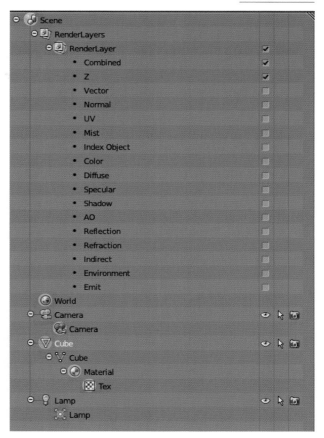

B.2.3 Step 3

Examine the data block for the cube object in the scene (Figure B.7). The first line represents the cube object, the second line the cube mesh, the third line the material, and the last line the texture. Each successive line or data block is linked to the next. When you open Blender, the cube object in the scene is selected (as shown in Figure B.8) by the orange outline in the 3D window. With your mouse cursor in the 3D window, press the A key to deselect the cube.

B.2.4 Step 4

In the outliner window, click on the cube line with the LMB and you will observe that the cube is again selected in the 3D window. Sometimes objects in the 3D window are obscured by other objects or they may even be inside other objects, making them difficult to select with the mouse—therefore, you can select them in the outliner window.

With the cursor in the 3D window, press the A key to deselect the cube. In the outliner window, click on the cube mesh data block with the LMB—the cube in the 3D window is now selected in edit mode. With the cursor in the 3D window, press the Tab key to go back to object mode.

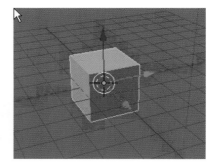

Figure B.7

Figure B.8

Figure B.9

B.2.5 Step 5

In the outliner window, look at the three icons at the right end of the data block line (Figure B.9). Click the eyeball to toggle between visible and invisible in the 3D window, click the white arrow to toggle between select and deselect in the 3D window, and click the camera to render an object. The three icons are grayed out if they're disengaged.

B.2.6 Step 6

In the properties window at the RHS of the screen, click on the "Material" button with the cube selected in the 3D window (Figure B.10). You will see that the default cube has a material applied to it, which is named "Material." While still in the properties window, click on

Figure B.10

Figure B.11

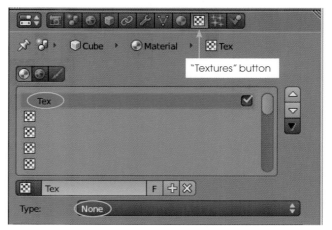

the "Textures" button and you will see that a texture is applied; note that the texture type is "None" (Figure B.11). In other words, there is a texture data block without any texture data in it. Blender is made up of data blocks and sometimes these data blocks do nothing until such time as you modify them—this is the case here.

The outliner window shows data blocks linked in a chain as demonstrated by the cube data block. In the outliner window, right click on the cube texture data block line. In the pop-up panel that displays, select "Unlink." You will see in the properties window that the cube's texture data is deleted. To reinstate the texture, go to the properties window – "Textures" button and click on the texture drop down icon (Figure B.12). In the drop down panel, select "Tex." If you right click on the cube's material data block in the outliner window and select "Unlink," both the material and texture are deleted. This occurs because a material must first be in place before a texture can be applied.

B.2.7 Step 7

In the 3D window, press the A key, deselect the cube, then press Shift + the A key and add a UV sphere (Figure B.13). You will see that a sphere data block is added into the outliner window (Figure B.14). Click on the + sign at the beginning of the line to display the sphere's mesh data block; note that there is no material and no texture.

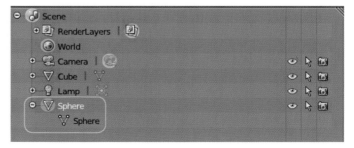

Figure B.12

Figure B.13

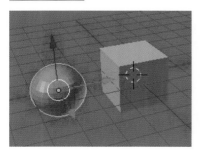

Figure B.14

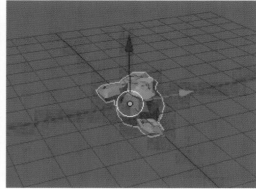

Click on the icon
to display a drop
down panel.

The monkey enters the scene lying on his back.

Go to the information window header at the top of the screen and click on the icon. In the drop down panel, you can see that the Blender file contains one scene named "Scene" (Figure B.15). Now press the + sign and select "New" to add a new scene to the file. You will then see "Scene.001" added to the outliner window. With the cursor in the new scene 3D window, press Shift + the A key and add a monkey object (Figure B.16). The monkey data block is added into the outliner window and by clicking on the + sign, you can expand the links. As with the UV sphere added to the previous scene, the monkey has no material or texture. When you click on the "Scene" icon in the information window header, you will see the two scenes in the file.

Figure B.17

B.2.8 Step 8

In the outliner window header, there is an "All Scenes" drop down selection button. If you select "Current Scene" in the drop down menu, only the data block for the scene showing in the 3D window is displayed (Figure B.17). This is very handy when you have a complicated file with many different scenes.

References

The following websites are recommended as sources of information for Blender 3D programming.

- Gryllus.net 3D Design: www.gryllus.net/Blender/3D.html.
- The Blender website: www.blender.org.
- The Wiki Users Manual: wiki.blender.org/index/php/Doc:Manual.
- Blender Nation: www.blendernation.com.

Additionally, here are some helpful sites that offer Blender tutorials (this is nowhere near an exhaustive list—there are literally hundreds more):

- Blender Guru: www.blenderguru.com.
- Blender 3D Tutorials: www.tutorialized.com/tutorials/Blender-3d/1.
- 555 Blender Tutorials: filmmakeriq.com/2009/04/555-blender-tutorials/.
- C G Tutorials: www.cgtutorials.com/c3/Blender.
- Blender Underground: blenderunderground.com.
- Blender Cookie: cgcookie.com/blender/get-started-with-blender.
- Blender Cycles: www.blendercycles.com.
- Blender Artist: www.blenderartist.org/forum/forumdisplay.php?32.

The following are a few examples of the many free graphics programs available on the internet. You may find them useful and/or interesting.

- FastStone Image Viewer (a useful tool for organizing your image files): www.faststone.org/download.htm.
- Make Human (creates the human figure): sites.google.com/site/makehuman docs/Home.

- Pov Ray (provides a way of creating graphics): www.povray.org.
- Serif Draw Plus (provides graphics drawing programs): www.freeserif software.com.
- Lohmüller (an interesting graphics site): www.f-lohmueller.de/.
- Ivy Generator (grow ivy on everything): graphics.uni-konstanz.de/~luft/ ivy_generator/.

Index

expansion button 19
expansion icon 25
extrapolation 154
  constant 154
  linear 154
extrusion 61

F

field of influence 319
file browser window 40
file formats 25
fire 261
fireworks 261–262
fluid simulation 329, 338–340
forward kinematics 320

G

game animation 363–364
gaming 359
gradient 92
graph editor window 149–152, 164, 171
graphical user interface xi–xii, 19
gravity 242

H

halo settings 93, 254
hardness value 91
horizon color 125
horizontal mid-plane 27

I

intensity 88
interpolation 144
  Bezier type 144, 153
  constant type 144
  linear type 144
inverse kinematics 320–321

K

key frames 144, 147, 157, 161, 304
keying sets 159–160
knife tool 72

L

lamps 131–133
  animation of 158
laptop users 20, 30
layers 29–30

lighting 131–133
logic blocks 361

M

Make Human models 315
manipulation widget 27, 61, 166
material
  animation 157
  button 85–87
  slots 99–107
meta shapes 188–189
mirror color 87
mist 127, 135
modifiers 66–71, 191
  armature 213, 312–313
  array 193–194
  bevel 67, 195
  Boolean 68, 196–197
  build 197
  cast 214
  cloth 223–225
  collision 225–226
  curve 214–215
  decimate 198
  displace 215–217
  edge split 198–200
  explode 226–227
  hook 217
  lattice 218
  mask 200
  mesh 219
  mirror 68, 201–202
  multiresolution 202–203
  particle instance 227–230
  screw 203–204
  shrinkwrap 220
  simple deform 221
  smoke 230–234
  smooth 222
  soft body 235–237
  solidify 205–206
  subdivision surface 67, 206–207, 337
  UV project 208–212
  wave 222–223
modifier stacks 192

N

node editor 343
nodes 341–344
  compositing 356–358